KANJI 1·2·3

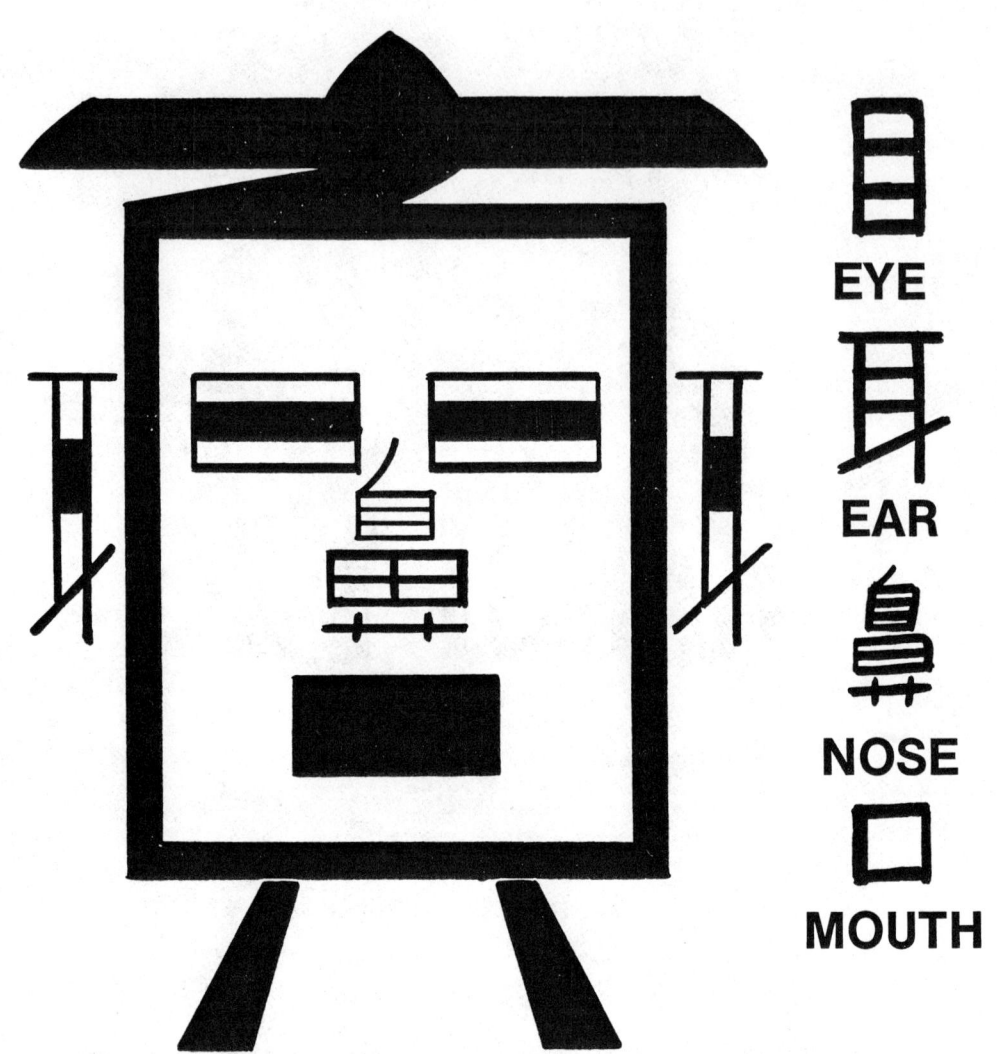

KANJI 1-2-3

ANDREW DYKSTRA

Associate Director
Kansai Gaidai Hawaii College

William Kaufmann, Inc.
Los Altos, California

Dedicated
With Love and Affection
to
Professor Susumu Winston Nakamura
"Grand Old Man of Japanese Studies"
at the
Navy Oriental Languages
Postgraduate School
University of California at Berkeley
Kansai Gaidai Hawaii College

Copyright © 1983 by Andrew Dykstra and Yoshiko Dykstra. All rights reserved. No part of this book may be reproduced in any manner whatsoever without the written permission of the publisher: William Kaufmann, Inc., 95 First Street, Los Altos, California 94022.

10 9 8 7 6 5 4 3 2 1

ISBN 0-86576-030-6

Library of Congress Cataloging in Publication Data

Dykstra, Andrew H.
    Kanji 1-2-3.

    1. Chinese characters—Japan.   2. Japanese language—Glossaries, vocabularies, etc.   3. Chinese characters—Miscellanea.   I. Title.   II. Title: Kanji one-two-three.
PL677.6.D9 1982   495.6'81   82-14007
ISBN 0-86576-030-6

Contents

Kanji 1-2-3 vii

Introduction ix

Volume Five: JME 339-543 339

214 Radicals With Meanings 544

Kanji Stroke Index for JME Numbers 548

Alphabetical Japanese Word Index for JME Numbers 555

Katakana and Hiragana 568

About the Author . . . . following 568

KANJI 1·2·3

This independent book is also a successor to *The Kanji ABC* and has been produced in answer to the many requests for an additional volume making it easy to learn more *kanji*.

As was said in *The Kanji ABC*, the *kanji* are the characters of Japan and China, invented by the Yellow Emperor in the legendary dawn of China's history. They are found in more primitive form on the oracle "dragon bones" of the Shang Dynasty. You can see them on the brightly colored signs of San Francisco's Chinatown and with the syllabic *kana* in the flashing neon lights of the Tokyo Ginza district.

The *kanji* are an international language of symbols. The people of Korea, Okinawa, Vietnam, and Japan, although speaking languages very different from Chinese, all accepted the *kanji* with the culture of China. Thus different peoples of the "World of Chopsticks" could communicate by writing *kanji*.

Japan's Ministry of Education has helped all students of the *kanji* by numbering the order of importance of the *kanji* which are necessary in reading Japanese. In general, they are as important for reading Chinese and have the same meaning. The *Kanji 1-2-3* gives you the Japanese Ministry of Education (JME or J) number, the radical (RAD or R) number for finding the *kanji* in the dictionary, and the number of strokes in the *kanji*, also for dictionary use. The little numbers with each *kanji* tell you the direction and order of the strokes. The Japanese words or sounds in large capital letters are of Chinese origin; those in small capital letters are of native origin. In the margin are the N (Nelson) dictionary number, the Chinese Wade-Giles romanization, the M (Mathews) dictionary number, and the Peoples' Republic of China romanization. Thus you can use this book to learn Japanese and Chinese and compare the two.

The purpose of the *Kanji 1-2-3* is to help you learn by overcoming the difficulties with which I am familiar. Some of the explanations of the *kanji* can be found in other books. Many are original with me, but seem obviously correct. I have observed and studied the *kanji* for more than a half-century, and studied them with Japanese and Chinese professors in several universities. You will notice that the explanations are usually easy and consistent.

The pictographic *kanji* are truly international and can be used for any language. I hope that by learning them in this book with its easy methods and associations, you will come to know and love the *kanji*. The ancient style of the *kanji* is often far superior to the alphabet writing of the Western world. Nowadays, for impact and retention as in international road signs and in advertisements, the Western world turns to the earlier picture writing, the symbolism that unites and belongs to all of us as human beings.

Introduction

The *kanji* and *kana* symbols of Japanese writing have contributed greatly to the flexibility, adaptability, ingenuity, and inventiveness of the Japanese mind which easily assimilates and incorporates foreign methods, ideas, and techniques.

Any Western bias that a nonalphabetic writing is cumbersome, ineffective, or wasteful must be discarded at the outset. The *kanji* are on a far higher plane of artistry, impact, composition, beauty, design, balance, imagery, and imagination than crude alphabetic letters. The *kanji* are the product of thousands of dynastic years of Chinese genius in art, poetry, music, and sculpture disciplined by the highest organizational talent personified in the rule of the First Emperor of the Ch'in who built the Great Wall.

The originally monosyllabic *kanji* were utilized by the Japanese with the aid of the simpler *kana* to write their native polysyllabic language. Nearly all foreigners are bewildered, frustrated, and handicapped by the apparent complexity of a system that seems unapproachably alien. And yet, whether perceived on an elementary or sophisticated level, the *kana* and *kanji* are warm, natural, and friendly.

The *kanji* should be regarded as an extensive clan with meaningful features in related faces. The features or radicals are 214 in number, presenting themselves in almost infinite variations, expanding or shrinking just as a forehead may be high or low, eyes wide-set or close-set, a nose pug or aquiline, a mouth turned up or down, a chin receding or prominent. And these features, although favoring certain positions, may be rearranged and modified.

The foreigner must realize that the Japanese and other *kanji* users in the "World of Chopsticks" comprising Japan, Korea, China, and Vietnam have been subjected to the perception of the *kanji* from infancy. The *kanji* of the Orient are everywhere present on hanging scrolls, on clothing, on shop signs, in newspapers, in books, in magazines, on placards, in earrings, in hair ornaments, in pendants, in fans, in street names, and in the decorative carvings of screens, of furniture, and of other woodwork. Having to a considerable degree subconsciously and effortlessly learned the *kanji,* the Japanese mind is generally unable to appreciate the foreigner's difficulty, slowness, and obtuseness. The adult foreigner can no longer learn as does the Japanese child. The foreigner must learn logically and systematically rather than spontaneously, and must benefit by all memory aids available.

The *Kanji 1-2-3*, which is an independent text as well as a continuation of *The Kanji ABC,* reduces these difficulties in several ways. The features or radicals or parts of each *kanji* are separated and identified in the initial explanation and are applied to the total meaning of the *kanji.* Related *kanji* are reviewed or introduced to reveal and clarify their connections.

The *kanji* with stroke order is shown in large size for greater mental impact. In your copying, follow the stroke order, tracing if necessary, and gradually increase your writing speed to improve your calligraphy, reproducing the original hundreds of times.

The spoken Japanese language may have several readings or sounds for a single *kanji.* The *on* reading, originally Chinese, is given in large capital letters. The *kun* reading for the native Japanese sounds is given in small capitals. Following each are the more frequent English readings.

In the margins of the pages from above to below are the Nelson (Japanese) dictionary number prefixed by an "N," the Wade-Giles romanization followed by the numerical tone, the Mathews (Chinese) dictionary number prefixed by an "M," and the PRC romanization with an accent for the tone (which you can check against the Wade-Giles tone number for identification). Note that the Chinese romanization is often related to the *on* sound. The *on* sound may be the same for certain *kanji* which share features or radicals or parts. This is rewarding but is undependable since the *kanji* were introduced to Japan at various times from different dialects and parts of China.

The prose and poetry often strikingly bare the essence of the *kanji* on a culturally sophisticated and international level. These are in small print so as to be available but unobtrusive.

These vivid texts are the product of more than a half-century of my love for the *kanji.* My purpose is to give you pleasure in your intimacy with the *kanji,* a pleasure that can become a passion of infinite depth and variety. Your reward will always be far greater than your investment in time or effort.

If any of you should wish to study Japanese language and culture in Japan, the Kansai University of Foreign Studies has an outstanding program in Osaka which is near the ancient capital of Kyoto and the temple city of Nara. For information please write:

Kansai University of Foreign Studies: Koryuka
333 Ogura, Hirakata City, Osaka, Japan 573

I am at present an administrator of the Kansai Gaidai Hawaii College which Kansai University is developing on the island of Oahu. I would appreciate your advising me through the publisher of errors which you may find in the text. If you should wish to obtain *The Kanji ABC*, it is also available through the publisher.

—Andrew Dykstra

Kage no Kanji
Yume no Kanji
Kage no Yume
Yume no Kage

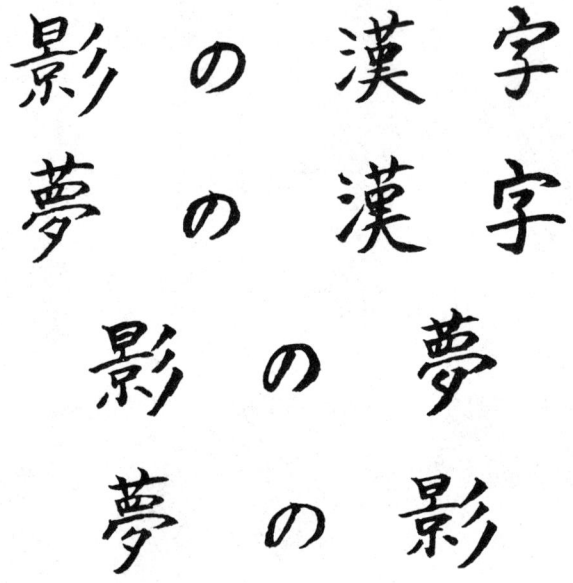

The Kanji of the Shadows:
The Kanji of Dreams;
The Dream of a Shadow:
The Shadow of a Dream.

339

JME	Stroke	Rad
339	13	61

AI, LOVE; AI SURU, TO LOVE.
LOVE 愛 IS THE PUNISHING ROD ／ IN HAND 又.
LOVE 愛 IS IN THE HEART, MIND 心 RECEIVING
THE CROWN ⌒ IN ITS CLAW HAND 爪.

For whom the Lord loveth he chasteneth...Hebrews 12:6.

So take me, daddy, to that old brass bed,
And beat me, daddy, till my face is cherry red.
    College Song (recalled from UC Berkeley of 1941)

N4499
ai4
M9
ài

love
like

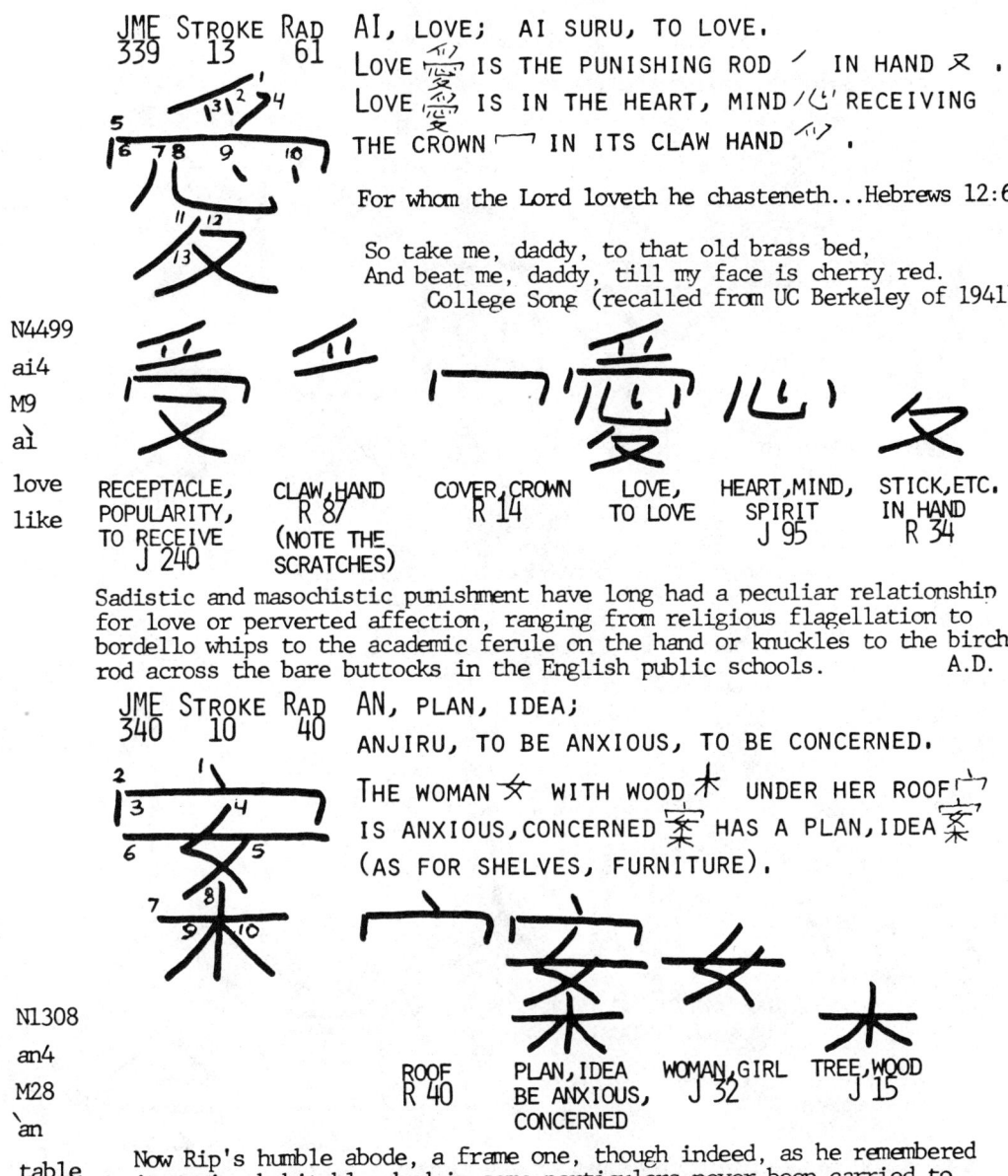

| RECEPTACLE, POPULARITY, TO RECEIVE J 240 | CLAW, HAND R 87 (NOTE THE SCRATCHES) | COVER, CROWN R 14 | LOVE, TO LOVE | HEART, MIND SPIRIT J 95 | STICK, ETC. IN HAND R 34 |

Sadistic and masochistic punishment have long had a peculiar relationship for love or perverted affection, ranging from religious flagellation to bordello whips to the academic ferule on the hand or knuckles to the birch rod across the bare buttocks in the English public schools.   A.D.

JME	Stroke	Rad
340	10	40

AN, PLAN, IDEA;
ANJIRU, TO BE ANXIOUS, TO BE CONCERNED.
THE WOMAN 女 WITH WOOD 木 UNDER HER ROOF ⌒
IS ANXIOUS, CONCERNED 案 HAS A PLAN, IDEA 案
(AS FOR SHELVES, FURNITURE).

N1308
an4
M28
àn

table

| ROOF R 40 | PLAN, IDEA BE ANXIOUS, CONCERNED | WOMAN, GIRL J 32 | TREE, WOOD J 15 |

Now Rip's humble abode, a frame one, though indeed, as he remembered it, quite habitable, had in some particulars never been carried to entire completion. Yes, the first occupants were Rip and his dame, then the bride.   Rip Van Winkle's Lilac   Herman Melville

The great error in Rip's composition was an insuperable aversion to all kinds of profitable labor. In a word, Rip was ready to attend to anybody's business but his own...His fences were continually falling to pieces...his wife kept dinning in his ears about his idleness, his carelessness, and the ruin he was bringing on his family. Morning, noon and night her tongue was incessantly going.
        Rip Van Winkle   The Sketch-Book   Washington Irving

341

I; KOROMO, CLOTHES, GARMENT, PRIEST'S ROBE. CLOTHES, GARMENT, PRIEST'S ROBE 衣 IS A PICTOGRAPH OF A SCHOLAR'S BIRETTA 亠 (HEAD AND SHOULDERS), FORWARD MOVING ARM ノ, BODY AND LEG LEADING ㇄, AND TRAILING BODY AND LEG ㇂ ALL MOVING LEFT.

Rad 145 Stroke 1 JME 341*

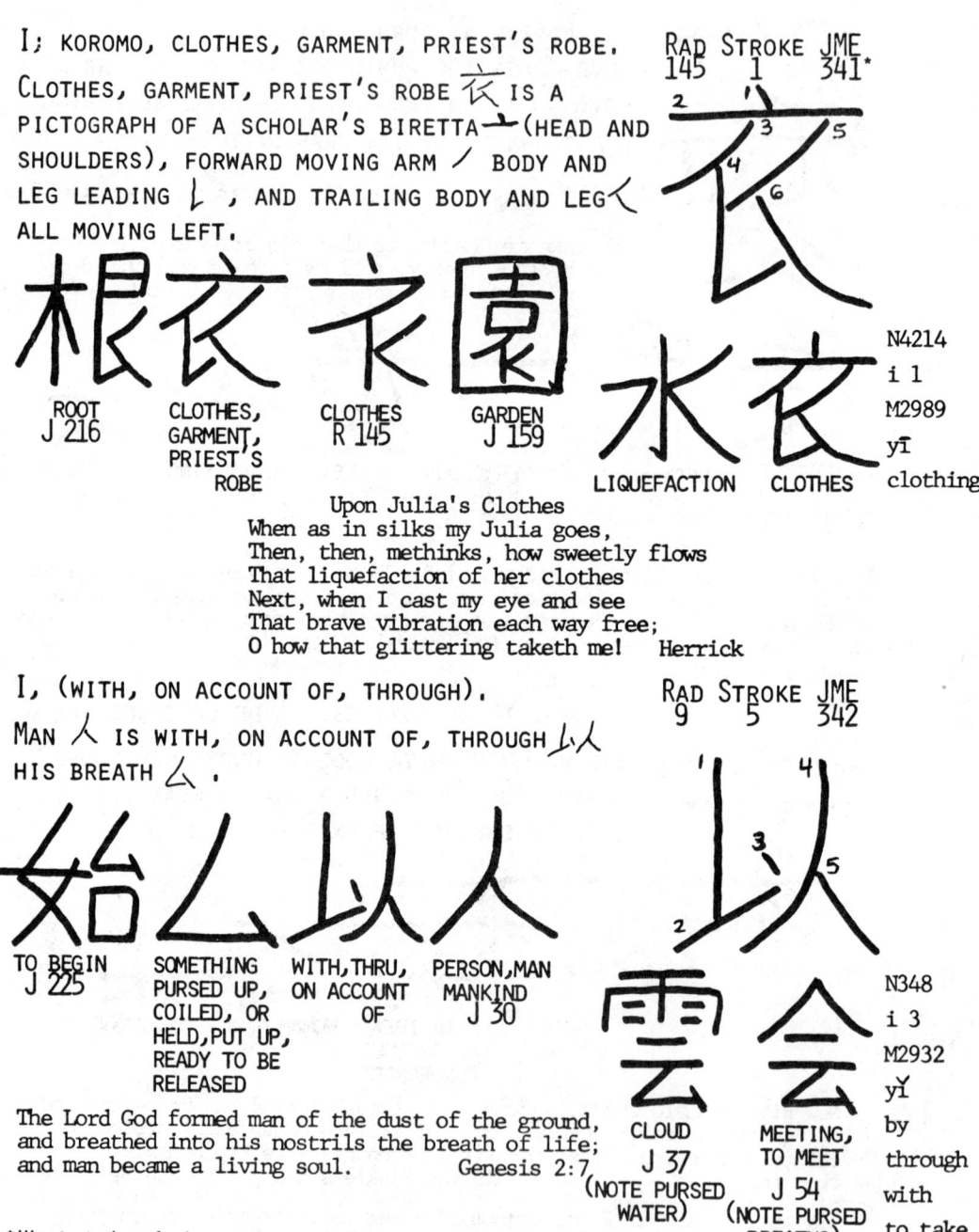

根 ROOT J 216

衣 CLOTHES, GARMENT, PRIEST'S ROBE R 145

衤 CLOTHES R 145

園 GARDEN J 159

水衣 LIQUEFACTION CLOTHES

N4214 i 1
M2989
yī
clothing

Upon Julia's Clothes
When as in silks my Julia goes,
Then, then, methinks, how sweetly flows
That liquefaction of her clothes
Next, when I cast my eye and see
That brave vibration each way free;
O how that glittering taketh me!   Herrick

I, (WITH, ON ACCOUNT OF, THROUGH).
MAN 人 IS WITH, ON ACCOUNT OF, THROUGH 以 HIS BREATH ㄙ.

Rad 9 Stroke 5 JME 342

始 TO BEGIN J 225

ㄙ SOMETHING PURSED UP, COILED, OR HELD, PUT UP, READY TO BE RELEASED

以 WITH, THRU, ON ACCOUNT OF

人 PERSON, MAN MANKIND J 30

以

雲 CLOUD J 37 (NOTE PURSED WATER)

会 MEETING, TO MEET J 54 (NOTE PURSED BREATHS)

N348 i 3
M2932
yǐ
by
through
with
to take

The Lord God formed man of the dust of the ground, and breathed into his nostrils the breath of life; and man became a living soul.   Genesis 2:7

*Illustrated on facing page

341X

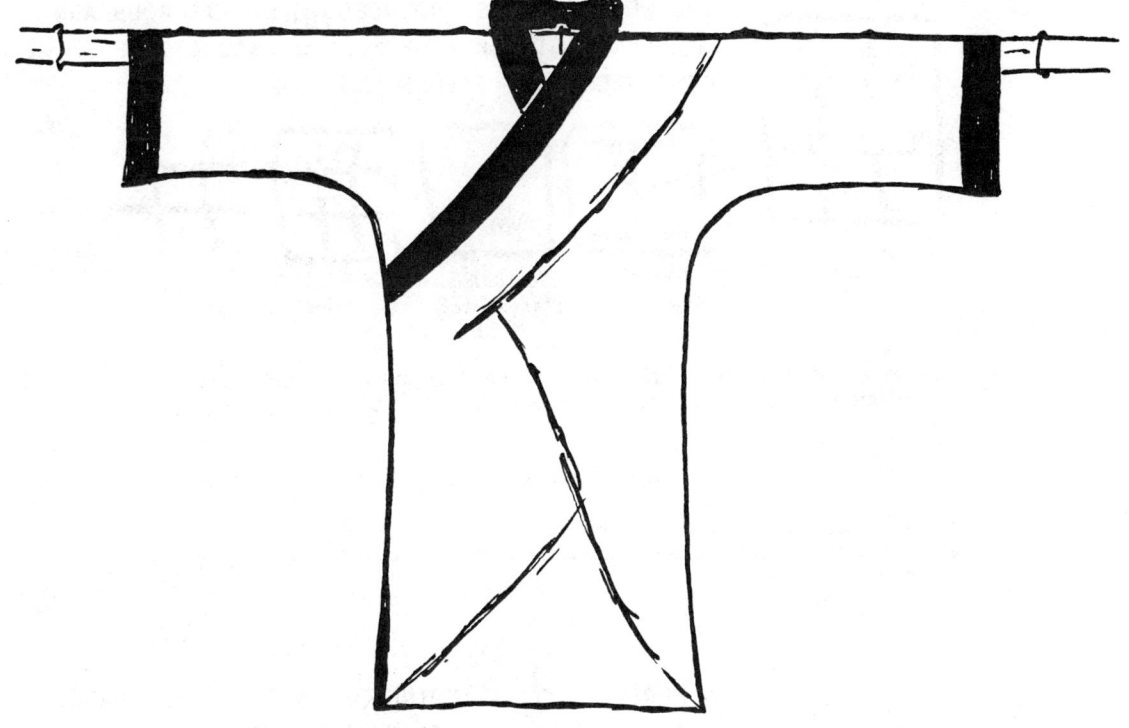

Rather than being hung on a clothesline with clothespins, laundered Chinese clothes traditionally have been pulled over a bamboo pole which enters the openings for arms and legs, making it difficult to steal the clothes unless the pole is taken down. On the pole, a jacket or tunic will have approximately the shape shown above.

343

JME 343 Stroke 4 Rad 31 I; KAKOMU, TO SURROUND

THE WELL 井 IS SURROUNDED 井 BY ITS BOUNDARY ☐. ORIGINALLY THE WELL 井 WAS AT THE CENTER OF NINE FIELDS 囲.

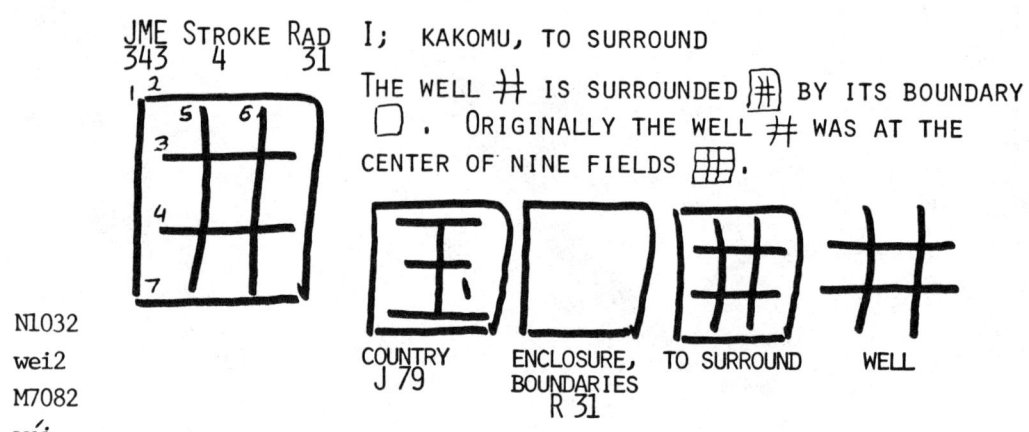

N1032
wei2
M7082

wéi
surround
besiege
invest

Summon archers against Babylon---; camp round about her; let none escape; her young men shall die in her squares... Jeremiah

Flodden   Sir Walter Scott
For still the Scots, around their king, Unbroken fought in desperate ring.

Thus Spake Zarathustra   Nietzsche
I draw circles and sacred boundaries which surround me.

JME 344 Stroke 7 Rad 9 I; KURAI, RANK, GRADE, POSITION, ABOUT.

A PERSON'S 亻 STANDING 立 IS BY RANK, GRADE, POSITION 位, AT LEAST ABOUT 位 SO.

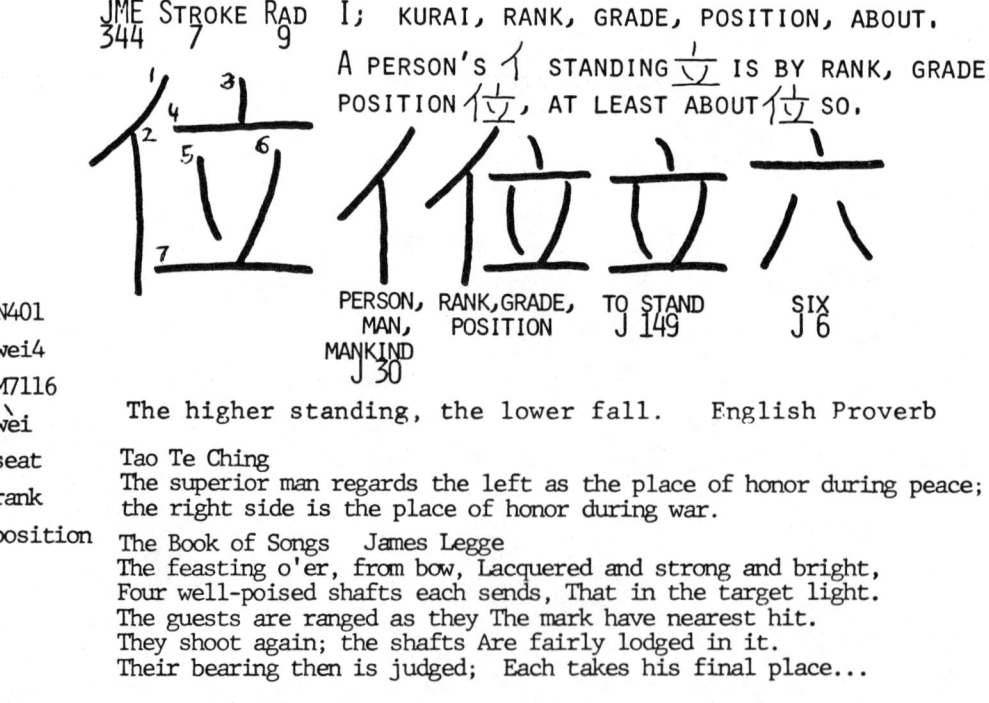

N401
wei4
M7116

wèi
seat
rank
position

The higher standing, the lower fall.   English Proverb

Tao Te Ching
The superior man regards the left as the place of honor during peace; the right side is the place of honor during war.

The Book of Songs   James Legge
The feasting o'er, from bow, Lacquered and strong and bright,
Four well-poised shafts each sends, That in the target light.
The guests are ranged as they The mark have nearest hit.
They shoot again; the shafts Are fairly lodged in it.
Their bearing then is judged; Each takes his final place...

I, (TO HEAL, TO CURE).
THE ARROW 矢 (AS THE NEEDLE IN ACUPUNCTURE) IS USED IN AN ENCLOSURE 匚 (SICK BAY) TO HEAL, TO CURE 医.

匚	医	矢	知
ENCLOSURE R 22	TO HEAL, TO CURE	ARROW	TO KNOW, TELL, TO INFORM J 112

RAD 22 STROKE 7 JME 345

医

POINTING HORN
GUIDING FEATHERS, FINS
NOCK
TAIL FEATHER

N763
i1
M2978
yī
to heal
to heal
a doctor

Sexy Laughing Stories of Old Japan   A. Dykstra
The acupuncturer heals or cures by tapping a needle through the skin and into the flesh, using a light mallet. The treatment is used particularly for rheumatism, sprains, and swellings in the joints. During the Sung Dynasty (A.D. 960-1279), copper manikins were made by order of the Throne and marked to illustrate the use of the needles and the relationship of the body surface to internal discomfort. Acupuncture was introduced into Europe in the seventeenth century by the Dutch surgeon, Ten Rhyne, and has recently been given considerable attention.

I, (TO ENTRUST WITH).
THE WOMAN 女 IS ENTRUSTED 委 WITH RICE 禾.

知	禾	委	女
HARMONY, PEACE, CALM, TO PACIFY J 338	RICE, GRAIN R 115	TO ENTRUST	WOMAN, GIRL, FEMALE J 32

RAD 115 STROKE 8 JME 346

委

N3267
wei3
M7098
wěi
depute
send
put in charge

347

JME 347　STROKE 8　RAD 130　IKU; SODATERU, TO BRING UP, TO RAISE, TO EDUCATE.

NEONATE OR NEW-BORN CHILD 厶 IS BROUGHT UP, RAISED, EDUCATED 育 TO A BODY 月.

N296
yu4
M7687
yù
give birth
nourish
bring up

方　子　厶　育　　　月

DIRECTION, WAY, SQUARE, PERSON, SIDE J 138　　CHILD J 31　　NEONATE (INVERTED CHILD)　　TO BRING UP, EDUCATE, RAISE　　BODY, MOON

PICTURE OF DIRECTION, COCOON & HEAD

JME 348　STROKE 6　RAD 26　IN, SEAL, STAMP; SHIRUSHI, (JIRUSHI), SIGN, SYMBOL, TRACE.

THE SEAL 卩 IS RAISED ON A STICK, CANE ノ . A ANIMAL CLAW 爪 , MIRROR-IMAGE OF THE HUMAN HAND ヨ , SUGGESTS THE BLOOD-RED COLOR AND PRESSING DOWN.

N102
yin4
M7451
yìn
print
stamp
seal
mark

ヨ　　　　　　印　　　卩

HAND, PIG'S HEAD R 58　　BEAST'S CLAW　　SEAL, STAMP, SIGN, TRACE, SYMBOL　　SEAL R 26

In Memoriam: Nature, red in tooth and claw.　Tennyson

　　　　Sohrab and Rustum
I tell thee, prick'd upon this arm I bear
That seal which Rustum to my mother gave...
And show'd a sign in faint vermilion points prick'd
So delicately prick'd the sign appeared
On Sohrab's arm, the sign of Rustum's seal.　Matthew Arnold

IN, (MEMBER, ONE IN CHARGE, OFFICIAL).

THE MOUTH 口 THAT HAS THE SEA SHELLS 貝 (COWRIE MONEY) IS THE MEMBER, ONE IN CHARGE, THE OFFICIAL 員.

RAD 30 STROKE 10 JME 349

口 — MOUTH J 27
員 — MEMBER, ONE IN CHARGE, OFFICIAL
貝 — SEA SHELL, COWRIE J 169
負 — TO DEFEAT, INDEBTED J 312

N928 yuan2
M7721 yuán
an official

A mollusc is a cheap edition of a man.   Ralph Waldo Emerson

The Chambered Nautilus   Oliver Wendell Holmes
Till thou at length art free,
Leaving thy outgrown shell by life's unresting sea.

IN, (TEMPLE, ACADEMY, BOARD), SUFFIX FOR INSTITUTION.

TEMPLE, ACADEMY, BOARD, INSTITUTION 院 IS ON A MOUND 阝 AND UNDER A ROOF 宀, AND IS THE BEGINNING, FOUNDATION, ORIGIN 元 (OF SOCIETY).

RAD 170 STROKE 10 JME 350

阝 — MOUND, HILL R 170
院 — TEMPLE, ACADEMY, BOARD
元 — BEGINNING, FOUNDATION, ORIGIN J 68
宀 — ROOF R 40

N4991 yuan
M7712 yuàn
courtyard
hall
college
public bldg.

351

JME	Stroke	Rad
351	12	184

飲

N5159
yin3
M7454
yǐn
to drink
swallow

IN; NOMU, TO DRINK.
ONE DRINKS 飲 THE FOOD 食 THAT ENTERS 入 THE WRAPPER 勹 (THE BODY) BY SIPPING THE LACKING 欠 NEXT 次 BREATH 欠 AS IN SINGING 哥欠.

食 飲 欠 歌

FOOD, TO EAT — TO DRINK — LACK, GAP — SINGING, SONG
J 253 — — J 597 — J 166

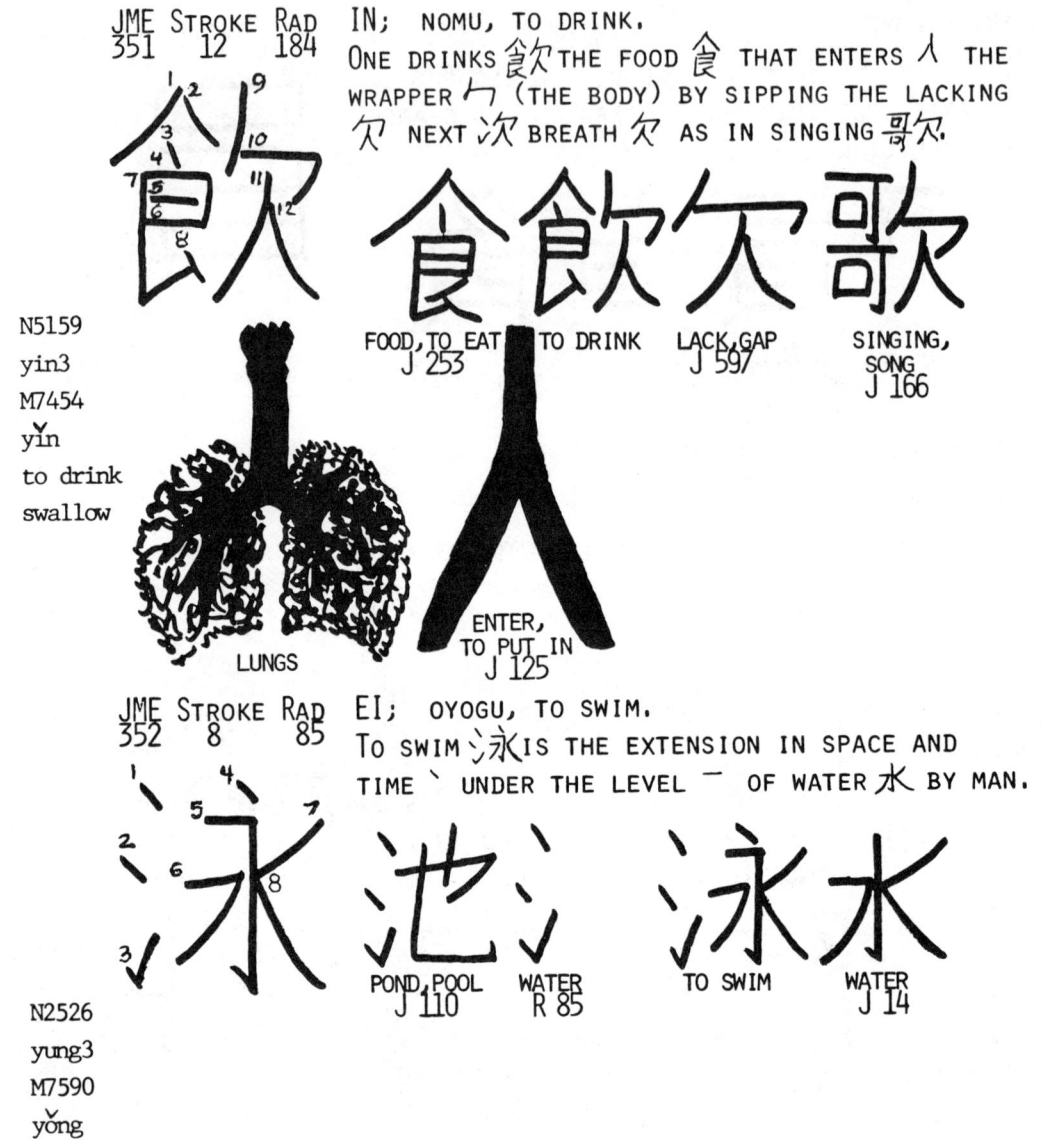

LUNGS

入

ENTER, TO PUT IN
J 125

JME	Stroke	Rad
352	8	85

泳

N2526
yung3
M7590
yǒng
to dive

EI; OYOGU, TO SWIM.
TO SWIM 泳 IS THE EXTENSION IN SPACE AND TIME ` UNDER THE LEVEL 一 OF WATER 水 BY MAN.

泳 池 泳 水

POND, POOL — WATER — TO SWIM — WATER
J 110 — R 85 — — J 14

353

EI, (ENGLAND, EXCELLENT).
A MAN 人 IN THE CENTER 夬 OF A GREAT 大
SPACE 冂 WITH GRASS 艹 IS IN EXCELLENT 英
(NOMADIC POSITION) LIKE ENGLAND (POLITICALLY)

RAD 140 STROKE 8 JME 353

英

N3927
ying 1
M7489
yīng
brave
heroic

艹 英 夬 中
GRASS EXCELLENT, CENTER, MIDDLE,
R 140 ENGLAND   MIDDLE   CENTER
              J 554   J 23

Excellent England!
Saints Andrew and George;
Middle central land
Holds line and the gorge.
          Victoriana   A.D.

EN; SHIO, SALT.
SALT 塩 SHOWS MAN 𠂉 ON EARTH 土 WITH MOUTH 口
TO DISH 皿 OF SALT 塩. DISH EVAPORATES
WATER FROM BRINE TO OBTAIN SALT.

RAD 32 STROKE 13 JME 354

塩

N1125
yen2
M7352
yán
salt
brine

土 塩 𠂉 口 皿 温
EARTH,SOIL SALT PERSON, MOUTH DISH WARM
J 17 J 354   MAN,   J 27   R 108 J 162
              MANKIND
              R 9

355

JME 355* Stroke 15 Rad 75 O; YOKO, THE SIDE, WIDTH.
THE TREE 木 IS ON ITS SIDE 横 FOR THE WIDTH 横 (OF A CROSSING) BY A TIGER 寅 AND MEN 廿.

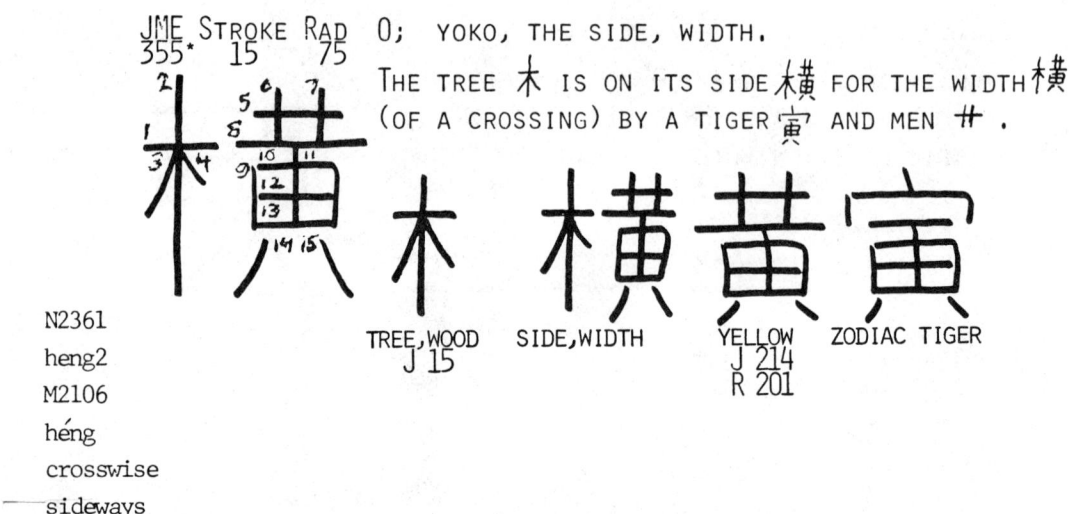

TREE, WOOD J 15
SIDE, WIDTH
YELLOW J 214 R 201
ZODIAC TIGER

N2361
heng2
M2106
héng
crosswise
sideways
horizontal

JME 356 Stroke 5 Rad 19 KA; KUWAERU, TO ADD, TO JOIN, TO INCREASE, T.V. KUWAWARU, TO JOIN IN, TO INCREASE, I.V.
THE MOUTH 口 OF STRENGTH, POWER 力 (CALLS TO OTHERS) TO ADD, TO JOIN, TO INCREASE 加.

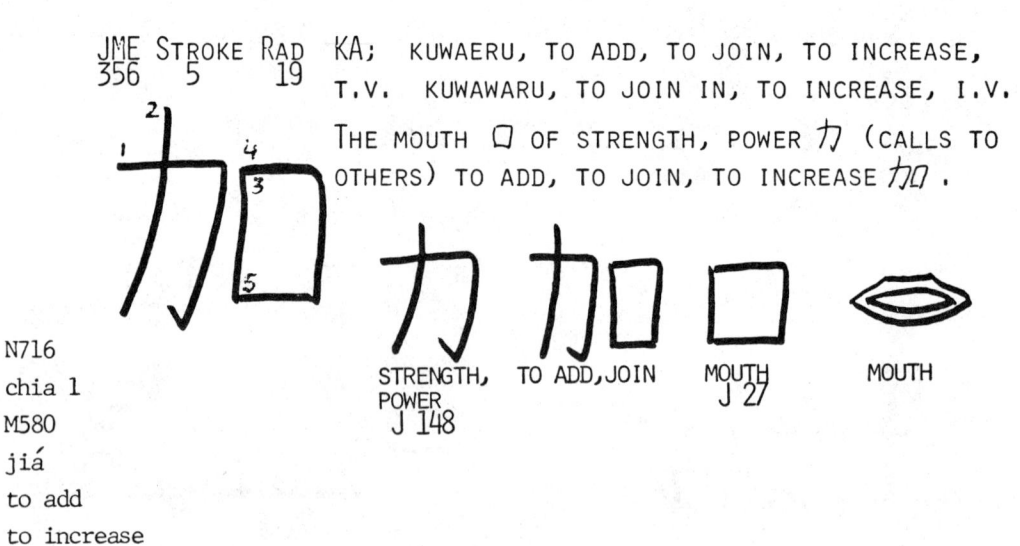

STRENGTH, POWER J 148
TO ADD, JOIN
MOUTH J 27
MOUTH

N716
chia 1
M580
jiá
to add
to increase

*Illustrated on facing page

355 X

A STRONG RESEMBLANCE TO THE KANJI FOR TREE IS SHOWN BY THE "WALKING TREE" OF HAWAII WITH ITS SPREADING AERIAL ROOTS AND SOMETIMES LATERAL BRANCHES. THE HAWAIIAN NAME IS HALA AND ITS BOTANIC NAME IS PANDANUS ODOPATISSIMUS.

357

KA, (TREASURE, GOODS).
TREASURE, GOODS 貨 LIKE SEA SHELLS 貝 (COWRIE) ARE CHANGED, TRANSFORMED 化 (BY BARTER).

RAD 154 STROKE 11 JME 357

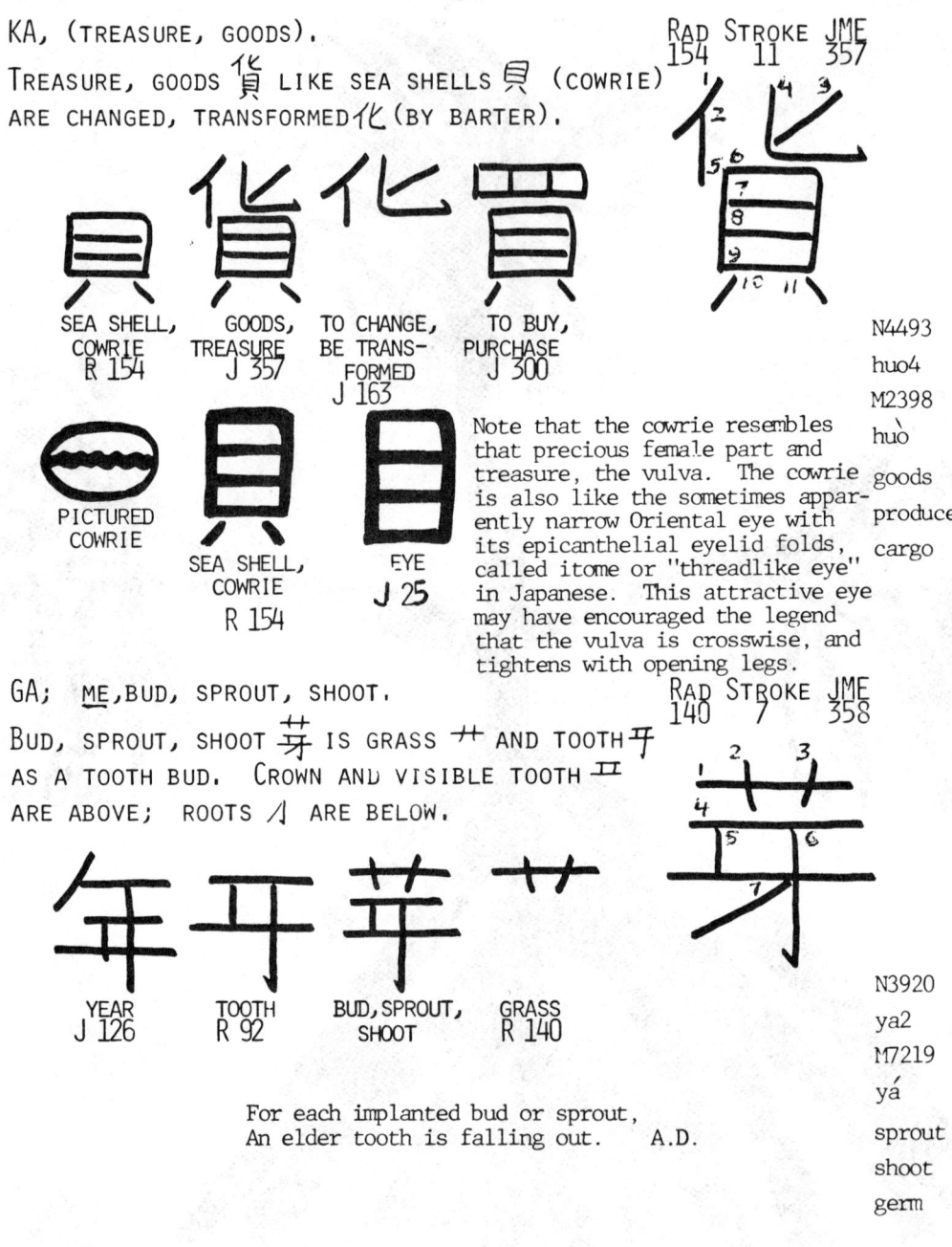

貝	貨	化	買
SEA SHELL, COWRIE R 154	GOODS, TREASURE J 357	TO CHANGE, BE TRANSFORMED J 163	TO BUY, PURCHASE J 300

N4493
huo4
M2398
huò
goods
produce
cargo

SEA SHELL, COWRIE R 154 — EYE J 25

Note that the cowrie resembles that precious female part and treasure, the vulva. The cowrie is also like the sometimes apparently narrow Oriental eye with its epicanthelial eyelid folds, called itome or "threadlike eye" in Japanese. This attractive eye may have encouraged the legend that the vulva is crosswise, and tightens with opening legs.

GA; ME, BUD, SPROUT, SHOOT.
BUD, SPROUT, SHOOT 芽 IS GRASS 艹 AND TOOTH 牙 AS A TOOTH BUD. CROWN AND VISIBLE TOOTH 丅 ARE ABOVE; ROOTS 丿 ARE BELOW.

RAD 140 STROKE 7 JME 358

年	牙	芽	艹
YEAR J 126	TOOTH R 92	BUD, SPROUT, SHOOT	GRASS R 140

N3920
ya2
M7219
yá
sprout
shoot
germ

For each implanted bud or sprout,
An elder tooth is falling out.   A.D.

JME 359   Stroke 7   Rad 49

KAI; ARATAMERU, TO CHANGE, TO REFORM, TO REVISE; ARATAMARU, TO BE REFORMED.

TO CHANGE, TO REFORM, TO REVISE 改 IS THE ZODIAC SERPENT 己 WHICH SHEDS OR MOULTS IN CHANGING, AND THE PERSON OR HAND 又 WITH THE STICK ノ FOR CHANGE, REFORMATION, REVISION 改

Don Quixote   Cervantes
Even a worm, when trod upon, will turn again.

N1464
kai3
M3196
gǎi
to alter
correct
to change
reform
repent

色 COLOR J 94
己 ZODIAC SNAKE
改 TO CHANGE, TO REFORM, TO REVISE, REFORMATION, REVISION
攵 (HAND OR BODY WITH STICK)

First Inaugural Address   Lincoln
This country, with its institutions, belongs to the people who inhabit it. Whenever they shall grow weary of the existing government, they can exercise their constitutional rights of amending it, or their revolutionary right to dismember or overthrow it.

JME 360   Stroke 11   Rad 75

KAI, (SHACKLES).

SHACKLES 械 SHACKLE THE HANDS 廾 TO THE TREE, WOOD 木 AND TO THE SPEAR 戈.

Captives, especially in the Arab north African slave traffic, often had their collaring neck irons chained to the same log which they carried as a collective burden which prevented their separate escape. Spears could also be placed on both sides of the captives' necks and utilized as stocks similar to those for hands and feet.   A.D.

N2264
hsieh4
M2538
xiè
weapons
fetter
imple-
ments

算 CALCULATION, RECKONING J 219
木 TREE, WOOD J 15
VEHICLE J 88 (TURNED 90°)
械 HANDS
戈 SHACKLES
SPEAR R 62
PICTURE OF SPEAR & THROWING ARM

361

KAI (GAI), STOREY, FLOOR, STAIR.

THE STORIES, FLOORS, STAIRS 階 ARE ALL 皆 COMPARABLE 比, AND RISE AS IF ON A MOUND 阝.

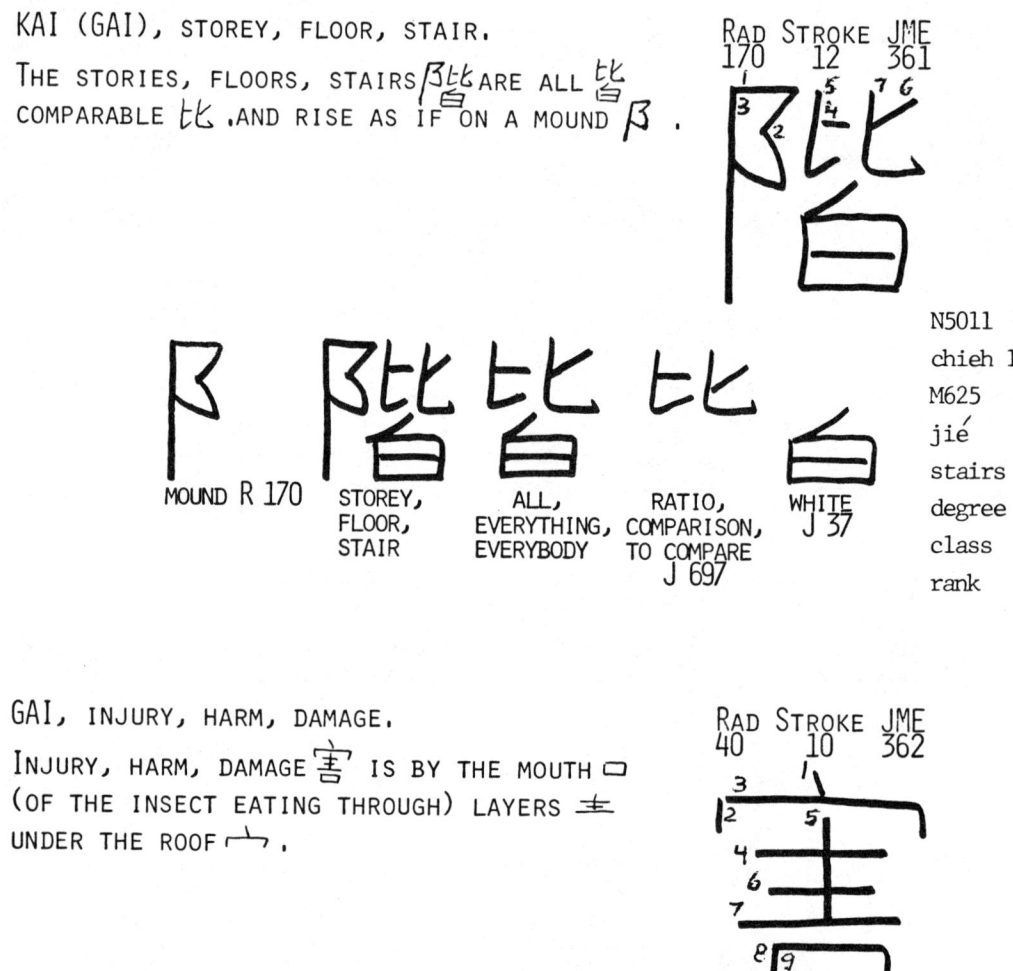

RAD 170 STROKE 12 JME 361

N5011
chieh 1
M625
jié
stairs
degree
class
rank

阝 MOUND R 170   階 STOREY, FLOOR, STAIR   皆 ALL, EVERYTHING, EVERYBODY   比 RATIO, COMPARISON, TO COMPARE J 697   白 WHITE J 37

GAI, INJURY, HARM, DAMAGE.

INJURY, HARM, DAMAGE 害 IS BY THE MOUTH 口 (OF THE INSECT EATING THROUGH) LAYERS 圭 UNDER THE ROOF 宀.

RAD 40 STROKE 10 JME 362

N1306
hai4
M2015
hài
injure
destroy
injury
suffer

青 BLUE, GREEN J 36   宀 ROOF J 40   害 INJURY, HARM, DAMAGE   三 THREE J 3 (LAYERS)   丨 (UP OR DOWN MOVEMENT) R 2   口 MOUTH R 27

363

JME 363 Stroke 12 Rad 147

KAKU; OBOERU, REMEMBER, MEMORIZE, LEARN. THE EYE 目 WHICH SEES, LOOKS 見 REMEMBERS, MEMORIZES, LEARNS 覚, WEARING THE CAP OF KNOWLEDGE 冖, AND BEARING THE BURDEN ⿱ OF LEARNING 学.

N4288 chuo3
M1178 jiào
perceive
be concious of

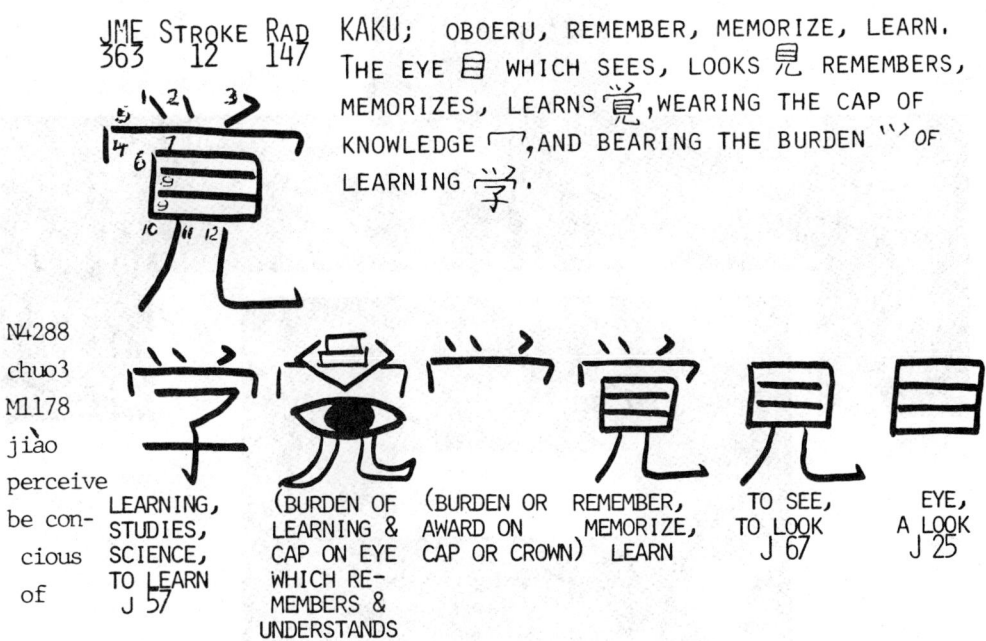

LEARNING, STUDIES, SCIENCE, TO LEARN J 57
(BURDEN OF LEARNING & CAP ON EYE WHICH REMEMBERS & UNDERSTANDS)
(BURDEN OR AWARD ON CAP OR CROWN)
REMEMBER, MEMORIZE, LEARN
TO SEE, TO LOOK J 67
EYE, A LOOK J 25

JME 364* Stroke 8 Rad 40

KAN, GOVERNMENT, GOVERNMENT POSITION. THE GOVERNMENT AND GOVERNMENT POSITIONS 官 ARE IN THE TWO- OR MULTI-STORIED BUILDINGS 呂 UNDER THE ROOF 宀.

...the keepers of the house shall tremble, and the strong men shall bow themselves, and the grinders shall cease because they are few, and those that look out of the window shall be darkened. Song of Solomon

(Body and building are analogous).

N1295 kuan 1
M3552 guān
mandarin
official
public

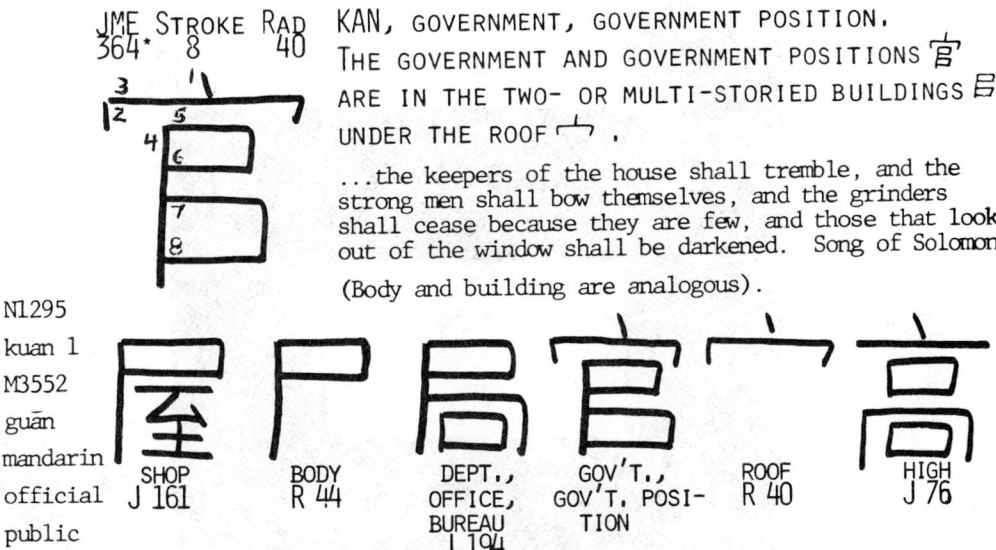

SHOP J 161
BODY R 44
DEPT., OFFICE, BUREAU J 194
GOV'T., GOV'T. POSITION
ROOF R 40
HIGH J 76

Tao Te Ching
Cut out the doors and cut out the windows
As you construct a building;
The building's use depends on space,
The space that is the emptiness within the walls.

*Illustrated on following page

364x

365

KAN; SEKI, BARRIER.
THE BARRIER 関 IS OF GATES 門 WITH A LARGE 大 BAR 一 (BLOCKING THE WAY) LIKE A RAM 丷.

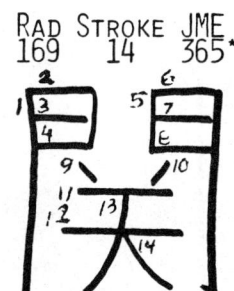

RAD 169 STROKE 14 JME 365*

N4950
kuan 1
M3571
guān
customs hse.
suburb

    Get Up and Bar the Door
They made a paction between them twa,
    They made it firm and sure,
That the first word whaeer should speak
    Should rise and bar the door.

GOAT'S HORNS (R 123) | ONE R 1 (BAR) | LARGE, BIG, GREAT J 22 | BARRIER | GATE J 143 | TO OPEN J 171

KAN, BUILDING, HALL.
IN A GOVERNMENT POSITION, GOVERNMENT 官 FOOD 食 IS EATEN 食 IN A BUILDING OR HALL 食官.

RAD 184 STROKE 16 JME 366*

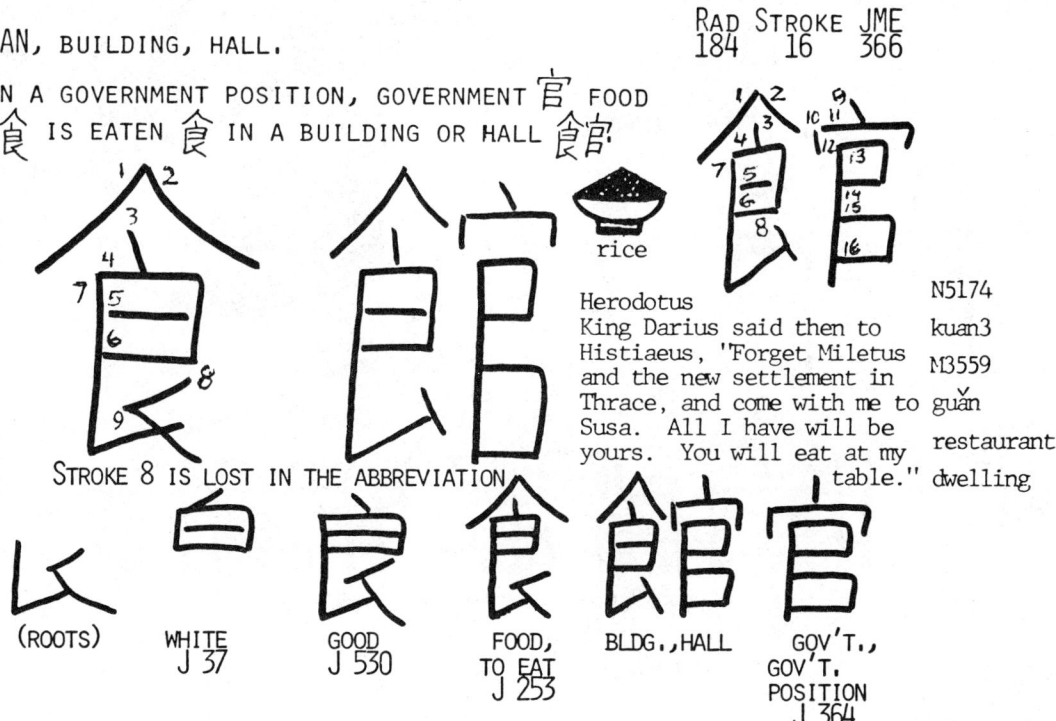

STROKE 8 IS LOST IN THE ABBREVIATION

Herodotus
King Darius said then to Histiaeus, "Forget Miletus and the new settlement in Thrace, and come with me to Susa. All I have will be yours. You will eat at my table."

N5174
kuan3
M3559
guǎn
restaurant
dwelling

(ROOTS) | WHITE J 37 | GOOD J 530 | FOOD, TO EAT J 253 | BLDG., HALL | GOV'T., GOV'T. POSITION J 364

*Illustrated on following page

365 X

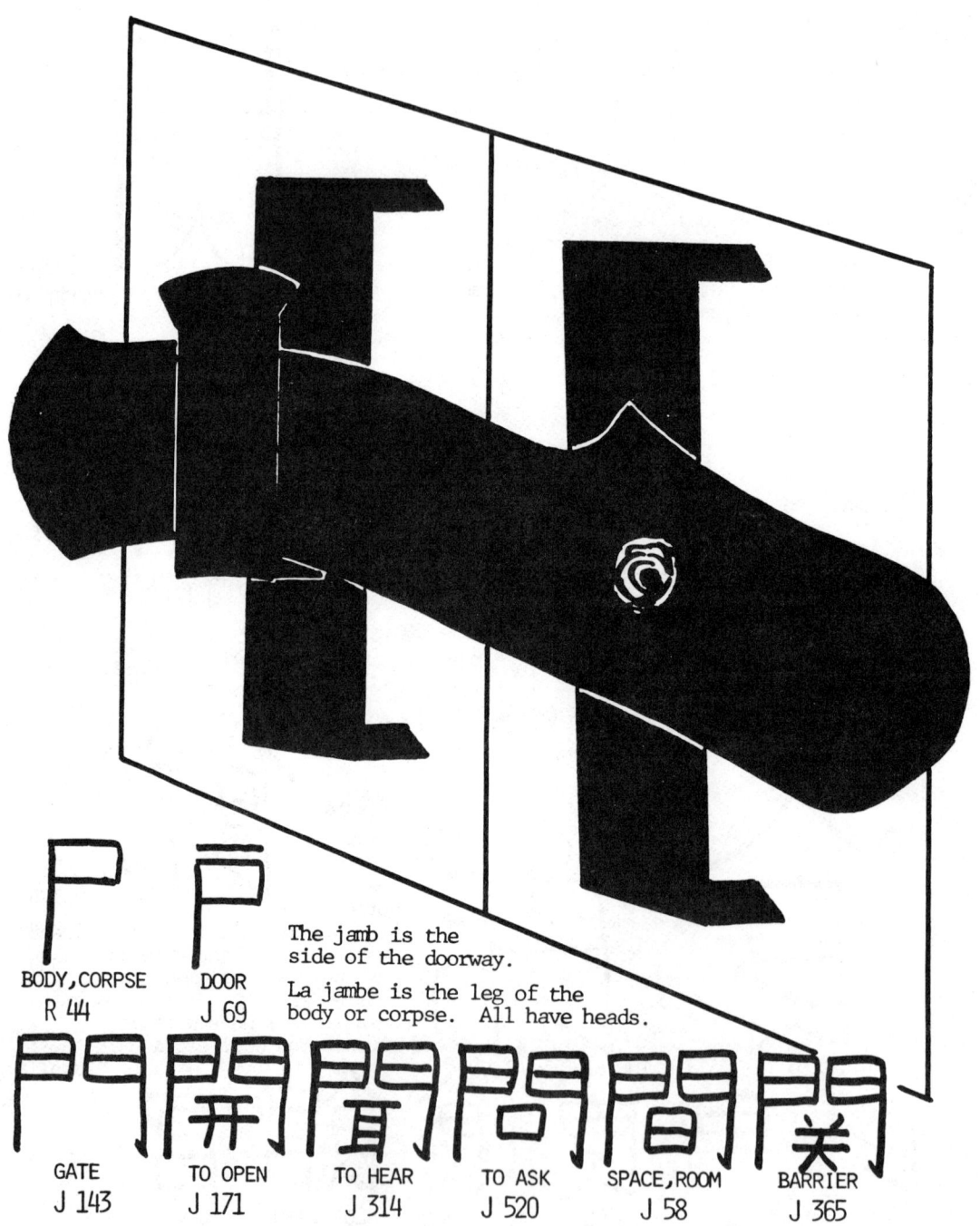

尸 BODY, CORPSE R 44

户 DOOR J 69

The jamb is the side of the doorway. La jambe is the leg of the body or corpse. All have heads.

門 GATE J 143

开 TO OPEN J 171

聞 TO HEAR J 314

問 TO ASK J 520

間 SPACE, ROOM J 58

关 BARRIER J 365

JME Stroke Rad
367* 18 147

觀

N4296
kuan 1
M3575
guān
gaze at
behold

KAN, (LOOK, APPEARANCE, VIEW, CONTEMPLATE).
THE SHORT-TAILED HERON HAS THE LOOK AND APPEARANCE OF VIEWING, CONTEMPLATING 觀 AS HE SEES, LOOKS 見 OVER THE WATER LEVEL 一 (READY TO STRIKE WITH HIS BEAK LIKE A BAMBOO SPIKE ケ

The Nilotenstellung is a one-legged stance usually of herons and male natives. This position is seen in many parts of the world, including the Upper Nile and Melanesia. The heron's bill is like a dagger and he may watch several hours before his lightning thrust.

The Haunted House: The moping heron, motionless and stiff,
That on a stone, as silently and stilly,
Stood, an apparent sentinel, as if
To guard the water-lily.   Thomas Hood

竹   ケ   ナ   隹   觀   見
BAMBOO (SINGLE,   HAND   SHORT-   LOOK,   TO SEE,
J 113   BAMBOO AS   TAILED   APPEARANCE, TO LOOK
        A SPIKE   BIRD   VIEW,   J 67
        OR STAKE)   R 172   CONTEMPLATE

JME Stroke Rad
368 19   181

願

N255
yuan4
M7729
yuàn
wish
desire

GAN; NEGAI, WISH, PETITION, REQUEST;
NEGAU, TO ASK, TO REQUEST, TO WISH, TO BEG.
THE HEAD 頁 OF THE ORIGIN, FIELD, MEADOW 原 IS ASKED, REQUESTED, BEGGED 願 AS BY A PETITION 願 FOR A LITTLE 小 WHITE 白 (SPRING WATER) FROM THE CLIFF 厂.

厂   原   願   頁   頁
CLIFF R 27 ORIGIN,   WISH,   HEAD, TOP, HEAD R 181 PICTURE
白   FIELD,   PETITION,   BRAIN   OF HEAD
WHITE J 37 MEADOW   REQUEST, BEG J 294
小   J 25
LITTLE,
SMALL J 24
(STREAM)

*Illustrated on following page

367X

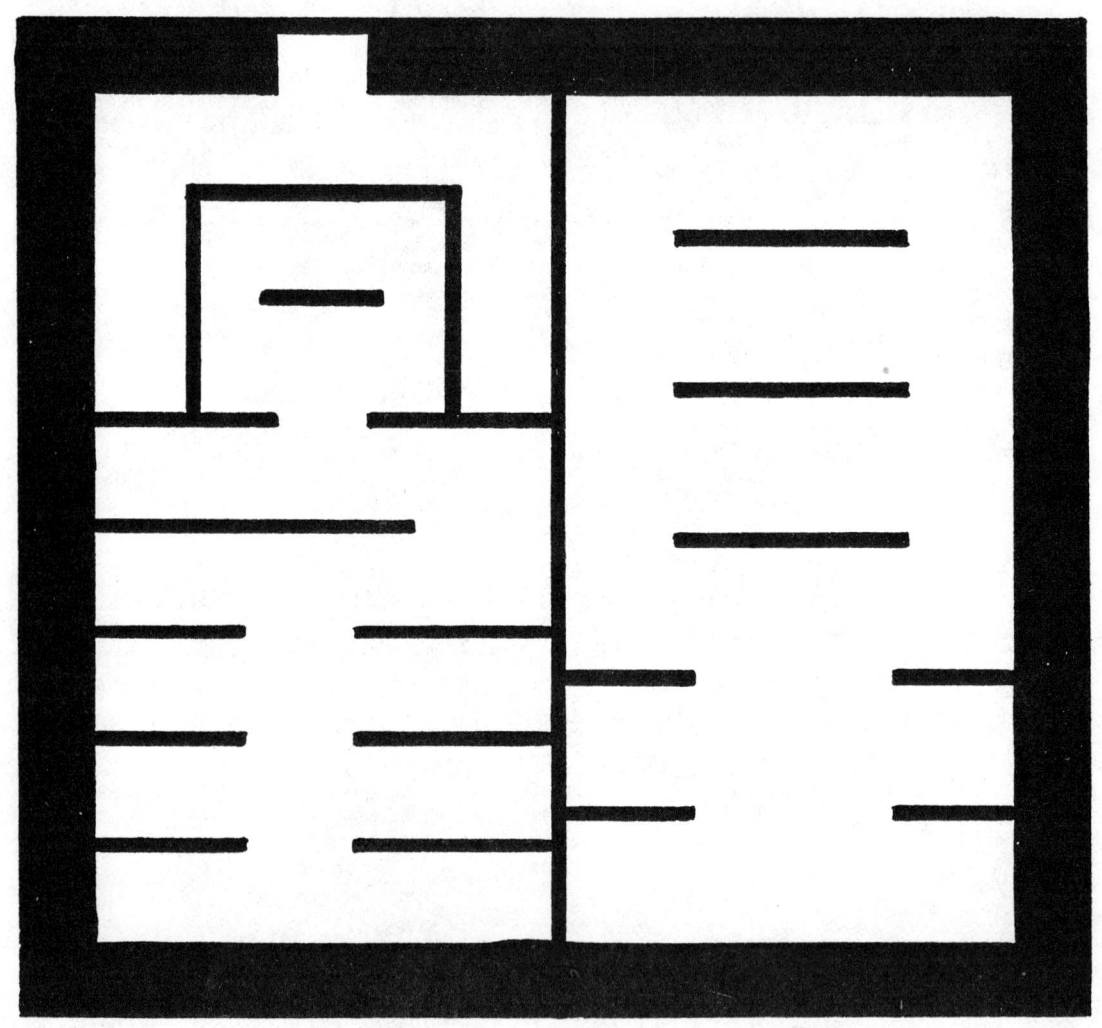

A STYLIZED SYMMETRICAL FORM OF THE KANJI J 367

367X

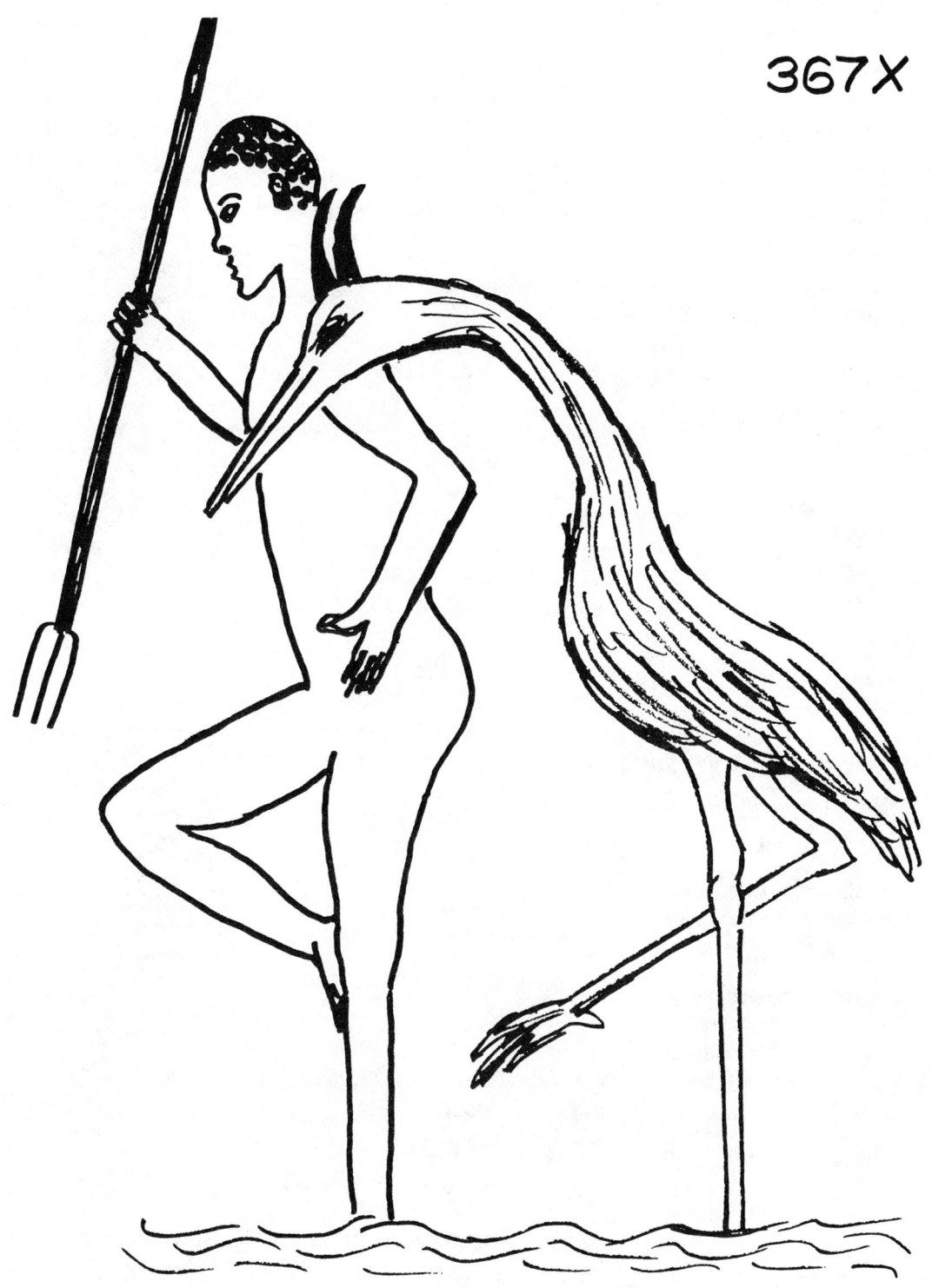

The Heron, Crane, etc. Looks, Views, Contemplates while Fishing

369

KI, SEASON.

SEASON 季 IS THE CHILD 子 IN THE RICE 禾 CROP. THE SEASON IS HARVEST TIME, AND THE GRAIN IS THE HEIGHT OF A CHILD.

Knee-high to a grasshopper is probably the American colloquial equivalent.

        Grain in season:
        Knee-high, a son.   A.D.

The corn is as high as an elephant's eye.   Oklahoma

RAD 115 STROKE 8 JME 369

N3266
chi4
M435
jì
tender
young
yngst. bro.

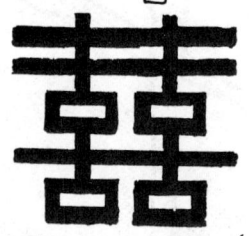

| RICE PICTURED | RICE, GRAIN R 115 | SEASON | CHILD J 31 |

KI; YOROKOBI, HAPPY EVENT, JOY, CONGRATULATIONS YOROKOBU, TO REJOICE, TO BE GLAD.

JOY, HAPPY EVENT, CONGRATULATIONS, TO REJOICE, TO BE GLAD 喜 WITH THE MOUTH 口 OF THE DRUM 鼓

RAD 30 STROKE 12 JME 370*

        Don Juan
        All who joy would win
        Must show it, --
        happiness was born a twin.
            Lord Byron

N1115
hsi3
M2434
xǐ
pleasure
joy
pleased w/

HAPPINESS SYMBOL (IS THE KANJI STYLIZED AND TWINNED).

MAN J 410
MOUTH R 30

PICTURE OF THE GOOD LUCK, GOOD OMEN (AS FROM AN ORACLE)

GOOD LUCK, GOOD OMEN

HAPPY EVENT, JOY, CONGRATULATIONS

(FLUTE OF REED OR OF GRASS)

MOUTH R 30

*Illustrated on facing page

370X

371

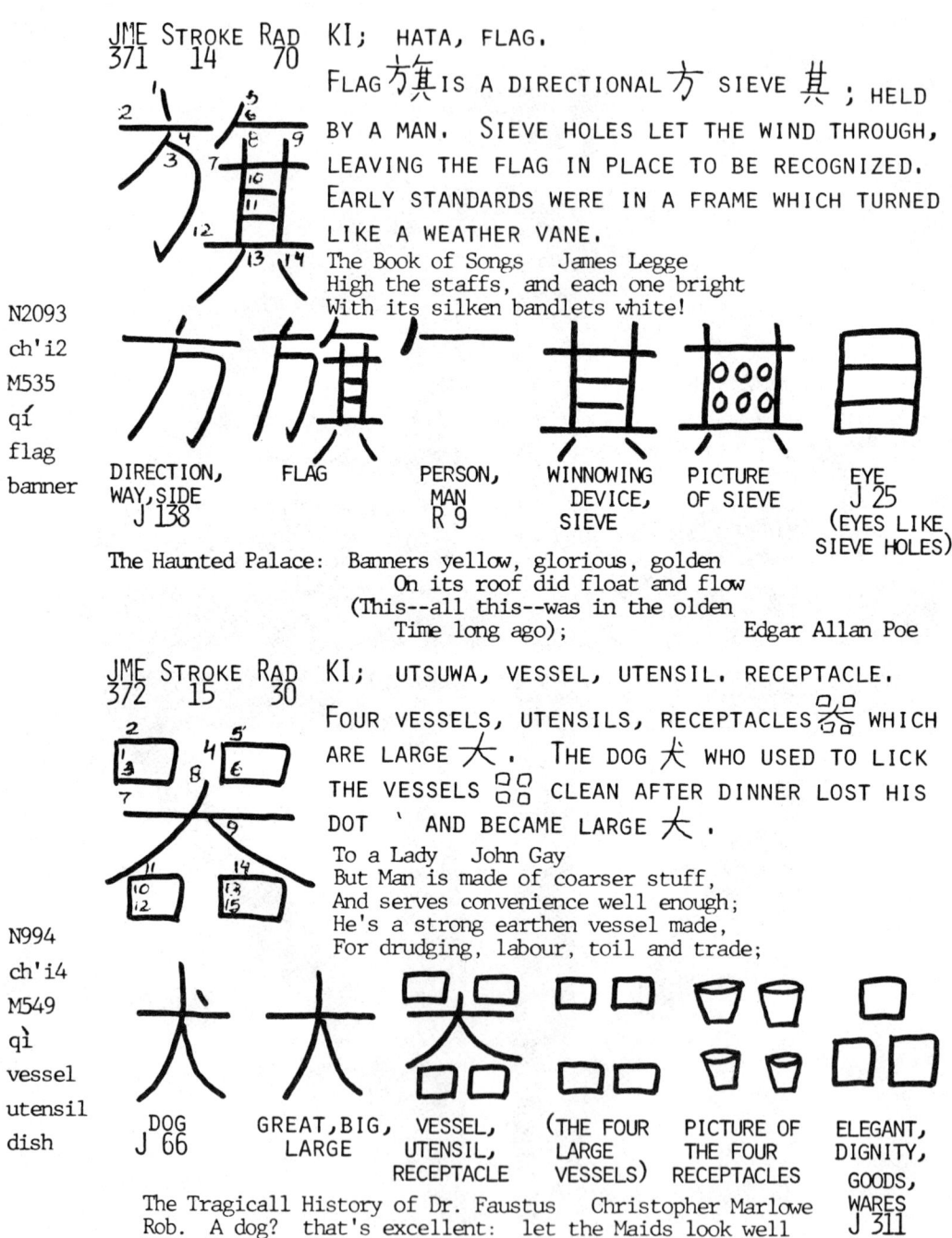

JME	Stroke	Rad
371	14	70

KI; HATA, FLAG.

FLAG 旗 IS A DIRECTIONAL 方 SIEVE 其; HELD BY A MAN. SIEVE HOLES LET THE WIND THROUGH, LEAVING THE FLAG IN PLACE TO BE RECOGNIZED. EARLY STANDARDS WERE IN A FRAME WHICH TURNED LIKE A WEATHER VANE.

The Book of Songs   James Legge
High the staffs, and each one bright
With its silken bandlets white!

N2093
ch'i2
M535
qí
flag
banner

方	旗	亻	其	其	目
DIRECTION, WAY, SIDE J 138	FLAG	PERSON, MAN R 9	WINNOWING DEVICE, SIEVE	PICTURE OF SIEVE	EYE J 25 (EYES LIKE SIEVE HOLES)

The Haunted Palace: Banners yellow, glorious, golden
                     On its roof did float and flow
                    (This--all this--was in the olden
                         Time long ago);   Edgar Allan Poe

JME	Stroke	Rad
372	15	30

KI; UTSUWA, VESSEL, UTENSIL. RECEPTACLE.

FOUR VESSELS, UTENSILS, RECEPTACLES 品 WHICH ARE LARGE 大. THE DOG 犬 WHO USED TO LICK THE VESSELS 品 CLEAN AFTER DINNER LOST HIS DOT ` AND BECAME LARGE 大.

To a Lady   John Gay
But Man is made of coarser stuff,
And serves convenience well enough;
He's a strong earthen vessel made,
For drudging, labour, toil and trade;

N994
ch'i4
M549
qì
vessel
utensil
dish

犬	大	器	□□ □□	□□ □□	品
DOG J 66	GREAT, BIG, LARGE	VESSEL, UTENSIL, RECEPTACLE	(THE FOUR LARGE VESSELS)	PICTURE OF THE FOUR RECEPTACLES	ELEGANT, DIGNITY, GOODS, WARES J 311

The Tragicall History of Dr. Faustus   Christopher Marlowe
Rob. A dog? that's excellent: let the Maids look well
to their porridge-pots, for I'le into the Kitchin presently.

373

KI; HATA, LOOM.

THE LOOM 機 IS THE WOOD 木 (OF THE LOOM), THE THREADS 幺幺 (ABBREVIATED), AND A PERSON 人 (OPERATING) WITH A LANCE 戈 (TO ROLL THE CLOTH)

...pin to which the cloth was fixed... Judges
...beam to which the warp was attached... II Samuel

RAD	STROKE	JME
75	16	373*

N2379
chi 1
M411
jī
changes
motions
mechanism

栈戈	木	機	人	幺幺	戈
SHACKLES J 360	TREE, WOOD J 15	LOOM	PERSON, MAN J 30	THREADS (DOUBLED) (OF COCOONS) SMALL R 52	SPEAR R 62

KYŪ, GŪ, KU; MIYA, SHRINE, PRINCE OF THE BLOOD, PALACE.

SHRINE, PALACE, PRINCE OF THE BLOOD 宮 IS A ROOFED 宀 TWO-STOREY BUILDING 呂. OBLIQUE LINE / CONNECTING THE STOREYS 呂 TO SHOW THE BUILDING IS MORE ORNATE. PEKING PALACES FOR PRINCES OF THE BLOOD WERE ON MOUNDS AND HAD SPECIFIED HEIGHT LIMITS ABOVE THE GROUND.

RAD	STROKE	JME
40	10	374*

N1310
kung 1
M3705
gōng
palace
temple
college
dwelling

官	宀	宮	呂	呂
GOV'T., GOV'T. POSITION J 364	ROOF R 40	SHRINE, PRINCE OF THE BLOOD, PALACE	2ND STOREY / LINK / 1ST STOREY (NOTE HOW THE BLDG. IS LIKE THE BACKBONE)	DISC SPINE DISC BACKBONE N 891

Fouvier proposed remodeling society into units called phalanges... "phalanxes" which would each have four hundred acres of land and five hundred to two thousand human beings. (Phalanges as bones in the hand are comparable to vertebrae in the kanji for backbone and palace).

Illustrated on following page

373 X

THE LOOM: THE UPRIGHTS ARE THE TREE IN THE KANJI; SPEARS CAN BE USED FOR THE HORIZONTAL RODS OR BARS; THE PERSON IN THE KANJI IS WEAVING ON THE LOOM WITH THE THREADS IN THE UPPER PART OF THE KANJI. THIS VERTICAL LOOM IS ASSOCIATED WITH WEAVERS FOR THOUSANDS OF YEARS.

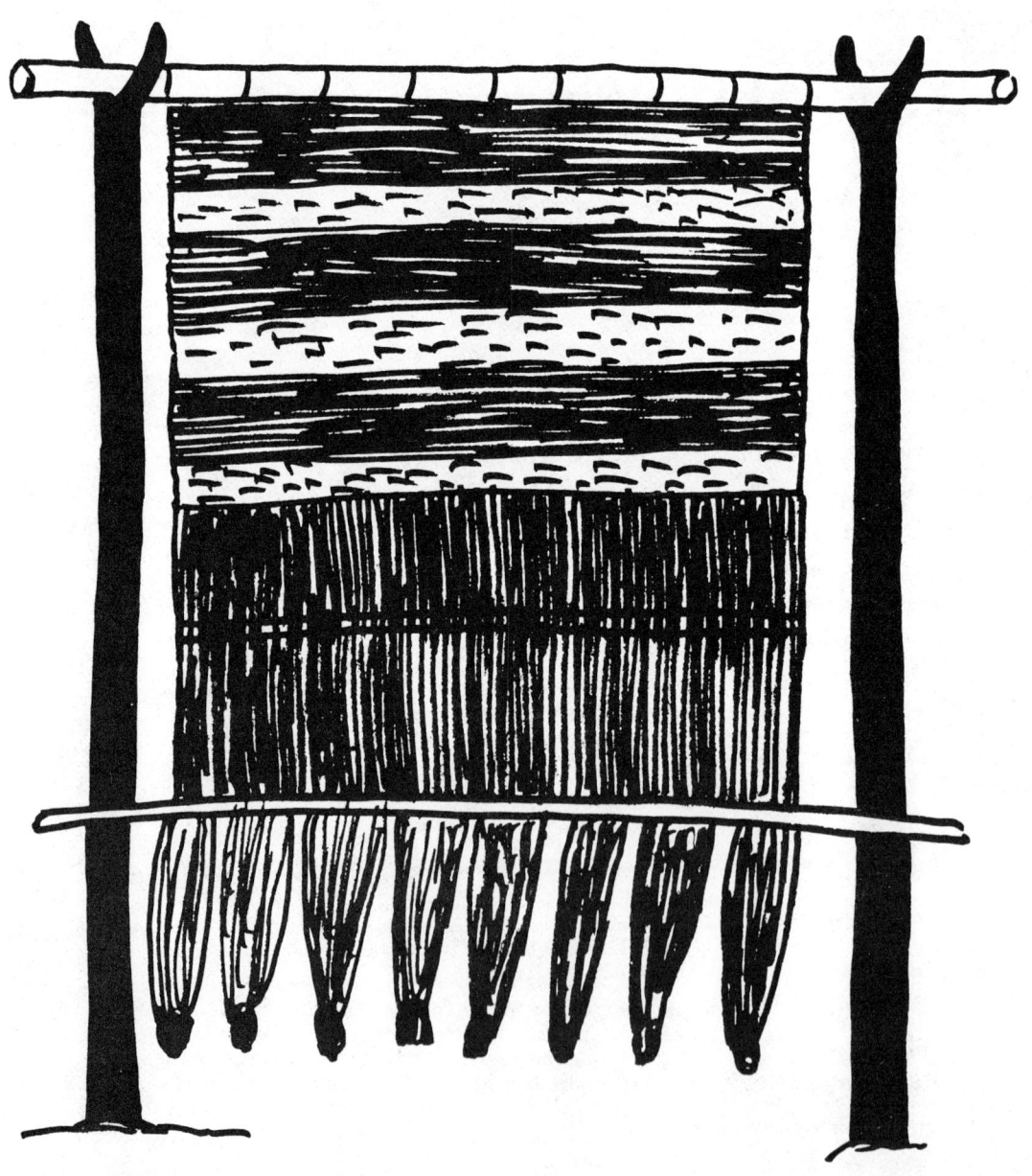

374 X

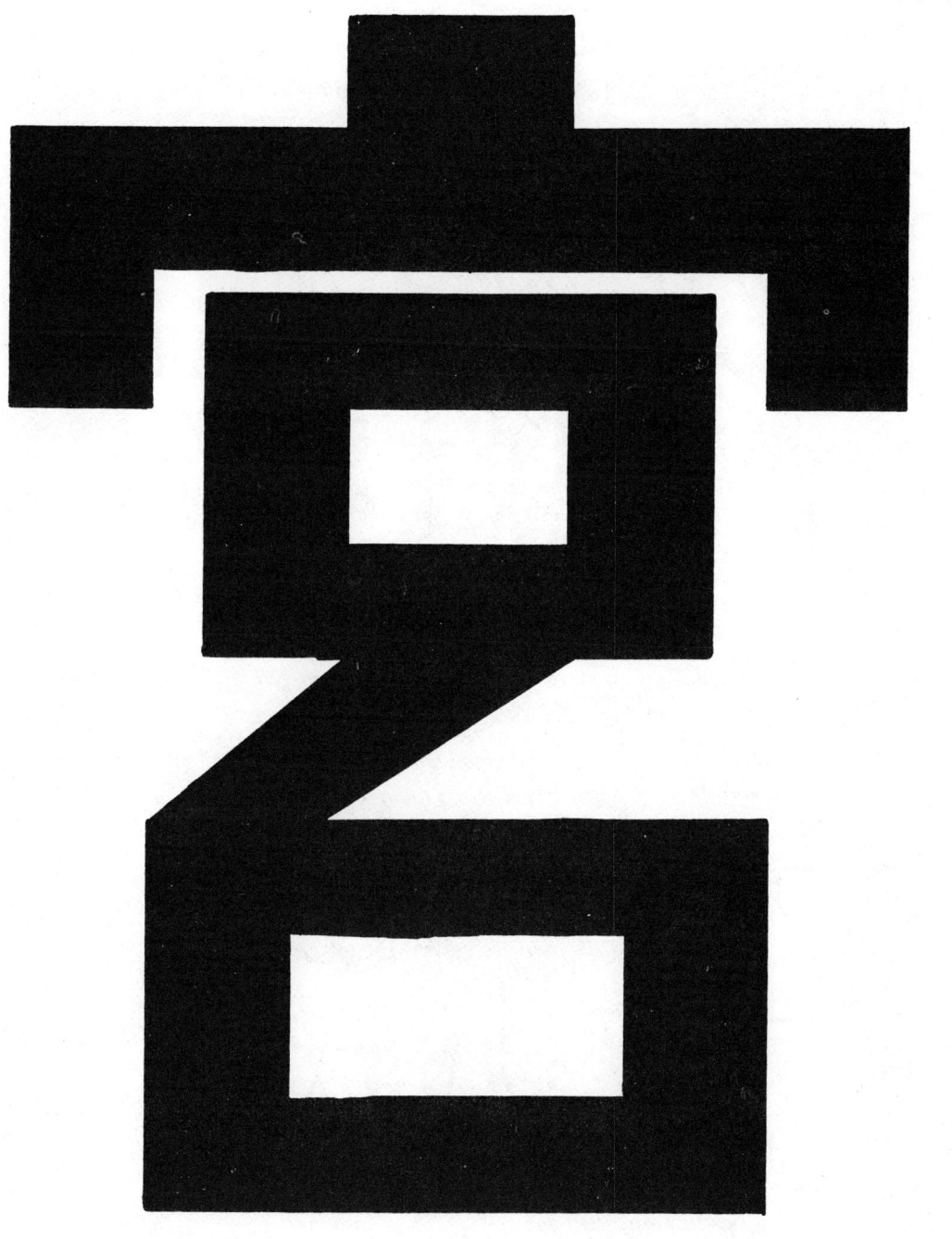

375

JME 375 Stroke 10 Rad 64

KYO, (TO CONDUCT, TO PERFORM).

IN CONDUCTING, PERFORMING 挙, THE ITEMS ⺌ ARE GIVEN BY THE HANDS 𠃌 (ABOVE) TO THE HAND 手 (BELOW), (AS FROM PODIUM TO ORCHESTRA).

> The constable with lifted hand
> Conducting the orchestral Strand
>   The Wife   Stephen Phillips

N1902 chu3
M1567 ju
to lift
raise

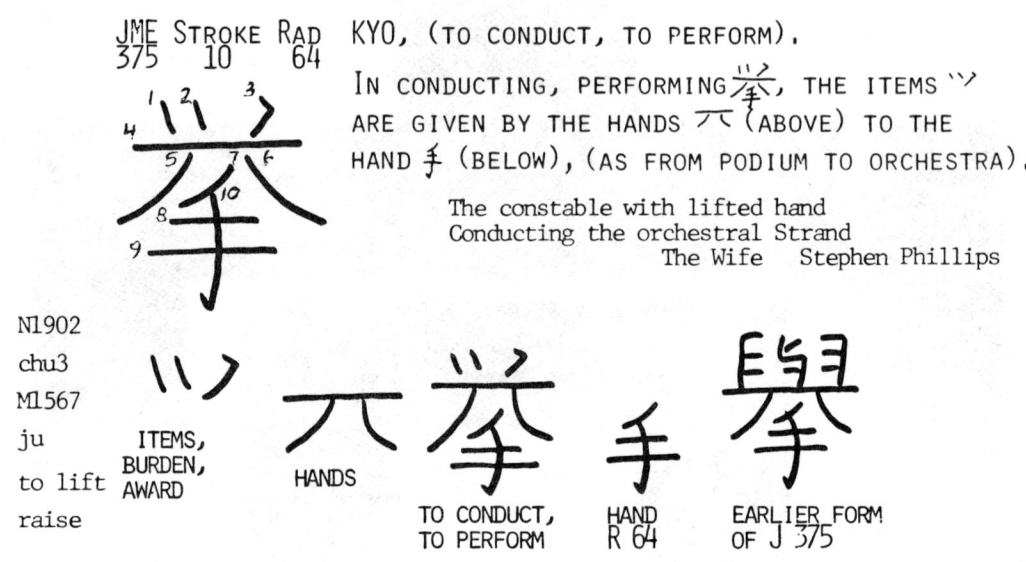

ITEMS, BURDEN, AWARD   HANDS   TO CONDUCT, TO PERFORM   HAND R 64   EARLIER FORM OF J 375

JME 376 Stroke 6 Rad 12

KYŌ; TOMO, BOTH, AS WELL AS, TOGETHER.

BOTH, AS WELL AS, TOGETHER 共 IS TWO BODIES // WITH LINKED ARMS 一 JOINED AT THE HIPS 一 AND ON TWO LEGS ハ.

Pastourelle   Anonymous
"Ye be so nice and so meet of age,
That ye greatly move my courage.
Sith I love you, love me again;
Let us make one, though we be twain."
"I pray you, sir, let me go milk my cow."

N581 kung 1
M3709 gong
all
whole
cooperate

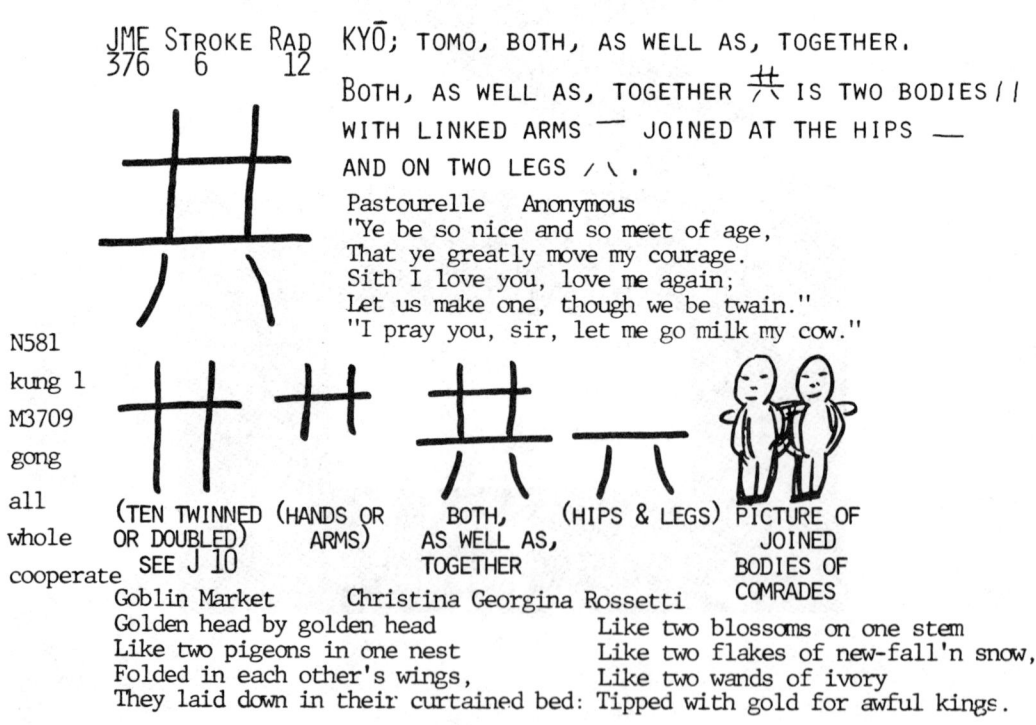

(TEN TWINNED OR DOUBLED) SEE J 10   (HANDS OR ARMS)   BOTH, AS WELL AS, TOGETHER   (HIPS & LEGS)   PICTURE OF JOINED BODIES OF COMRADES

Goblin Market   Christina Georgina Rossetti
Golden head by golden head   Like two blossoms on one stem
Like two pigeons in one nest   Like two flakes of new-fall'n snow,
Folded in each other's wings,   Like two wands of ivory
They laid down in their curtained bed: Tipped with gold for awful kings.

KYŌ, (TO BE IN HARMONY).

To be in harmony 协 is ten-tenths 十 (for completeness), and strength, power 力 tripled 力力. There is a suggestion of the dipper whose stars move in harmony 协, and of Orion's belt of three major stars.

RAD 24　STROKE 8　JME 377

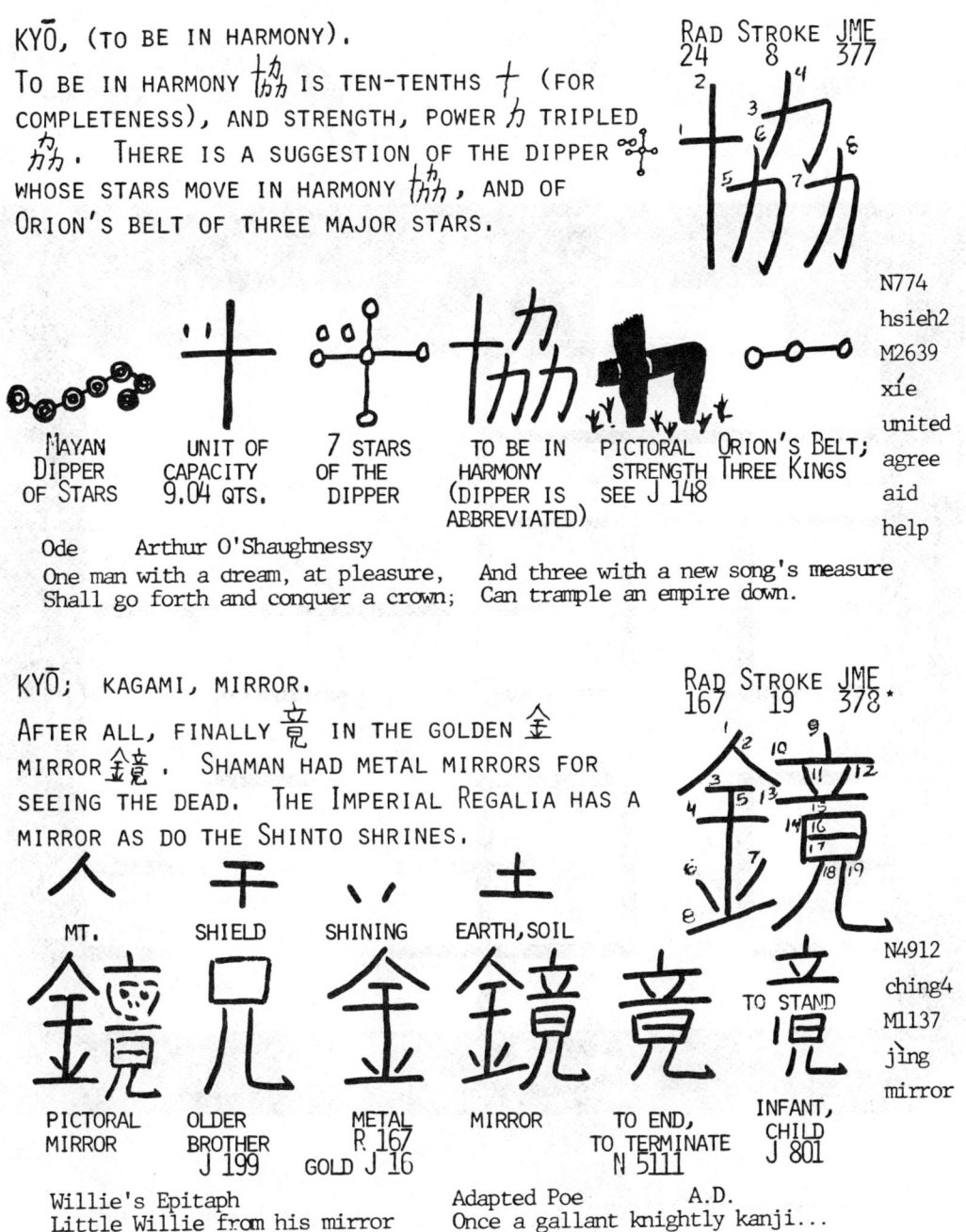

N774
hsieh2
M2639
xié
united
agree
aid
help

| Mayan Dipper of Stars | Unit of Capacity 9.04 qts. | 7 Stars of the Dipper | To be in Harmony (Dipper is abbreviated) | Pictoral Strength see J 148 | Orion's Belt; Three Kings |

Ode　Arthur O'Shaughnessy
One man with a dream, at pleasure,　And three with a new song's measure
Shall go forth and conquer a crown;　Can trample an empire down.

KYŌ; KAGAMI, MIRROR.

After all, finally 竟 in the golden 金 mirror 鏡. Shaman had metal mirrors for seeing the dead. The Imperial Regalia has a mirror as do the Shinto shrines.

RAD 167　STROKE 19　JME 378*

N4912
ching4
M1137
jìng
mirror

人	干	ヽ	土		
MT.	SHIELD	SHINING	EARTH, SOIL		
鏡	兄	金	鏡	竟	竟
PICTORAL MIRROR	OLDER BROTHER J 199	METAL R. 167 GOLD J 16	MIRROR	TO END, TO TERMINATE N 5111	TO STAND / INFANT, CHILD J 801

Willie's Epitaph
Little Willie from his mirror
Licked the mercury right off,
Thinking in his childish error,
It could cure the whooping cough.

Adapted Poe　A.D.
Once a gallant knightly kanji...
Now an Eldorado shadow
Reflects the further wester valley...
Land beyond the golden mirror.

*Illustrated on following page

378X

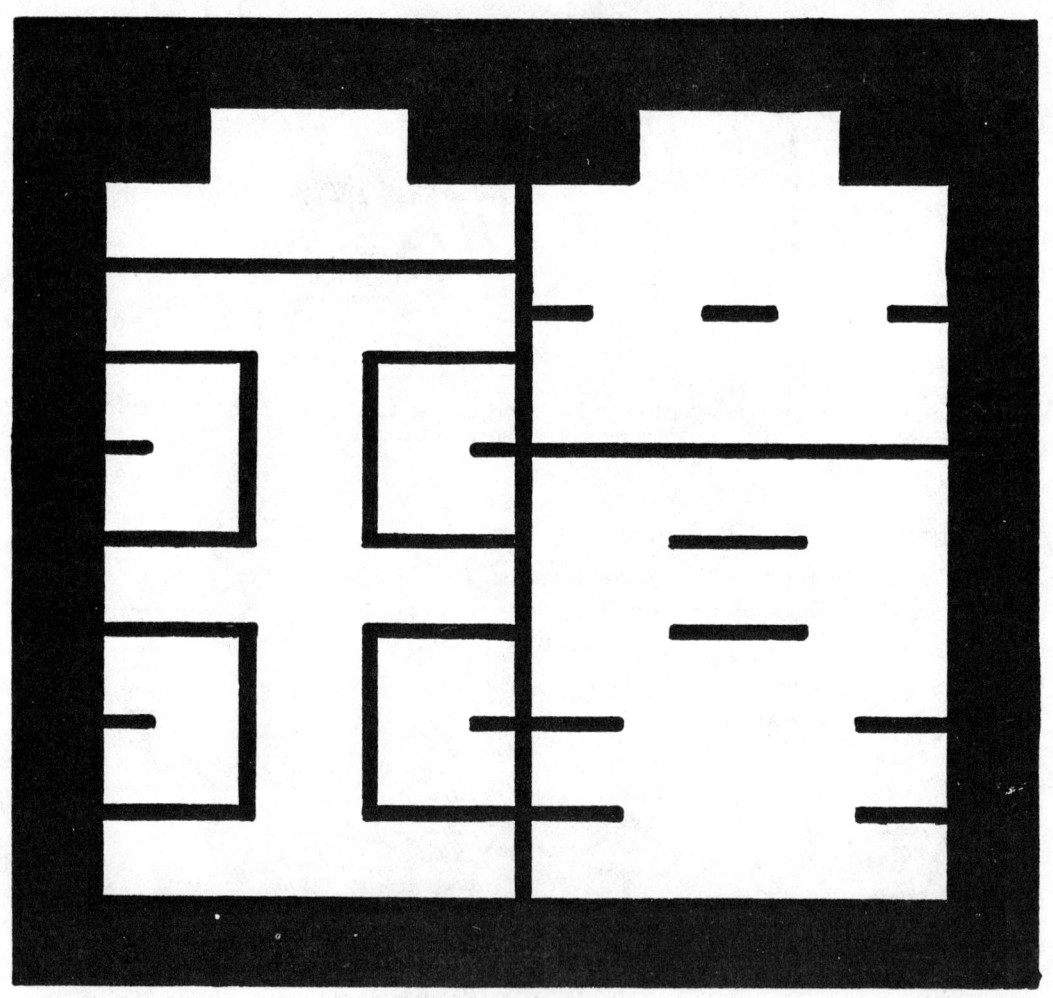

A STYLIZED BUT RECOGNIZABLE FORM OF THE KANJI FOR MIRROR

JME 379　STROKE 20　RAD 117　KYŌ, KEI; KISOU, TO RIVAL, TO COMPETE.

TO RIVAL, TO COMPETE 竞竞 IS A PICTOGRAPH OF TWINS OR BROTHERS READY TO RACE OR COMPETE.

N3364
ching4
M1133
jìng
quarrel

Dum and Dee　Lewis Carroll

Tweedledum and Tweedledee
Agreed to have a battle
Cause Tweedledum said Tweedledee
Had spoiled his nice new rattle.

Like the rivalry we see　　A.D.
In the great University
Where Dee needles Dum
Who's tweedling Dee
All for some small notoriety.

Strange this difference should be
'Twixt such alikes as Dum and Dee.

TWEEDLEDUM AND TWEEDLEDEE

JME 380　STROKE 13　RAD 75　GYŌ, OCCUPATION, INDUSTRY, BUSINESS, STUDIES. GŌ, KARMA.

OCCUPATION, INDUSTRY, BUSINESS, STUDIES, AND KARMA 業 FLOURISH LIKE ANTLERS 业 OR NEW GROWTH 业 BY THE PLOW 耒 & FROM A SINGLE TREE 木   NOTE FUSED MALE 羊 & FEMALE GOATS 耒

N143
yeh4
M7321
yè
property
trade
business

木	耒	業	羊	未	业
TREE, WOOD J 15	PLOW R 127	OCCUPATION, INDUSTRY, BUSINESS, STUDIES, KARMA	GOAT R 123	ZODIAC EWE	CONCEPT OF LUXURIANT GROWTH AS ANTLERS OR VEGETATION

The Garden　Andrew Marvell
How vainly men themselves amaze,
To win the palm, the oak, or bays,
And their incessant labors see
Crowned from some single herb or tree.

381

KYOKU, MELODY; MAGARU, TO BEND, TO TWIST, TO TURN, I.V.; MAGERU, TO BEND, TO TWIST, TO TURN, T.V.

MELODY, TO BEND, TO TWIST, TO TURN 曲 IS THE CONVOLUTED PIPES OF A MUSICAL INSTRUMENT.

RAD 2 STROKE 6 JME 381

N103 ch'u 1
M1623 qǔ
crooked
bent
wrong
false

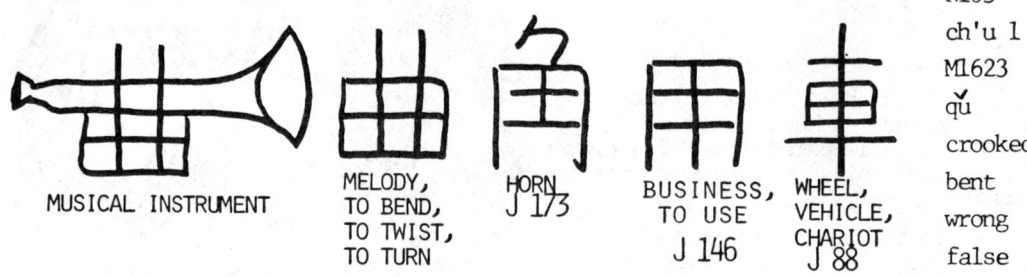

MUSICAL INSTRUMENT | MELODY, TO BEND, TO TWIST, TO TURN | HORN J 173 | BUSINESS, TO USE J 146 | WHEEL, VEHICLE, CHARIOT J 88

A convoluted melody of pipes all twisting in their glee.

KYOKU, TERRESTRIAL POLES, MAGNETIC POLES, ZENITH; GOKU, VERY, EXTREMELY.

THE TERRESTRIAL POLES, MAGNETIC POLES, ZENITH 極 ARE VERY, THE EXTREMES 極 BETWEEN HEAVEN AND EARTH 二 . THE TREE IS LIKE THE ASH TREE YGGDRASIL. THE SOUND OF THE BOWSTRING 弓 FILLS ALL BETWEEN SHOUTING MOUTH 口 AND PULLING HAND 又 .

RAD 2 STROKE 12 JME 382

N2305 chi2
M484 jí
ridgepole
very
Poles

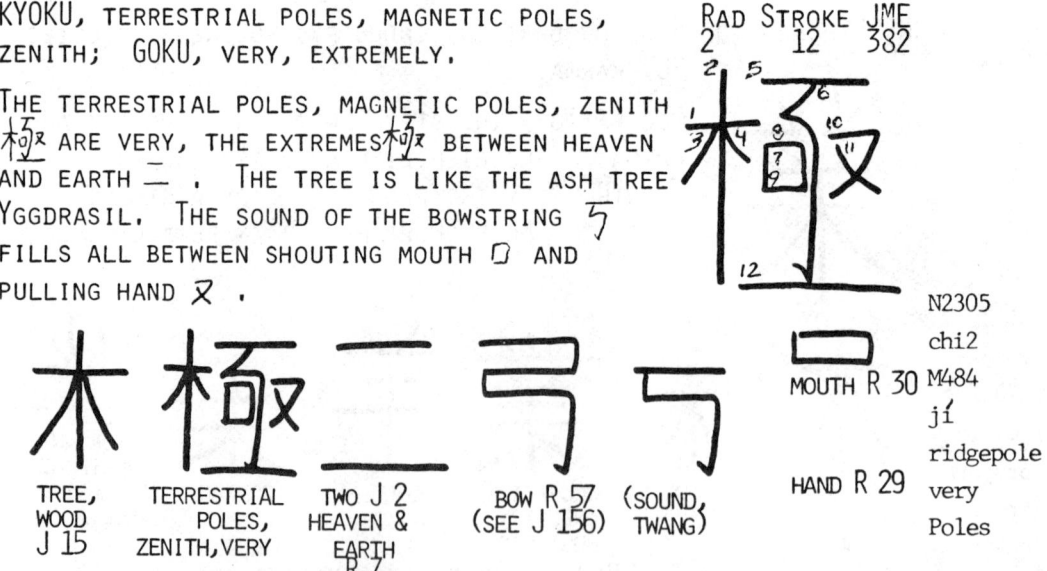

TREE, WOOD J 15 | TERRESTRIAL POLES, ZENITH, VERY | TWO J 2 HEAVEN & EARTH R 7 | BOW R 57 (SEE J 156) | (SOUND TWANG) | MOUTH R 30 | HAND R 29

The Definition of Love   Andrew Marvell
And therefore her Decrees of Steel,
Us as the distant poles has plac'd,
(Though Love's whole World doth on us wheel)
Not by themselves to be embrac'd.

383

JME 383 Stroke 8 Rad 109

GU, TOOL, UTENSIL, INGREDIENTS.

THE TOOL, UTENSIL 具 IS LIKE A SIEVE 其 WHOSE INGREDIENTS 具 ARE HANDLED WITH TWO HANDS 八 JAPANESE SCRAPE HORSERADISH WITH A GRATER LIKE STAIRSTEPS.

A Cinder-Sifter   Mother Goose
A riddle, a riddle, as I suppose,
A hundred eyes and never a nose.

His answer trickled through my head, Like water through a sieve. Carroll

N3128
chu4
M1556
jú
tool
utensil

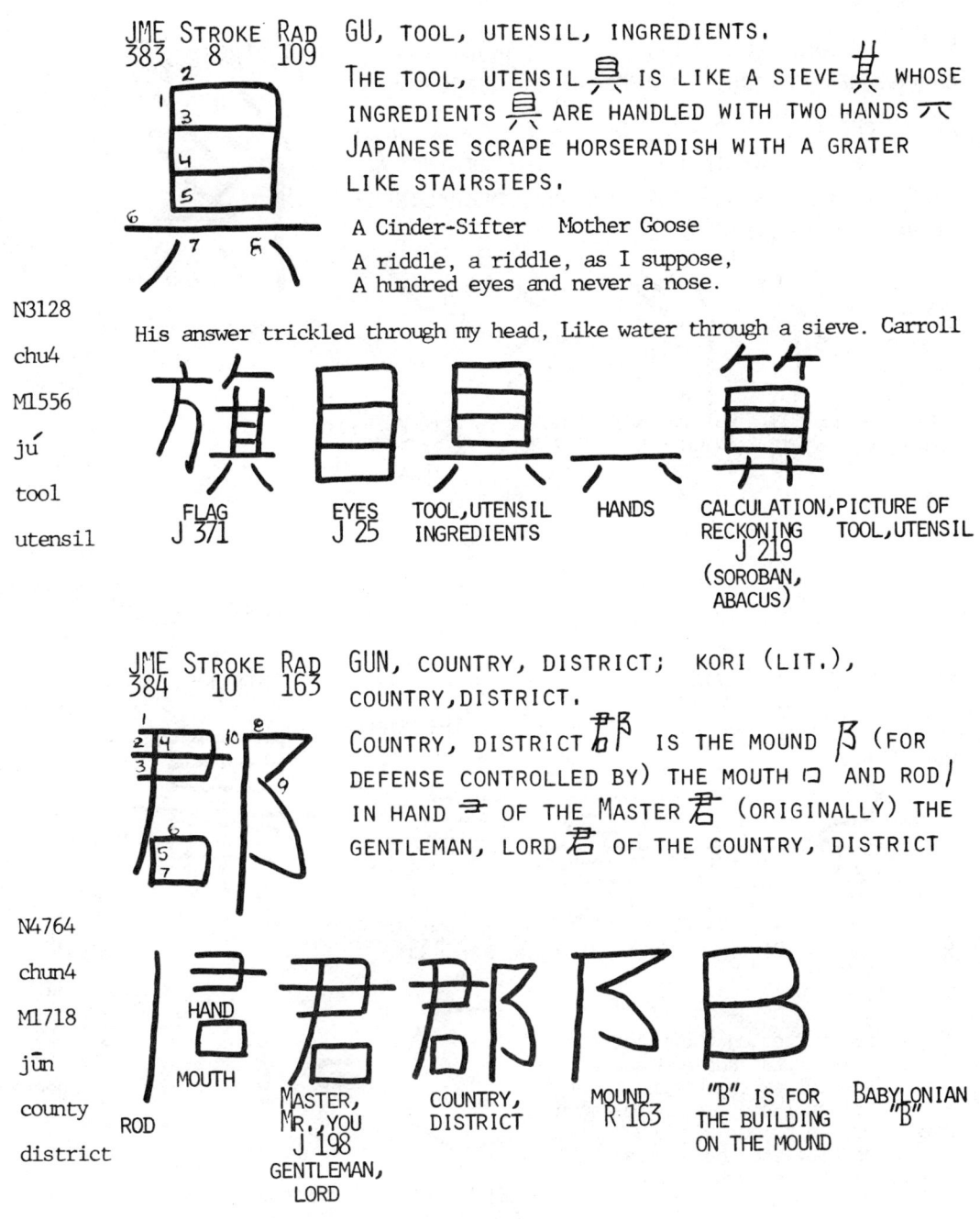

旗 — FLAG J 371
目 — EYES J 25
具 — TOOL, UTENSIL INGREDIENTS
八 — HANDS
算 — CALCULATION, PICTURE OF RECKONING TOOL, UTENSIL J 219 (SOROBAN, ABACUS)

JME 384 Stroke 10 Rad 163

GUN, COUNTRY, DISTRICT; KORI (LIT.), COUNTRY, DISTRICT.

COUNTRY, DISTRICT 郡 IS THE MOUND 阝 (FOR DEFENSE CONTROLLED BY) THE MOUTH 口 AND ROD ノ IN HAND ヨ OF THE MASTER 君 (ORIGINALLY) THE GENTLEMAN, LORD 君 OF THE COUNTRY, DISTRICT

N4764
chun4
M1718
jūn
county
district

HAND
MOUTH
ROD
君 — MASTER, MR., YOU J 198 GENTLEMAN, LORD
郡 — COUNTRY, DISTRICT
阝 — MOUND R 163
"B" IS FOR THE BUILDING ON THE MOUND
BABYLONIAN "B"

385

KEI; KAKARI, (GAKARI), DUTY, CHARGE, IN CHARGE OF; HAKARU, TO AFFECT, TO CONCERN.

DUTY, CHARGE, IN CHARGE OF, TO CONCERN 係 IS THE PERSON 亻 IN CHARGE OF THE STRINGS 糸 (FAMILY SUCCESSION, CONNECTIONS, BLOODLINES) OF HORNED ノ (ANIMALS).

RAD 9 STROKE 9 JME 385

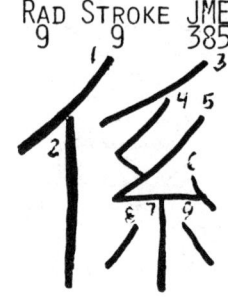

  ノ

| PERSON PICTURED | PERSON, MAN J 30 | DUTY, CHARGE, IN CHARGE OF TO AFFECT, TO CONCERN | THREAD, STRING J 83 | HORN (COMPONENT) J 62 |

N449
hsi4
M2424
xì
belong

KEI, KE, (SCENE, VIEW).

SCENE, VIEW 景 IS THE CAPITAL 京 IN THE SUN 日 (SHINE).

RAD 72 STROKE 12 JME 386

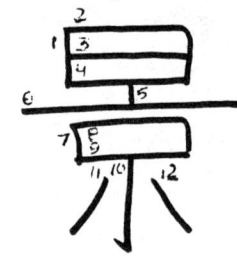

| PICTURE OF STONE LAMP IN CAPITAL | CAPITAL J 63 | SCENE, VIEW | SUN J 11 |

N2142
ching3
M1129
jǐn
prospects
view

The Gothic letter on the right is the symbol for the sun and has the sound HV which is the beginning of the Gothic hvil and the Anglo-Saxon hweol related to our English wheel, the Dutch wiel and the Frisian fial. The wheel is the symbol of the sun.

GOTHIC LETTER HV FOR WHEEL

SUN

THE KANJI SUN IS ALSO PART OF THE KANJI FOR CHARIOT, VEHICLE, CARRIAGE

387

JME 387 **Stroke** 12 **Rad** 159

KEI; KARU, (GARU), KARUI, LIGHT, TRIFLING, UNIMPORTANT, SLIGHT.

LIGHT, TRIFLING, UNIMPORTANT 軽 IS THE LIGHT, SLIGHT 軽 CHARIOT, CARRIAGE 車 (GUIDED OVER) THE EARTH, GROUND 土 BY A HAND 又.

N4620
ch'ing 1
M1156
qīn
light (wt.)

重 DOUBLE WHEELS, CHASSIS, DOUBLE WHEELS — HEAVY, WEIGHTY, SERIOUS J 245

車 SINGLE WHEEL, CHASSIS SINGLE WHEEL, AXLE — WHEEL, VEHICLE J 88

軽 LIGHT, TRIFLING, UNIMPORTANT, SLIGHT, EASY

土 EARTH, SOIL J 17

又 HAND R 29

JME 388 **Stroke** 7 **Rad** 140

GEI, ARTS, ACCOMPLISHMENTS.

ARTS, ACCOMPLISHMENTS 芸 ARE BY HANDS 艹 AND BY MOUTH ム SPEAKING 云.

The Temple of Nature   Erasmus Darwin
The hand, first gift of Heaven! to man belongs;
Untipt with claws the circling fingers close,
With rival joints the bending thumbs oppose,
Trace the nice lines of form with sense refined,
And clear ideas charm the thinking mind.

N3908
i4
M3014
yi
skill
ability
craft

艹 HANDS   芸 ARTS, ACCOMPLISHMENTS   云 (MOUTH SPEAKING)   会 MEETING, TO MEET J 54   雲 CLOUD J 47

The Hand: It might well be regarded by the reflective mind as the teacher of the arts....   Lewis Burdick

389

ETSU; CHI, BLOOD.

BLOOD 血 OF HORNED ╱ (ANIMALS IS CAUGHT) IN A BOWL 皿 (LIKE A TAUROBOLIUM). BLOOD 血, POURED OR AS CAKES, WAS A PRIMITIVE DELICACY.

Rad	Stroke	JME
143	6	389

Their blood contains the animus, spirit, life, soul when creatures are sacrificed or killed. The blood in sacred temple vessels represented the creatures and their qualities. Eating or drinking conveyed the powers of the blood and its original owner.

There is power, power, wonder-working power..In the blood, in the blood,
There is power, power, wonder-working power..In the precious blood of
   the Lamb.   Hymn

N4205
hsueh3
M2901
xuè
xiě
blood

牛   ╱   血   皿   温

CATTLE,COW, HORN   BLOOD BOWL,DISH   WARM J 162
BULL,OX   R 143   R 108
J 62

flood

                            Hymn
There is a fountain filled with blood | And sinners plunged beneath that ╱
Drawn from Immanuel's veins, | Lose all their guilty stains.

KETSU; MUSUBI, END, KNOT. MUSUBU, TO TIE, TO BIND, TO CONCLUDE, TO LINK; YUU, TO DRESS.

Rad	Stroke	JME
120	12	390*

THE GENTLEMAN 士 USES THE STRING 糸 AS THE END, KNOT 結 TO TIE, TO BIND, TO CONCLUDE, TO LINK, TO DRESS 結 THE HAIR.

Divorce me, untie, or break that knot again,
Take me to you, imprison me, for I,
Except you enthrall me, never shall be free,
Nor ever chaste except you ravish me.   John Donne

N3540
chieh2
M782
jié
to contract

糸   結   吉   士   口   壴

THREADS, END,KNOT, GOOD LUCK, MAN,FIGURE, MOUTH (VASE WITH
STRINGS TO TIE,BIND, GOOD OMEN GENTLEMAN, R 32   PLUG OR LID)
J 83   TO CONCLUDE, N 1053   SAMURAI
         TO LINK,DRESS   J 410

The Highwayman   Alfred Noyes
He whistles a tune to the window and who should be waiting there
But the landlord's black-eyed daughter, Bess the landlord's daughter,
Plaiting a dark red love knot into her long black hair.

*Illustrated on facing page

390X

Before vandalizing, the Easter Island statues had topknots.

391

JME 391 Stroke 9 Rad 54

KEN; TATERU, TO BUILD, TO ESTABLISH; TATSU TO BE BUILD, -DATE, -STORIED BUILDING.

THE LONG STRIDE 廴 OF THE BRUSH 聿 (AS IN A BLUEPRINT) BUILDS, ESTABLISHES 建 THE STORIED BUILDING 建.

N1549
chien4
M853
jiàn
establish
to erect
to found

延	廴	建	聿	筆	書
TO POSTPONE, TO EXTEND J 743	TO STRETCH, TO LENTHEN, LONG STRIDE R 54	TO BUILD, ESTABLISH, TO BE BUILT, -STORIED BLDG.	BRUSH R 129	WRITING BRUSH J 701	TO WRITE J 92

JME 392 Stroke 7 Rad 149

GEN, GON, SPEECH, STATEMENT; KOTO, WORD, SPEECH, EXPRESSION; IU, TO SAY.

SPEECH, STATEMENTS, WORDS, EXPRESSIONS 言 ARE VIBRATIONS 二 FROM THE MOUTH 口.

SPEECH CARRIES BEST UP, BUT PHYSICS TEXTS SHOW THE VIBRATIONS TRAVELLING SIDEWISE.

N4309
yen2
M7334
yán
words
speech
talk

云	音	語	話	舌	読
(MOUTH SPEAKING)	SOUND J 50	WORD, SPEECH, TO SPEAK, TALK J 209	STORY, TO SPEAK J 151	TONGUE R 135 J 827	TO READ J 123

The Theogony   Hesiod
They pour sweet dew on his tongue and gentle words flow from his mouth.

KO; KATAMERU, TO HARDEN, TO MAKE HARD, T.V.
KATAMARU, TO BECOME HARD; KATAI, HARD, FIRM.

RAD 31　STROKE 8　JME 393

THE EARTH 土 IN AN OLD 古 ENCLOSURE 囗 IS
HARD, HARDENS, IS MADE HARD, BECOMES HARD 固
(AS WITH A POTTED PLANT).

TEN J 10
MOUTH R 32

古 OLD, ANCIENT J 70

固 TO HARDEN, TO MAKE HARD, HARD, FIRM

囗 ENCLOSURE, BOUNDARIES R 31

国 COUNTRY J 79

園 GARDEN J 159

N1036
ku4
M3450
gù
firm
strong

KO; MIZU-UMI, LAKE.

RAD 85　STROKE 12　JME 394

AN OLD 古 MOON 月 ON THE WATER 氵 (SHINES ON)
A LAKE 湖 LIKE A DEWLAP 胡.
(DEWLAPS ARE THE DOUBLE CHINS BELOW THE
THROATS OF OLD CATTLE, BLOODHOUNDS, AND OLD
PEOPLE LIKE WATER LAPPING AT THE SHORES).

PICTORAL WATER DROPLETS

WATER R 85

湖 LAKE

胡 DEWLAPS

古 ANCIENT, OLD J 70

月 MOON, BODY J 12

N2628
hu2
M2168
hú
lake

Antique Lake   A.D.
Antient shore and antique lake
Ten mouths a mocking mirror make;
Ten generations; yet so soon;
Timeless waters and ageless moon.

When we were boys, Who
would believe that there were mountain-
eers Dew-lapp'd like bulls, whose
throats had hanging at 'em wallets of
flesh?* The Tempest   Wm. Shakespear
*goiter

395

JME 395　STROKE 8　RAD 51

KŌ; SAIWAI, BLESSINGS, GOOD LUCK, FORTUNE, HAPPINESS.

BLESSINGS, GOOD LUCK, FORTUNE, HAPPINESS 幸 IS THE SHINING SHIELD 干 (OF PEACE) 平 (SUSTAINING) THE EARTH 土.

N1073
hsing4
M2764
xìn

rejoice
fortunate
prosperous

走 TO RUN J 105
土 EARTH, SOIL J 32
幸 BLESSINGS, GOOD LUCK, FORTUNE, HAPPINESS
平 LEVEL, PEACEFUL J 315
丷 SHINING, GLEAMING SEE J 16
干 SHIELD, WEAPON R 51

JME 396*　STROKE 10　RAD 137

KŌ, (TO SAIL ON WATER).

TO SAIL 航 IS THE DIRECTIONAL 一 WING 几 OF THE SAIL 亢.

Anthony and Cleopatra　Wm. Shakespear
SCARBUS　She once being looft,
The Noble ruine of her Magicke, Anthony,
Claps on his Sea-wing, and (like a doting Mallard)
Leaving the Fight in heighth, flyes after her:

N3867
hang2
M2059
háng

sail
navigation
2 lashed boats

船 SHIP, BOAT, LINER J 266
舟 BOAT N 3863
航 TO SAIL
亢 HIGH SPIRITS N 282
方 DIRECTION, WAY, SIDE, PERSON J 138
風 WIND J 132

Sea-Fever　John Masefield
All I ask is a tall ship and a star to steer her by,
And the wheel's kick and the wind's song and the white sail's shaking,

*Illustrated on facing page

As with other examples in primitive and in modern art, the location of the parts of a kanji may have little relation to their position in the article represented. In picturing the sailing craft below, the boat and the sail are returned to a more customary relationship from their juxtaposition in the kanji for sailing on the water.

397

KŌ; MINATO, HARBOR.
HARBOR 港 IS WATER 氵 WITH TURNING, REFLEXIVE 己 (MOVEMENT) AS OF THE ZODIAC SERPENT 己 BETWEEN THE LEGS 八 (OF THE POINTS OF LAND OR BREAKWATERS), AND LEGS 八 OF PERSONS WORKING TOGETHER 共.

RAD 85 STROKE 12 JME 397

N2630
kang3
M3267
gǎng
port
creek

氵	港	巷	己	共	改
WATER R 85	HARBOR	FORKING ROAD, QUARTERS, ARENA N 1465	ZODIAC SNAKE TURN, CYCLE, I, MYSELF, ONESELF J 777	TOGETHER, BOTH J 376	CHANGE, REFORM, REVISE J 359

KOKU; TSUGERU, TO INFORM, TO TELL.
THE MOUTH 口 OF THE BULL, COW 牛 TELLS AND INFORMS 告 AS OF ITS LOCATION.

RAD 30 STROKE 7 JME 398

N900
kao4
M3287
gào
tell
inform

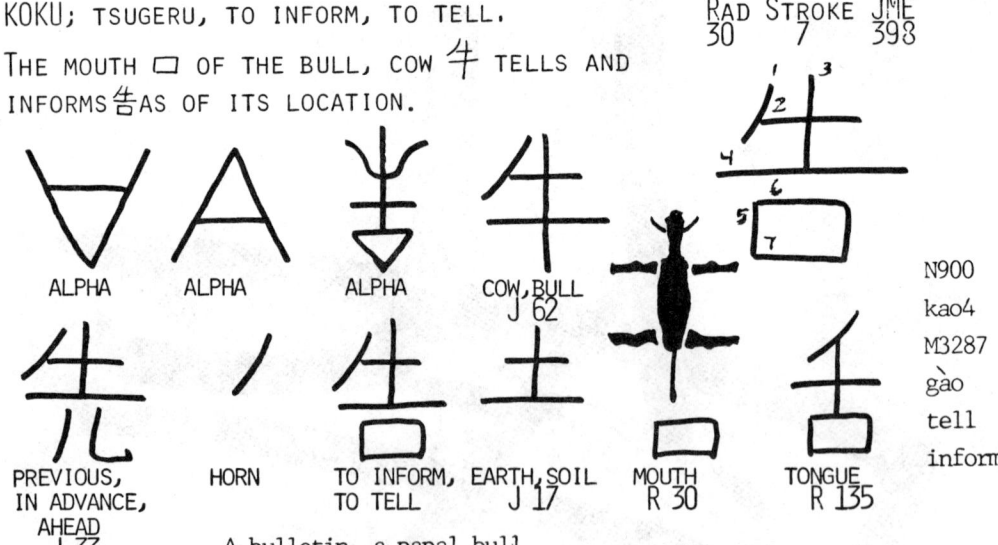

∀	A	ᴛ	牛		告
ALPHA	ALPHA	ALPHA	COW, BULL J 62		

先	ノ	告	土	口	舌
PREVIOUS, IN ADVANCE, AHEAD J 33	HORN	TO INFORM, TO TELL	EARTH, SOIL J 17	MOUTH R 30	TONGUE R 135

A bulletin, a papal bull.

As roars a bull grazing in a meadow.   Odyssey

The bull-roarer, a noise device made of a thong attached to an elliptical bone, was created by Stone Age man twenty-five thousand years ago.

399

JME 399 **Stroke** 10 **Rad** 48

SA, DIFFERENCE, REMAINDER (IN MATH). SASU, TO INSERT, TO THRUST.

DIFFERENCE, REMAINDER 差 IS THE (CONTRACTOR-LIKE ESTIMATE) SUPPORTED ノ BY THE SQUARE 工 WHEN THE GOAT 羊 LEAPS UP AND DOWN THE CLIFFS 厂. THE GOAT 羊 THRUSTS, INSERTS 差 (HIS FEET).

N3662
ch'a 1
M105
chā
to err
differ
error

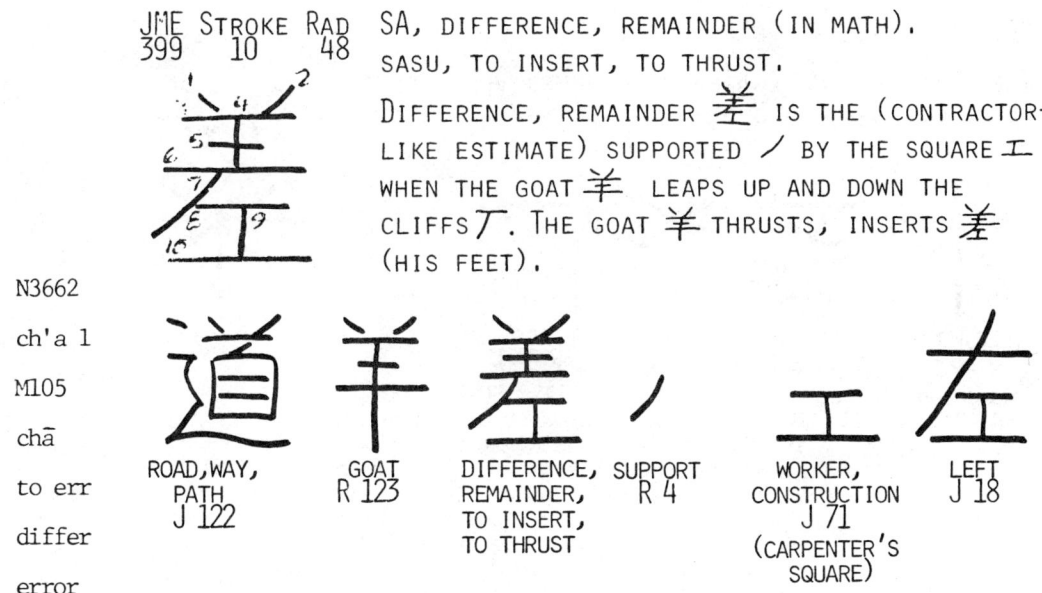

道	羊	差	ノ	工	左
ROAD, WAY, PATH J 122	GOAT R 123	DIFFERENCE, REMAINDER, TO INSERT, TO THRUST	SUPPORT R 4	WORKER, CONSTRUCTION J 71 (CARPENTER'S SQUARE)	LEFT J 18

JME 400 **Stroke** 11 **Rad** 113

SAI; MATSURI, FESTIVAL; MATSURU, TO DEIFY, TO WORSHIP AS A GOD, TO OFFER PRAYERS FOR THE SAKE OF.

AT THE FESTIVAL WHEN WORSHIPPING, DEIFYING, OFFERING PRAYERS 祭, THE HANDS 又 (SACRIFICE) THE BODY 夕 (TO THE GODS) WHO SHOW, POINT OUT 示 (IN RESPONSE).

N3247
chi4
M465
jì
sacrifice

夕	祭	又	示	二	小
BODY, MOON J 12	FESTIVAL, TO DEIFY, OFFER PRAYERS	HAND 29	TO SHOW, POINT OUT J 622	HEAVEN & EARTH R 7	INSTRUCTION FROM THREE RAYS AS THE SUN, MOON & STARS

The Chinese called the sun, moon, and stars "The Three Lights."

The Principal Chief...took in one hand some of the most Delicate Parts of the Dog...prepared for the feast and made a Sacrifice to the flag.
Journals of the Lewis and Clark Expedition

401

SAI; NA, GREENS, VEGETABLES.
THE CLAW HAND 爫 (GATHERS) GREENS, VEGETABLES
菜 OF THE GRASSES, HERBS 艹 AND TREES 木.

RAD 140 STROKE 11 JME 401

木 菜 爫 艹   菜

TREE, WOOD GREENS,   CLAW,   GRASS
J 15   VEGETABLES HAND   R 140
                      R 87

N3982
ts'ai4
M6671
cǎi
greens
herbs
food

Romeo and Juliet   William Shakespear
FRIAR LAURENCE. Now, ere the sun advance his burning eye,
                The day to cheer and night's dank dew to dry,
                I must up-fill this osier cage of ours
                With baleful weeds and precious-juiced flowers.
                The earth that's nature's mother is her tomb;
                What is her burying grave, that is her womb:
                And from her womb children of divers kind
                We sucking on her natural bosom find,
                Many for many virtues excellent,
                None but for some, and yet all different.
                O, mickle is the powerful grace that lies
                In herbs, plants, stones, and their true qualities:

SAI; MOTTOMO, MOST; SAI-, MOST, EXTREME.
TAKING 取 (UNDER THE HIGH) SUN 日 IS MOST 最
WITH MAXIMUM 最 (ILLUMINATION).

RAD 72 STROKE 12 JME 402

日   最   取   耳   又   最

SUN MOST, TO TAKE EAR   HAND
J 11 EXTREME J 238   R 128 R 29

N2146
tsui4
M6858
zuì
very
most

The Song of Wandering Aengus   Yeats   The Superlative   A.D.
And pluck till time and times are done   To seize the sun by his halo
The silver apples of the moon,   And take the moon by her horns.
The golden apples of the sun.

JME	Stroke	Rad
403	7	75

ZAI, LOG, TIMBER, LUMBER, MATERIAL, ABILITY.

A TREE 木 (TRIMMED) TO 才 FOR LOGS, TIMBER, LUMBER, MATERIAL 材 IS ANALOGOUS TO TRAINING A PERSON TO DEVELOP HIS ABILITY 材.

N2189
ts'ai2
M6661
cái
materials
stuff
quality

木	材	才
TREE, WOOD J 15	LUMBER, LOG, TIMBER, MATERIAL, ABILITY	TALENT, SUFFIX TO COUNT AGE J 217

JME	Stroke	Rad
404	9	72

SAKU, (THE PAST, YESTERDAY).

THE PAST, YESTERDAY 昨, THE DAY 日 THE BAMBOO 𠂉 HORN ノ OR SPIKE 丁 WAS MOVED = (IN PLANTING).

N2119
tso2
M6782
zuó
yesterday
lately

日	昨	竹	ノ HORN 丁 NAIL, SPIKE	作	=
SUN J 11	THE PAST, YESTERDAY	BAMBOO J 113		TO MAKE J 82	MOVEMENT IN MAKING

405

SATSU; SURU, PRINT.

TO PRINT 刷 (A NEGATIVE IMPRESSION OR MOULD IS SHAPED) WITH A KNIFE 刂 (AS A CLOTH 巾 OR CLOTHES TAKE A NEGATIVE IMPRESSION FROM THE BODY 尸. THIS WAS THE METHOD IN WOODBLOCK PRINTING WHERE THE WOOD WAS CUT AWAY FROM THE NEGATIVE IMAGE.

RAD 4 STROKE 8 JME 405

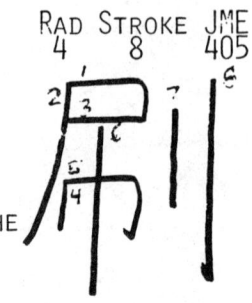

N210 shua 1
M5905 shuā
print
scrub
cleanse

尸 　　　巾 　　　刷 　　　刂 　　　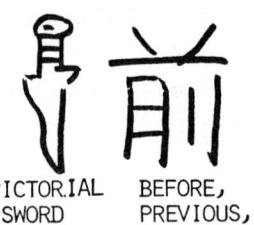

BODY
R 44

CLOTH,
KERCHIEF
R 50

TO PRINT

KNIFE,
SWORD
R 16

PICTORIAL
SWORD

BEFORE,
PREVIOUS,
IN FRONT OF
J 102

SATSU; SASSURU, SASSHIRU, PRESUME, JUDGE, UNDERSTAND, IMAGINE.

TO PRESUME, JUDGE, UNDERSTAND, IMAGINE 察 (WHAT THE GODS) SHOW, POINT OUT 示 AT THE FESTIVAL 祭 AS THE BODY 夕 IS HANDED 又 (IN SACRIFICE) UNDER THE ROOF 宀.

RAD 40 STROKE 14 JME 406

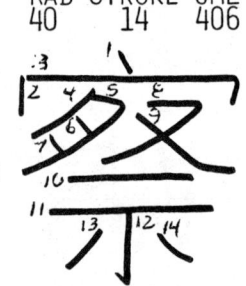

N1334 ch'a2
M111 chá
find out

然 　　夕 　　察 　　又 　　示 　　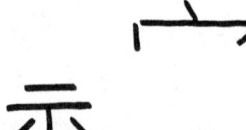

YES, BUT,
HOWEVER
J 450

BODY,
MOON
J 12

TO PRESUME,
TO JUDGE,
TO IMAGINE

HAND
J 29

TO SHOW,
TO POINT OUT
J 622

ROOF
J 40

JME	Stroke	Rad
407	12	66

SAN; CHIRU, TO FALL, BE SCATTERED, TO BE DISPERSED I.V.; CHIRASU TO SCATTER, TO DISPERSE T.V.; -SAN, MEDICINAL POWDERS.

THE STICK 丿 IN HAND 又 STRIKES 攵 THE MEAT FIBERS 丗 OF THE BODY 月 WHICH FALL, SCATTER, ARE DISPERSED 散 BECOME LIKE PEMMICAN OR MEDICINAL POWDERS 散.

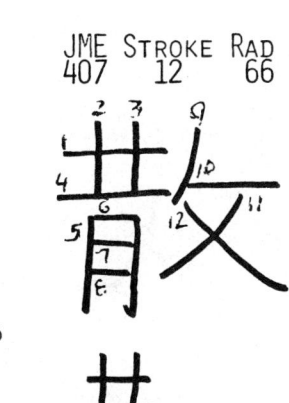

N2056
san4
M5421
sàn
scatter
disperse

丗	月	散	攵	丿
FIBERS	BODY, MOON J 12	TO FALL, BE SCATTERED, BE DISPERSED, TO SCATTER, TO DISPERSE, MEDICINAL POWDER	STICK IN HAND R 66	HAND	STICK R 4

JME	Stroke	Rad
408	11	117

SAN, CHILDBIRTH, PRODUCT, PROPERTY; UMU TO GIVE BIRTH TO, TO PRODUCE.

PICTOGRAPH WITH TO STAND 立 (AS THE HEAD) AND A CLIFF 厂 (AS THE BODY) WITH THE KANJI FOR EXISTENCE, LIFE, TO BE BORN 生 AS THE CHILDBIRTH, PRODUCT, PROPERTY 産 GIVEN BIRTH 産 OR PRODUCED 産.

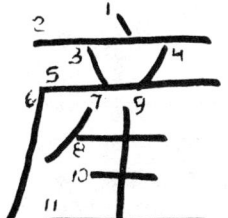

N3354
ch'an3
M163
chǎn
give
birth

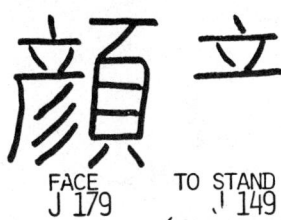

顔	立	産	厂	厂	生
FACE J 179	TO STAND J 149 (ALSO USED AS A HEAD)	CHILDBIRTH, PRODUCT, PROPERTY, GIVE BIRTH TO, TO PRODUCE	CLIFF R 27	BODY R 44	EXISTENCE, TO GIVE LIFE, TO GIVE BIRTH, TO LIVE, RAW, GENUINE, PURE J 34

409

ZAN; NOKORI, REMAINDER, BALANCE; NOKORU, TO REMAIN, TO STAY; NOKOSU, TO LEAVE BEHIND, TO SAVE, TO BEQUEATH.

DEATH, CORPSES, DRIED BONES 歹 AND LAYERS 三 OF ARMS 戈 REMAIN, ARE LEFT BEHIND, ARE BEQUEATHED, ARE SAVED, ARE THE BALANCE 歹戈.

Apocrypha   Book of Judith   my marching armies will fill the ravines with his wounded and fill the streams and rivers with his corpses...

RAD 78 STROKE 10 JME 409

N2445 ts'an2
M6689 cán
injure
spoil
destroy
oppress
remnant

| BODY, MOON J 12 | DEATH, BAD, EVIL R 78 (Remnant of body hangs on bar or hook like a chrysalis or pupa) | REMAINDER, BALANCE, TO REMAIN, TO STAY, TO LEAVE BEHIND, TO SAVE, TO BEQUEATH | THREE LAYERS (PILED UP) | SPEAR R 62 | ARM OR HAND HOLDING THE SPEAR |

The Rape of the Lock   Alexander Pope
The pierced battalions disunited fall,
In heaps on heaps;
    one fate o'erwhelms them all.

SHI, MAN, FIGURE, SAMURAI.

MAN, FIGURE, SAMURAI 士 IS AN INVERTED SHIELD 干. IN JAPAN THE SAMURAI 士, IN CHINA THE SCHOLAR 士, WAS THE HIGHEST CLASS.

RAD 33 STROKE 3 JME 410*

N1160 shih4
M5776 shì
scholar
gentleman
officer
soldier

| THOUSAND J 101 | SHIELD R 51 | MAN, FIGURE, SAMURAI J 33 | PICTORIAL SAMURAI |

Ballade of a Tayokuni Colour-Print
Was I a Samurai renowned,
Two-sworded, fierce, immense of bow?
A histrion angular and profound?
A priest, A porter? --Child although
I have forgotten clean, I know
That in the shade of Fujisan
What time the cherry orchards blow,
I loved you once in old Japan.
            Wm. Ernest Henley

The Canterbury Tales
A KNIGHT there was, and that
            a worthy man,
That from the time that
            he first began
To riden out, he loved chivalry,
Truth and honour, freedom and
            courtesy.
            Geoffrey Chaucer

*Illustrated on facing page

410 X

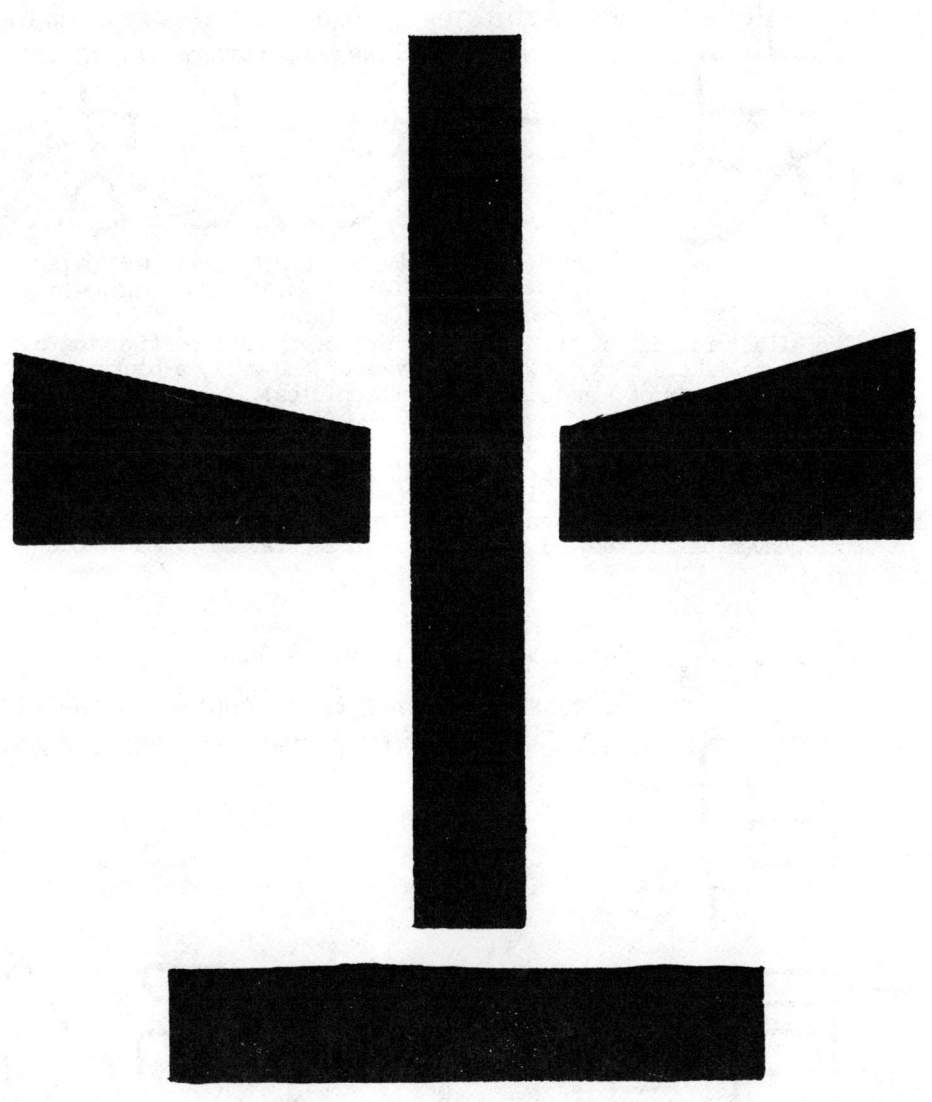

411

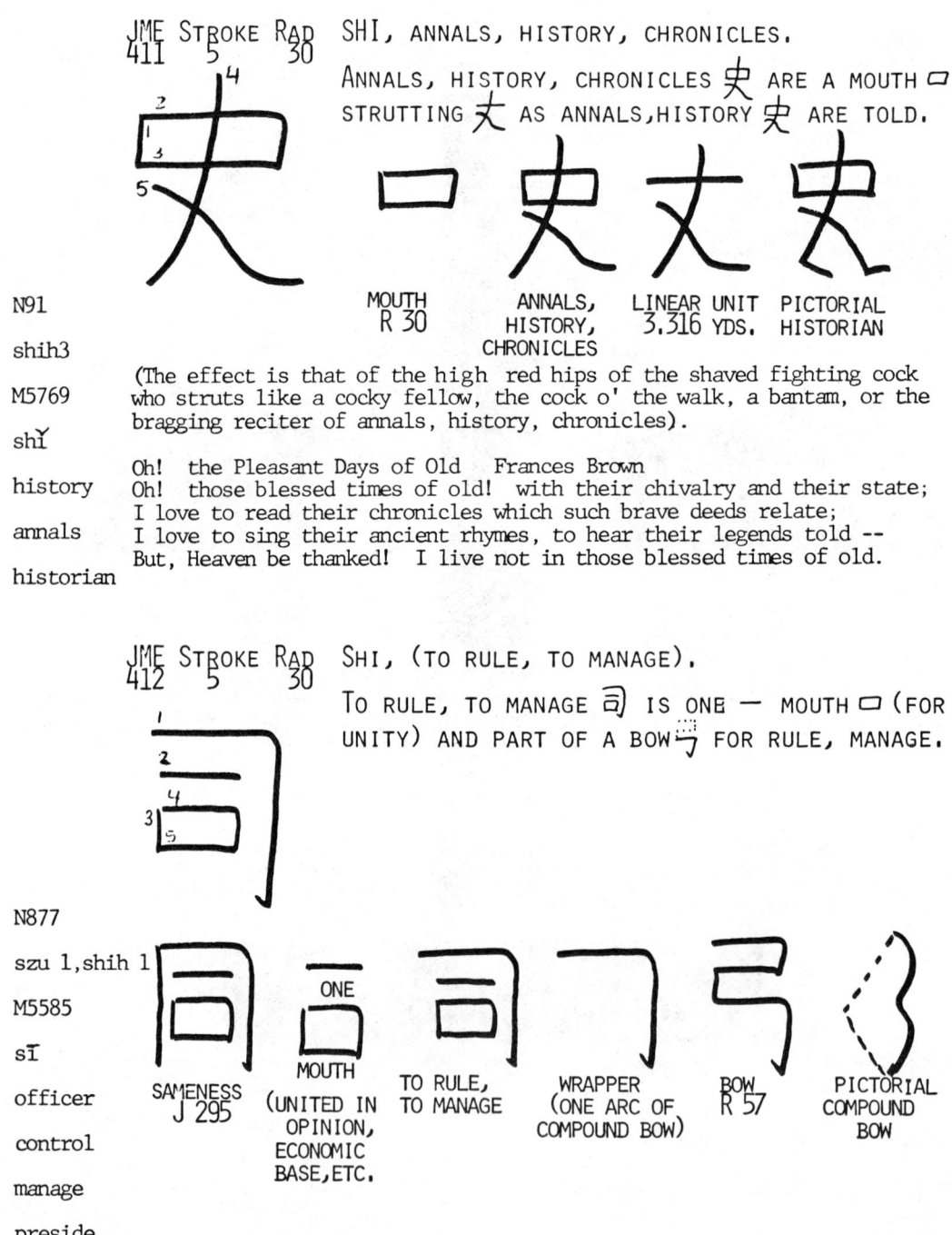

JME 411 STROKE 5 RAD 30

SHI, ANNALS, HISTORY, CHRONICLES.

ANNALS, HISTORY, CHRONICLES 史 ARE A MOUTH 口 STRUTTING 丈 AS ANNALS, HISTORY 史 ARE TOLD.

N91
shih3
M5769
shǐ
history
annals
historian

MOUTH R 30

ANNALS, HISTORY, CHRONICLES

LINEAR UNIT 3.316 YDS.

PICTORIAL HISTORIAN

(The effect is that of the high red hips of the shaved fighting cock who struts like a cocky fellow, the cock o' the walk, a bantam, or the bragging reciter of annals, history, chronicles).

Oh! the Pleasant Days of Old   Frances Brown
Oh! those blessed times of old! with their chivalry and their state;
I love to read their chronicles which such brave deeds relate;
I love to sing their ancient rhymes, to hear their legends told --
But, Heaven be thanked! I live not in those blessed times of old.

JME 412 STROKE 5 RAD 30

SHI, (TO RULE, TO MANAGE).

TO RULE, TO MANAGE 司 IS ONE 一 MOUTH 口 (FOR UNITY) AND PART OF A BOW ㇆ FOR RULE, MANAGE.

N877
szu 1, shih 1
M5585
sī
officer
control
manage
preside

SAMENESS J 295

ONE
MOUTH
(UNITED IN OPINION, ECONOMIC BASE, ETC.

TO RULE, TO MANAGE

WRAPPER (ONE ARC OF COMPOUND BOW)

BOW R 57

PICTORIAL COMPOUND BOW

413

SHI; ANE, ELDER SISTER.

ELDER SISTER 姉 IS THE WOMAN 女 (WHO GOES TO) THE CITY 市 TO MARKET 市.

RAD 38 STROKE 8 JME 413

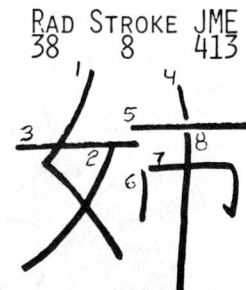

Tam o'Shanter   Robert Burns
Her cutty sark, o' Paisley harn,
That while a lassie she had worn,
In longitude tho' sorely scanty,
It was her best, and she was vauntie,

女	女	姉	市	巾	(duster)
PICTORIAL WOMAN	WOMAN, GIRL, FEMALE J 32	ELDER SISTER	CITY, MARKET J 222	CLOTH, KERCHIEF R 50	PICTORIAL DUSTER

N1207
chieh3
M6948
jiě
elder sister

SHI; HA, (BA), TOOTH.

TEETH 歯 ARE LIKE RICE 米 GRAINS IN AN OPEN VESSEL 凵. THEY (CLOSE AND) STOP 止.

RAD 211 STROKE 12 JME 414

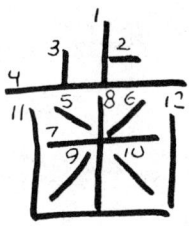

Upon Lucie: Epigram   Robert Herrick
Sound teeth has Lucie, pure as pearl, and small,
With mellow lips, and lucious therewithall.

Mother Goose
Thirty white horses upon a red hill,
Now they tramp, now they champ, Now they stand still.

N5428
ch'ih3
M1037
chǐ
upper incisors

止	凵	歯	米	十	
TO STOP, A STOP J 220	OPEN VESSEL R 17	TOOTH, TEETH	RICE J 135	TEN J 10	GRAINS OF RICE CENTERED ON TEN FOR COMPLETENESS

The Book of Songs   James Legge
Her even teeth, behind their screen concealed,
Like melon seeds. Her forehead cicada-square...

In the Shih Ching (Classic of Songs), teeth are like a row of melon seeds. The same description is used in Japanese literature.

415

JME 415 **Stroke** 13 **Rad** 149

SHI, POETRY, POEM.

POETRY, A POEM 詩 IS SPEECH, WORDS 言 SAID AT A TEMPLE 寺, (A FAVORITE PLACE FOR VERSE-COMPOSING, DRINKING, FEASTING, & VIEWING).

Outre-Mer Henry Wadsworth Longfellow
Music is the universal language of mankind, --
poetry their universal pastime and delight.

N4360
shih 1
M5783
shī
poetry
ode

言	詩	寺	土	寸	丶
SPEECH, WORDS, TO SAY J 392	POETRY, POEM	TEMPLE J 228	EARTH, SOIL R 32	PULSE, INCH R 41	DOT R 3 EXTENSION OF POWER, AUTHORITY, ETC.

JME 416 **Stroke** 13 **Rad** 149

SHI; KOKOROMI, TRIAL, TEST; KOKOROMIRU, TO TRY.

TRIAL, TEST 試 TO TRY 試 BY WORDS 言 AS THE DART'S FORM, MOULD 式 WORK 工 IS TESTED 試.

N4361
shih4
M5798
shì
to test
try
examine
to use

言	試	式	工	弋	朿
SPEECH, WORDS, TO SAY J 392	TRIAL, TEST, TO TRY	CEREMONY, FORM, MODEL, -STYLE, -TYPE J 417	WORKER, ENGINEERING, CONSTRUCTION J 71	DART R 56	PICTORIAL METAL THROWING DART (VAJRA)

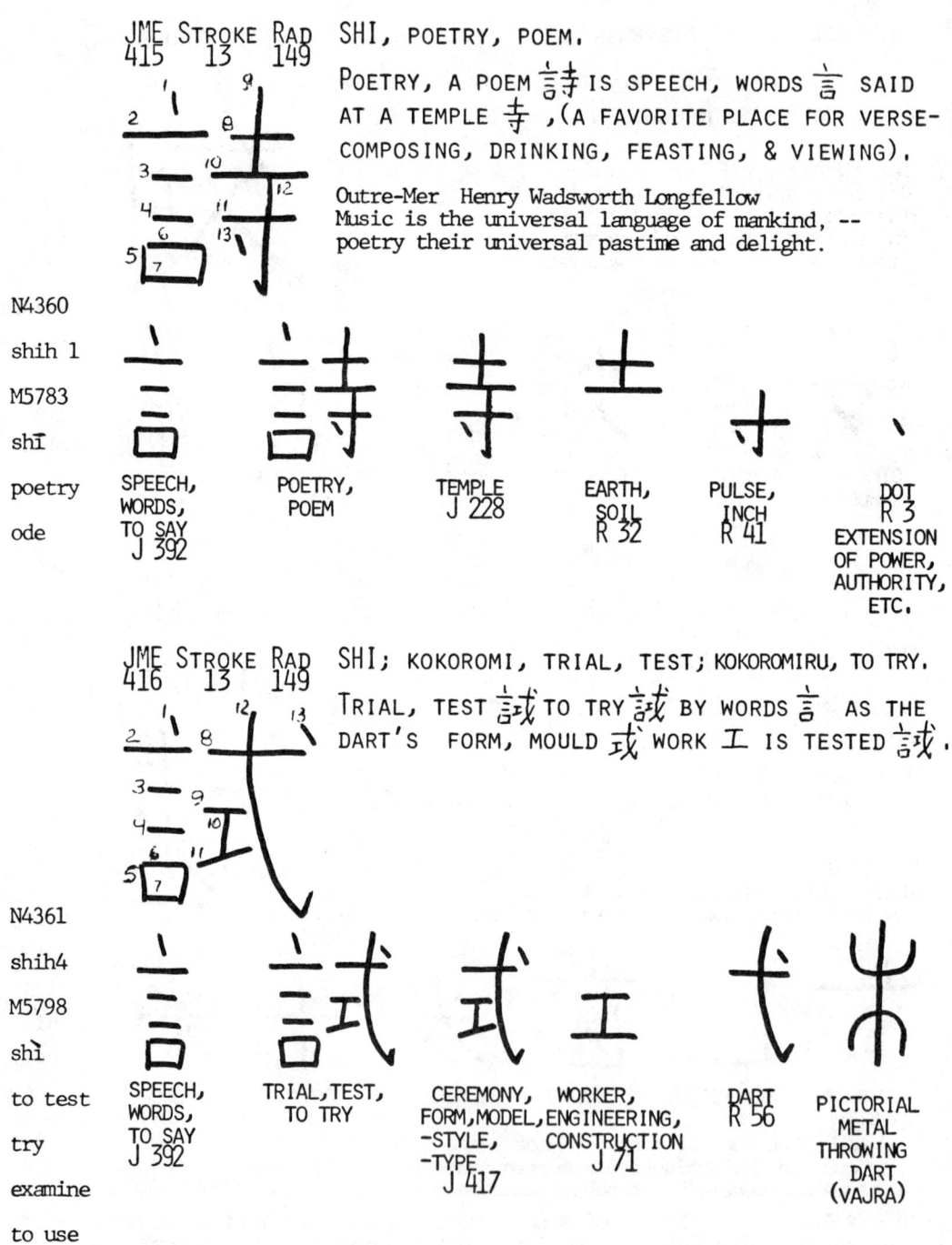

417

SHIKI, CEREMONY, FORM, MODEL; -SHIKI, -STYLE, RAD 56 STROKE 6 JME 417

THE FORM, MODEL, STYLE, TYPE 式 OF THE CONSTRUCTION, ENGINEERING 工 OF THE DART 弋 USED ALSO CEREMONIALLY 戎.

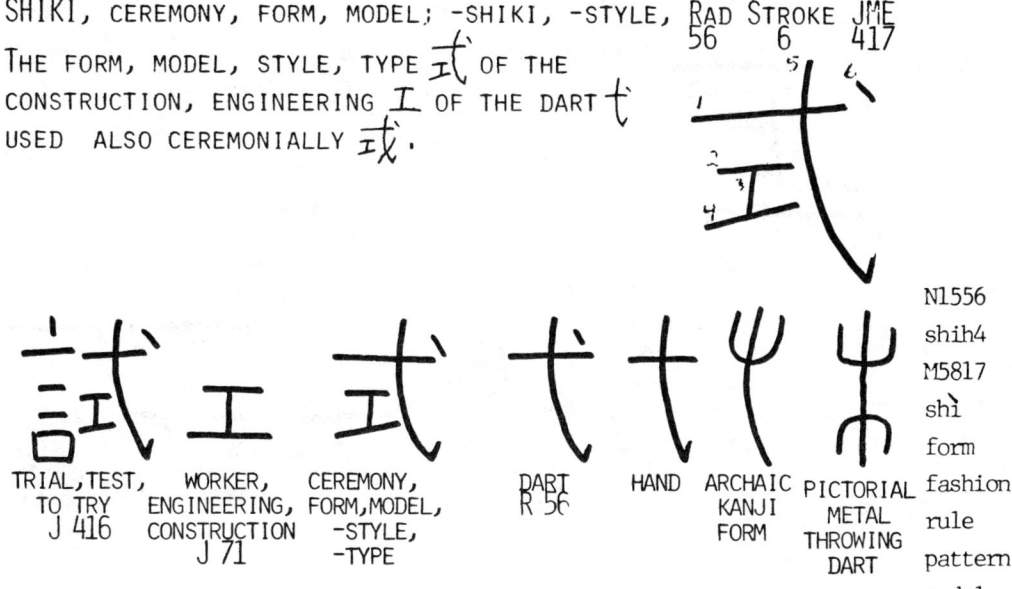

試	工	式	弋	弋	丫	朱
TRIAL, TEST, TO TRY J 416	WORKER, ENGINEERING, CONSTRUCTION J 71	CEREMONY, FORM, MODEL, -STYLE, -TYPE	DART R 56	HAND	ARCHAIC KANJI FORM	PICTORIAL METAL THROWING DART

N1556
shih4
M5817
shì
form
fashion
rule
pattern
model

SHITSU; USHINAU, TO LOSE, TO MISS.

A FUSION OF THE ARROW 矢 AND COW 牛 LOST, MISSED 失 BY THE HUSBAND 夫. PERHAPS HUMOR OF HUSBAND WANDERING ALL ABOUT LIKE A LOST COW AS HE SEARCHES FOR HIS ARROW.

RAD 37 STROKE 5 JME 418

失

矢	失	牛
ARROW R 111	TO LOSE J 418	BULL, COW J 62

N178
shih 1
M5806
shī
to lose
to slip
to neglect
to miss
to err

```
        The Merchant of Venice   Wm. Shakespear
    In my schooldays when I had lost one shaft,
    I shot his fellow of the selfsame flight
    The selfsame way, with more advised watch,
    To find the other forth; and by adventuring both,
    I oft found both.
```

419

| JME 419 | Stroke 5 | Rad 14 | SHA, UTSUSU, TO COPY, IMITATE, TO PHOTOGRAPH. |

ONE COPIES, IMITATES, TAKES A PHOTOGRAPH 写 UNDER A CAP OF DARKNESS 冖 (TARNHELM) IN THE CAMERA OBSCURO BY PULLING THE BOW'S 弓 STRING 一

N626

hsieh3

M2627

xiě

to write

to sketch

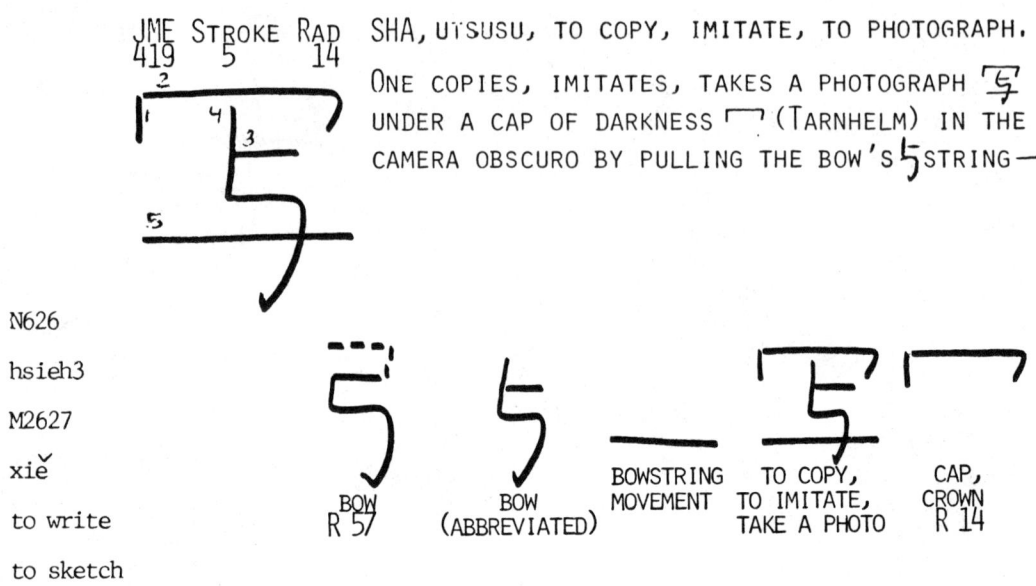

| JME 420 | Stroke 10 | Rad 9 | SHAKU; KARI, BORROWING, DEBT, LOAN; KARIRU, KARU, TO BORROW, BUY ON CREDIT, RENT. |

PERSONS 亻 SINCE ANCIENT TIMES 昔 BORROW, BUY ON CREDIT, RENT 借.

N490

chieh4

M765

jiè

borrow

lend

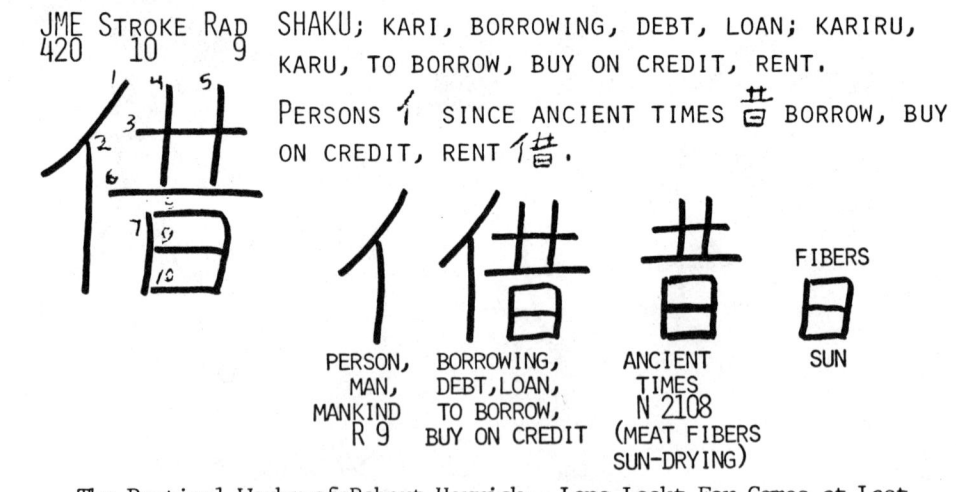

The Poetical Works of Robert Herrick: Long Lookt For Comes at Last
Though long it be, yeeres may repay the debt;
None loseth that which he in time may get.

SHU, SU; MAMORU, TO PROTECT, TO GUARD, TO DEFEND, TO OBEY.

THE **PULSE** 寸 (AS A LEGAL CONTROL) UNDER THE ROOF 宀 PROTECTS, DEFENDS, GUARDS, (CAUSES) TO OBEY 守.

Rad 40 Stroke 6 JME 421

家	宀	守	寸	寺	ヽ
HOUSE, HOME J 53	ROOF R 40	TO PROTECT, TO GUARD, TO DEFEND, TO OBEY	INCH, PULSE, R 41 (CONTROL)	TEMPLE J 228	DOT P. 3 EXTENSION OF RANGE, POWER, AUTHORITY

N1282 shou3 M5844 shǒu to guard protect observe maintain

SHU; SAKE, SAKA, RICE WINE, LIQUOR.

RICE WINE, LIQUOR 酒 IS A FLUID 氵 IN A CORKED 丙 CONTAINER 口 WITH THE WINE LEVEL —

Rad 85 Stroke 10 JME 422

The Little Brown Jug
Ha -- ha -- ha, you and me,
Little brown jug, don't I love thee?

...the people of Cathay drink wine...a liquor which they brew of rice...with spice...being very hot, it makes one drunk sooner   The Travels of Marco Polo

氵	酒	酉	兀	口	一
WATER R 85	SAKE, SAKA	ZODIAC COCK (COCK'S RED-AS-WINE BLOOD USED IN SACRIFICE LIKE LIQUOR)	PICTOGRAPHIC CORK OR BIRD-ON-EGGS SEE J 96	CONTAINER OR NEST	LEVEL OF LIQUOR OR BLOOD IN CONTAINER

N2573 chiu3 M1208 jiǔ wine liquor

Drinking Song
Back and side go bare, go bare,   But, belly, God send thee good ale enough,
   Both hand and foot go cold: Whether it be new or old.

423

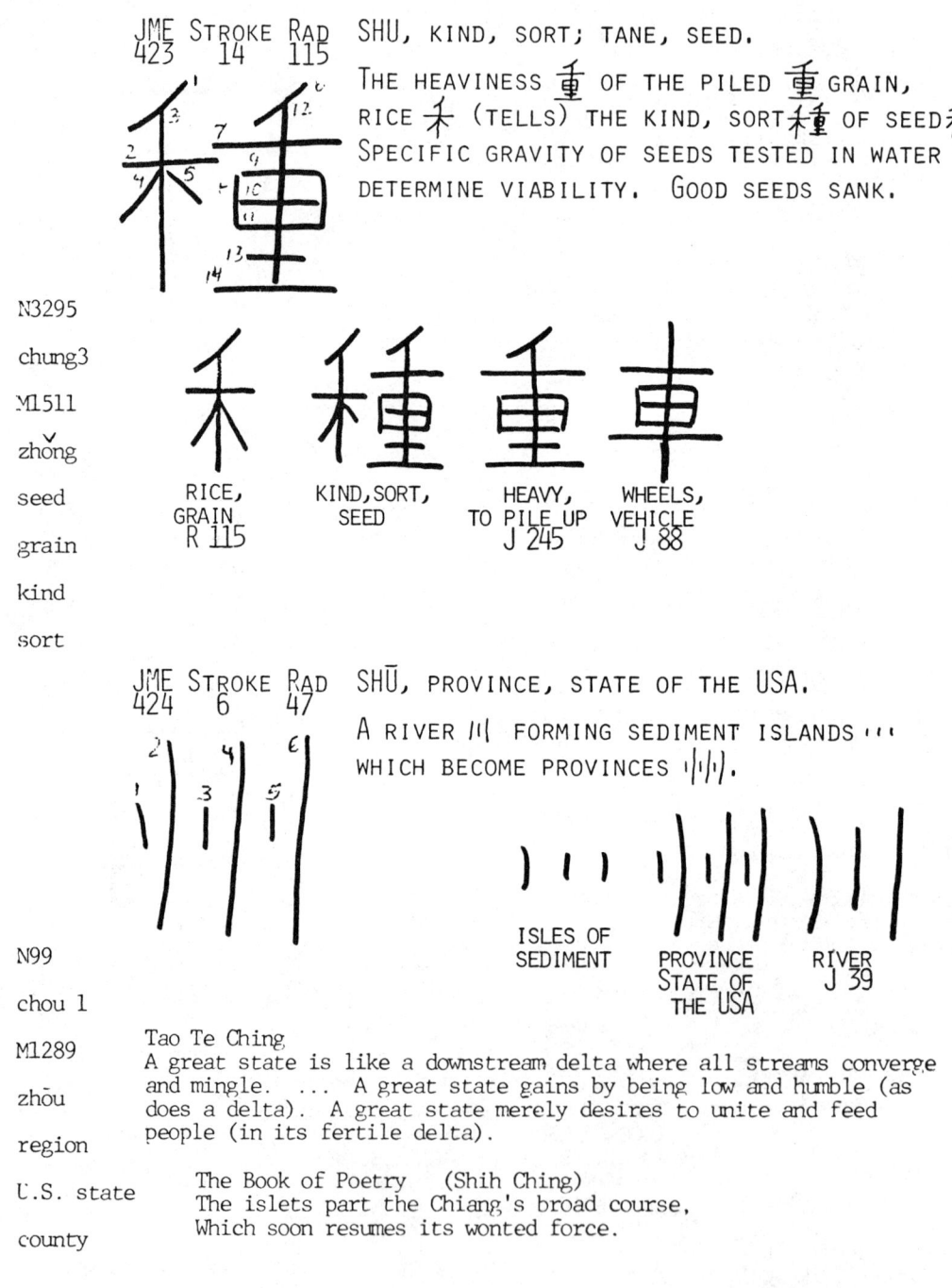

JME 423 STROKE 14 RAD 115

SHU, KIND, SORT; TANE, SEED.

THE HEAVINESS 重 OF THE PILED 重 GRAIN, RICE 禾 (TELLS) THE KIND, SORT 種 OF SEED 種. SPECIFIC GRAVITY OF SEEDS TESTED IN WATER TO DETERMINE VIABILITY. GOOD SEEDS SANK.

N3295
chung3
M1511
zhǒng
seed
grain
kind
sort

禾 RICE, GRAIN R 115
種 KIND, SORT, SEED
重 HEAVY, TO PILE UP J 245
車 WHEELS, VEHICLE J 88

JME 424 STROKE 6 RAD 47

SHŪ, PROVINCE, STATE OF THE USA.

A RIVER 川 FORMING SEDIMENT ISLANDS ··· WHICH BECOME PROVINCES 州.

ISLES OF SEDIMENT
PROVINCE STATE OF THE USA
RIVER J 39

N99
chou 1
M1289
zhōu
region
U.S. state
county

Tao Te Ching
A great state is like a downstream delta where all streams converge and mingle. ... A great state gains by being low and humble (as does a delta). A great state merely desires to unite and feed people (in its fertile delta).

The Book of Poetry (Shih Ching)
The islets part the Chiang's broad course,
Which soon resumes its wonted force.

SHŪ, JŪ, TEN (AS IN LEGAL DOCUMENTS).
HIROU, TO PICK UP, GATHER.

THE HAND 扌 PICKS UP, GATHERS 拾 WHAT FITS, SUITS, BELONGS, IS TOGETHER 合 AS BY TENS 拾

Rad 64 Stroke 9 JME 425

| HAND | HAND | TEN, | FITS, |
| R 64 | R 64 (AS A COMPONENT) | TO PICK UP, TO GATHER | SUITS, TOGETHER J 77 |

NN1901
shih 1
M5809
shī
pick up
collect
ten

SHŪ,; NARAU, TO LEARN, TO STUDY.

THE WHITE 白 WINGED 羽 (FLEDGLINGS) LEARN, STUDY 習.

Rad 124 Stroke 11 JME 426

| WEAK J 236 | PINFEATHERS | WINGS R 124 | TO LEARN, TO STUDY | WHITE J 37 |

N3675
hsi 2
M2499
xí
practice
study
practices
customs

427

JUN, ORDER, TURN.

THE ORDER, TURNS 順 FOR THE RIVER 川 (WATER) ARE GIVEN BY THE HEAD 頁. (RIPARIAN RIGHTS).

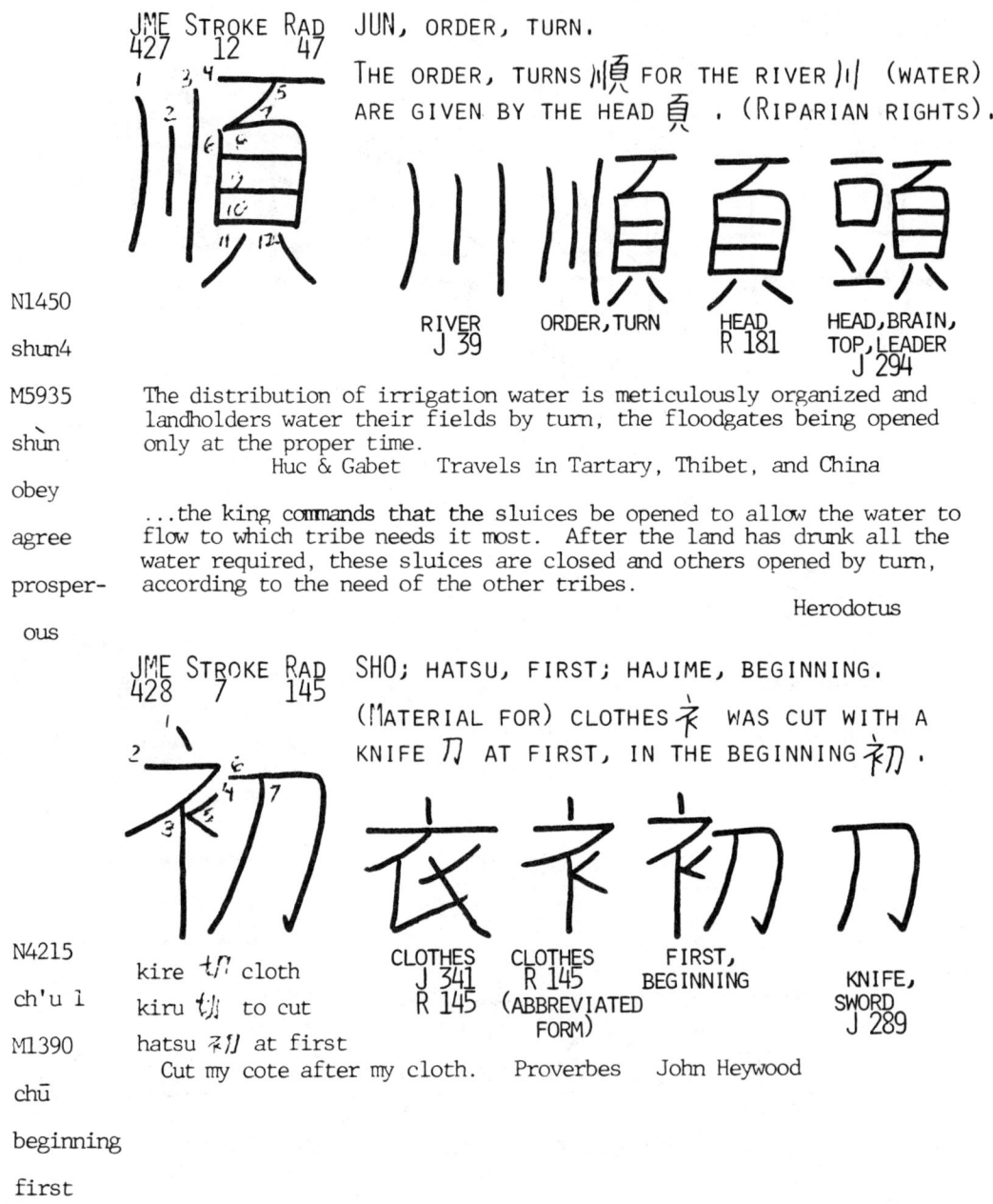

N1450
shun4
M5935
shùn
obey
agree
prosperous

RIVER J 39 — ORDER, TURN — HEAD R 181 — HEAD, BRAIN, TOP, LEADER J 294

The distribution of irrigation water is meticulously organized and landholders water their fields by turn, the floodgates being opened only at the proper time.
       Huc & Gabet   Travels in Tartary, Thibet, and China

...the king commands that the sluices be opened to allow the water to flow to which tribe needs it most. After the land has drunk all the water required, these sluices are closed and others opened by turn, according to the need of the other tribes.
       Herodotus

SHO; HATSU, FIRST; HAJIME, BEGINNING.

(MATERIAL FOR) CLOTHES 衣 WAS CUT WITH A KNIFE 刀 AT FIRST, IN THE BEGINNING 初.

N4215
ch'u 1
M1390
chū
beginning
first

kire 切 cloth
kiru 切 to cut
hatsu 初 at first

CLOTHES J 341 R 145 — CLOTHES R 145 (ABBREVIATED FORM) — FIRST, BEGINNING — KNIFE, SWORD J 289

Cut my cote after my cloth.   Proverbes   John Heywood

SHŌ; KIERU, TO VANISH, TO GO OUT, TO MELT AWAY; KESU, TO EXTINGUISH, TO SWITCH OFF.

To vanish, to go out, to melt away, to switch off, to extinguish, to put out a light 消 is the last gleams ⺡ of the moon 月 vanishing 消 in the water ⺡.

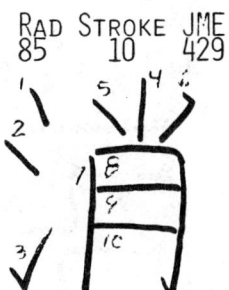

RAD	STROKE	JME
85	10	429

N2574
hsiao 1
M2607
xiāo
melt
thaw
disperse

⺡	消	光	月
WATER R 85	TO VANISH, TO GO OUT, MELT AWAY, EXTINGUISH, SWITCH OFF	LIGHT, BRILLIANCE, TO SHINE J 72	MOON J 12

Faust   Goethe
No crash of shipwreck shall have power to affright me
Clouds gather above me
The moon hides her light
The lamp goes out! Angry red rays dart about my head!

SHŌ; TONAERU, TO CHANT, TO RECITE, TO SAY.

To chant, to recite, to say 唱 is a mouth 口 on the left and two speaking mouths 昌 on the right...antiphonal singing as by turns.

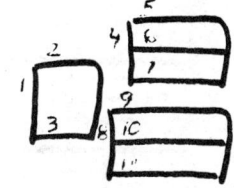

RAD	STROKE	JME
30	11	430

N941
ch'ang4
M208
chàng
to sing

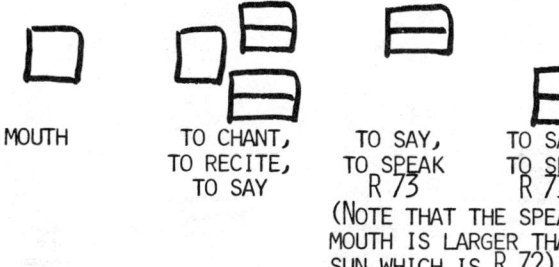

口	唱	曰	曰
MOUTH	TO CHANT, TO RECITE, TO SAY	TO SAY, TO SPEAK R 73	TO SAY, TO SPEAK R 73

(Note that the speaking mouth is larger than sun which is R 72)

431

JME 431* Stroke 11 Rad 30

N321
shang 1
M5673
shāng
trade
commerce

SHŌ; AKINAU, SELL, DEAL IN.

TO SELL, DEAL IN 商 IS A PICTOGRAPH OF THE PEDLAR'S HEAD 立, SHOULDERS AND POLE ⌐¬, ARMS 儿, TIED-ON LOADS ⌐¬, AND PELVIS □, OR MOUTH.

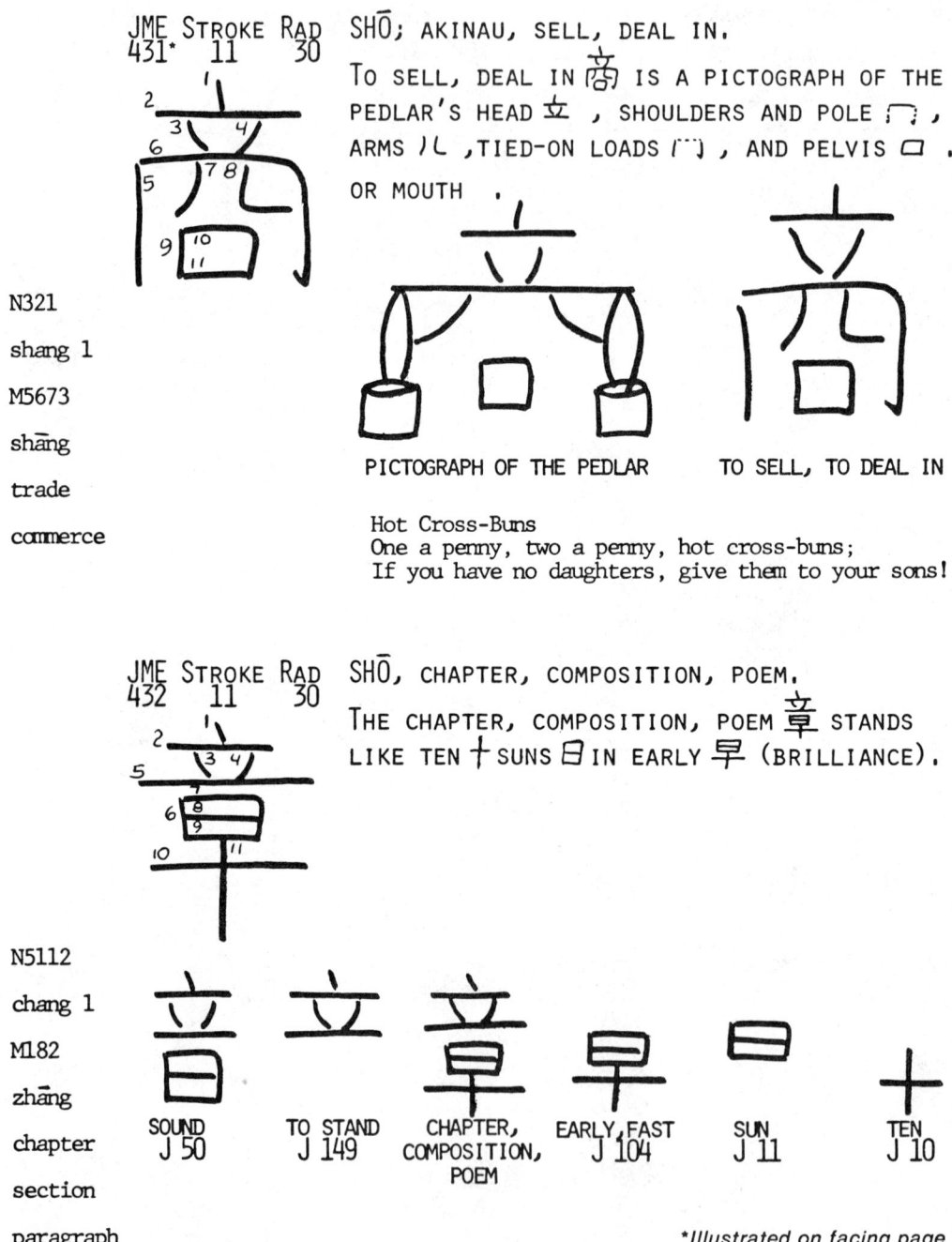

PICTOGRAPH OF THE PEDLAR   TO SELL, TO DEAL IN

Hot Cross-Buns
One a penny, two a penny, hot cross-buns;
If you have no daughters, give them to your sons!

JME 432 Stroke 11 Rad 30

N5112
chang 1
M182
zhāng
chapter
section
paragraph

SHŌ, CHAPTER, COMPOSITION, POEM.

THE CHAPTER, COMPOSITION, POEM 章 STANDS LIKE TEN 十 SUNS 日 IN EARLY 早 (BRILLIANCE).

音 立 章 早 日 十
SOUND TO STAND CHAPTER, EARLY, FAST SUN TEN
J 50   J 149   COMPOSITION, J 104   J 11 J 10
                POEM

*Illustrated on facing page

431 X

433

SHŌ; TERASU, SHINE ON, SHED LIGHT ON, ILLUMINATE, TO COMPARE WITH; TERU, TO SHINE.

As the bright 昭 fire 灬 under the sun 日 sheds light 照, we are summoned 召 as mouth 口 calls and knife 刀. (Shares and generosity are compared 昭 as in potlach).

RAD 86 STROKE 13 JME 433

NN2785
chao4
M238
zhāo
illumine
reflect

灬	日	昭	照	召	刀	口
FIRE R 86	SUN J 11	BRIGHT J 249	SHINE ON, SHED LIGHT ON, ILLUMINATE, COMPARE WITH, TO SHINE	TO WEAR, TO SUMMON N 668	KNIFE	MOUTH

SHŌ; YAKU, TO BURN, TO BAKE, TO GRILL, TO TOAST T.V.; YAKERU, TO BE BURNED, TO BE ROASTED, TO BE JEALOUS OF.

The fire 火 in an earthen 垚 (oven) on a stand 兀 burns, bakes, grills, toasts, roasts, 焼 as one burns with jealousy 焼.

RAD 86 STROKE 12 JME 434

N2772
shao 1
M5692
shāo
burn
heat
roast
bake
faver

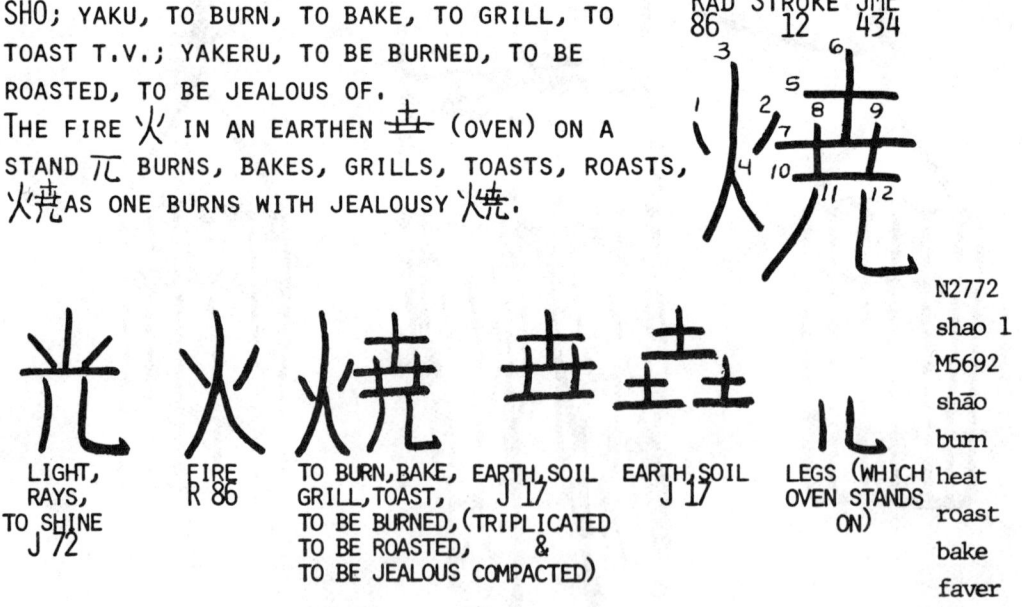

光	火	焼	垚	垚	兀
LIGHT, RAYS, TO SHINE J 72	FIRE R 86	TO BURN, BAKE, GRILL, TOAST, TO BE BURNED, TO BE ROASTED, TO BE JEALOUS	EARTH, SOIL J 17 (TRIPLICATED & COMPACTED)	EARTH, SOIL J 17	LEGS (WHICH OVEN STANDS ON)

435

JME 435 Stroke 10 Rad 75

SHOKU; UERU, TO PLANT, TO SET TYPE.

TREE OR WOOD 木 (USED) TO PLANT, TO SET TYPE 植. EYES 目 MUST BE TEN-TENTHS 十 ON THE SQUARE ㄴ (FOR ACCURACY).

N2303 chih2
M1007 zhí
trees
plants

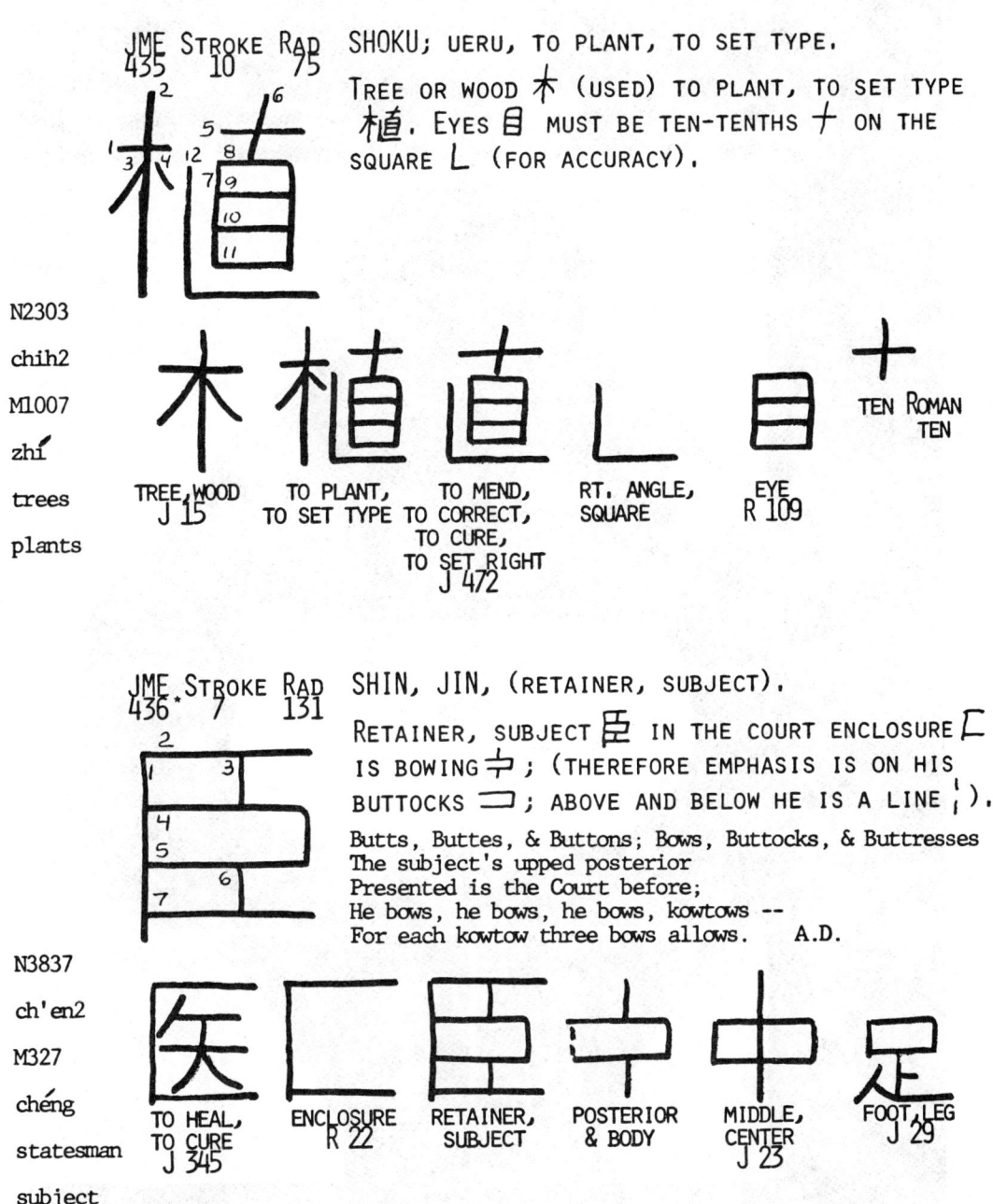

木	植	直	ㄴ	目	十
TREE, WOOD J 15	TO PLANT, TO SET TYPE	TO MEND, TO CORRECT, TO CURE, TO SET RIGHT J 472	RT. ANGLE, SQUARE	EYE R 109	TEN ROMAN TEN

JME 436* Stroke 7 Rad 131

SHIN, JIN, (RETAINER, SUBJECT).

RETAINER, SUBJECT 臣 IN THE COURT ENCLOSURE ㄷ IS BOWING 中; (THEREFORE EMPHASIS IS ON HIS BUTTOCKS ⊐; ABOVE AND BELOW HE IS A LINE ¦).

Butts, Buttes, & Buttons; Bows, Buttocks, & Buttresses
The subject's upped posterior
Presented is the Court before;
He bows, he bows, he bows, kowtows —
For each kowtow three bows allows.   A.D.

N3837 ch'en2
M327 chéng
statesman
subject

医	ㄷ	臣	中	中	足
TO HEAL, TO CURE J 345	ENCLOSURE R 22	RETAINER, SUBJECT	POSTERIOR & BODY	MIDDLE, CENTER J 23	FOOT, LEG J 29

(The kowtow was a prostration or series of prostrations before the Emperor of China in which the forehead was brought to the ground).

*Illustrated on following page

436 X

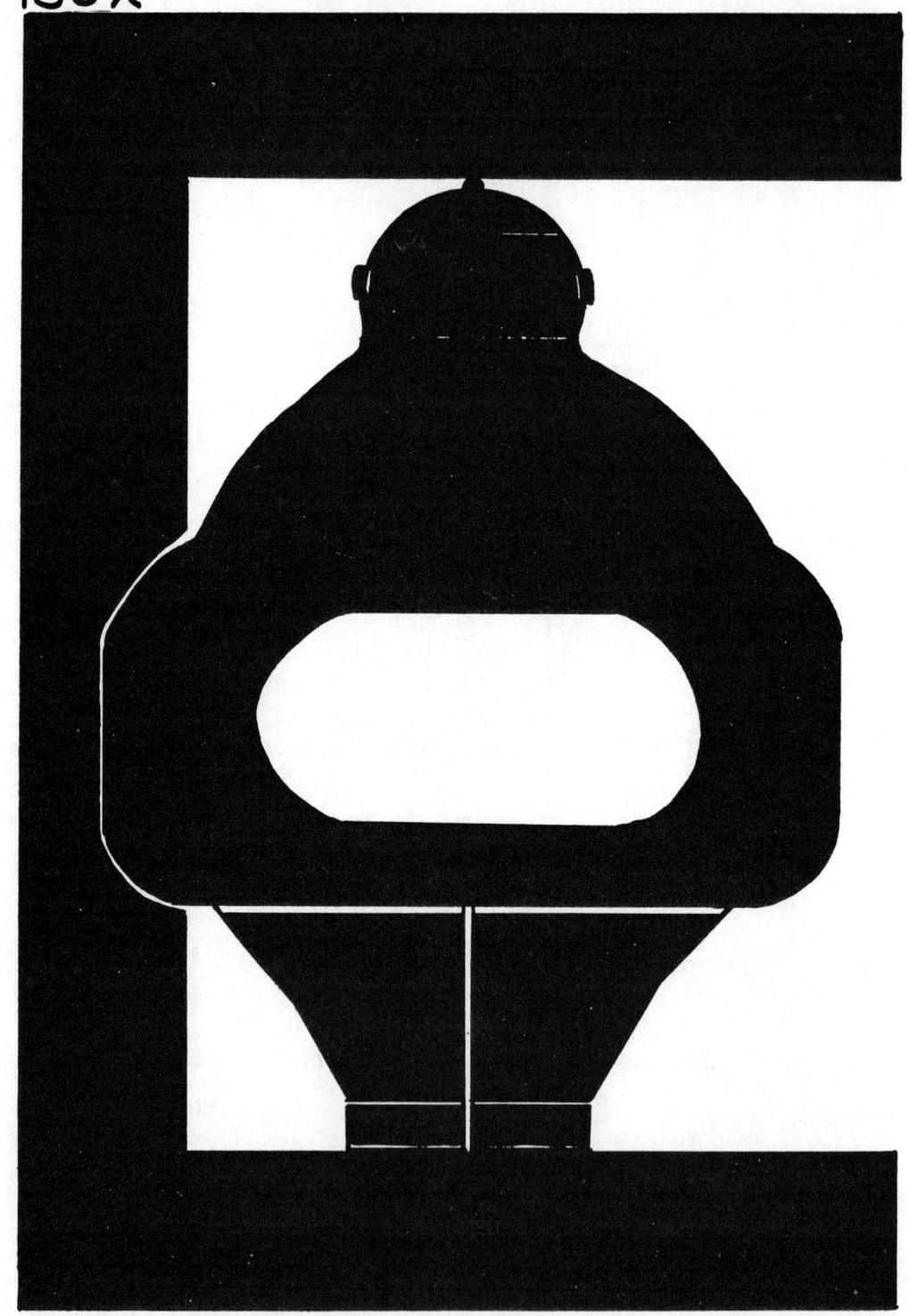

SHIN, SINCERITY, TRUST, FAITH;
SHINZURU, TO BELIEVE, TO TRUST, TO BELIEVE IN.

A PERSON'S 亻 WORDS STATEMENT 言 HAVE TRUST, SINCERITY, FAITH 信, ARE BELIEVED, TRUSTED, BELIEVED IN 信.

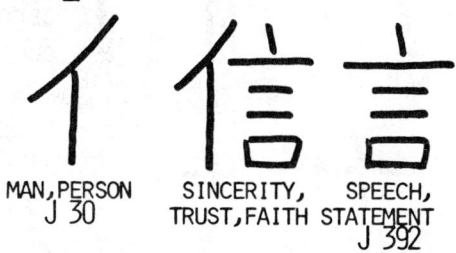

亻 MAN, PERSON J 30

信 SINCERITY, TRUST, FAITH

言 SPEECH, STATEMENT J 392

JME 9 STROKE 9 RAD 437

N454
hsin4
M2748
xìn
believe
trust
truth
sincerity
confidence

An honest man's word is as good as his bond.
          Don Quixote   Miguel de Cervantes

SHIN, MA, TRUTH, REALITY.
EYES 目 MUST BE TEN-TENTHS 十 (ACCURATE IN GIVING TO THE RECEIVING) HANDS 六.

JME 24 STROKE 10 RAD 438

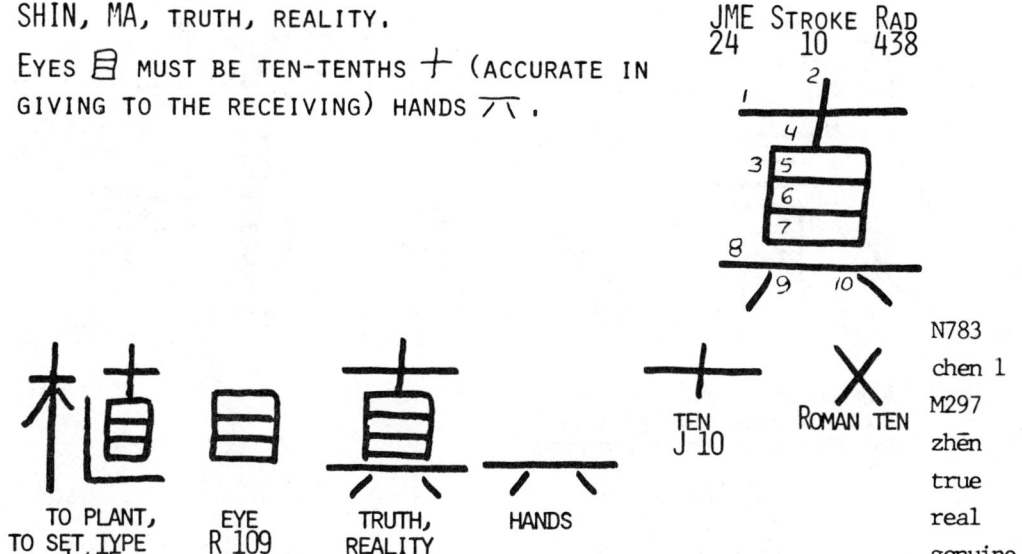

植 TO PLANT, TO SET TYPE J 435

目 EYE R 109

真 TRUTH, REALITY

六 HANDS

十 TEN J 10

✕ ROMAN TEN

N783
chen 1
M297
zhēn
true
real
genuine

439

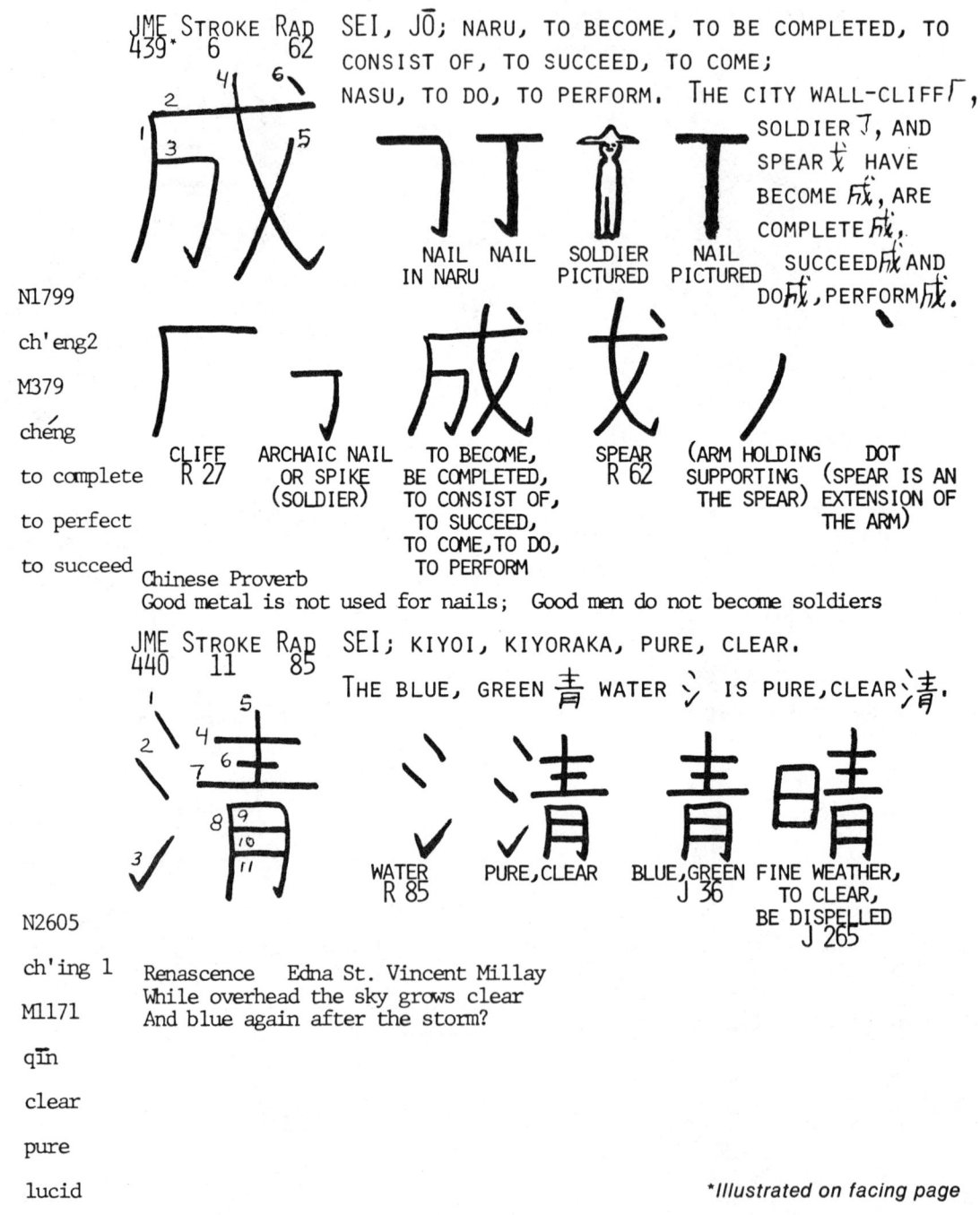

439

JME 439* Stroke 6 Rad 62

SEI, JŌ; NARU, TO BECOME, TO BE COMPLETED, TO CONSIST OF, TO SUCCEED, TO COME; NASU, TO DO, TO PERFORM. THE CITY WALL-CLIFF 厂, SOLDIER 丁, AND SPEAR 戈 HAVE BECOME 成, ARE COMPLETE 成, SUCCEED 成 AND DO 成, PERFORM 成.

N1799
ch'eng2
M379
chéng

to complete
to perfect
to succeed

NAIL IN NARU — NAIL PICTURED — SOLDIER PICTURED — NAIL PICTURED

CLIFF R 27 — ARCHAIC NAIL OR SPIKE (SOLDIER) — TO BECOME, BE COMPLETED, TO CONSIST OF, TO SUCCEED, TO COME, TO DO, TO PERFORM — SPEAR R 62 — (ARM HOLDING THE SPEAR) — DOT (SPEAR IS AN EXTENSION OF THE ARM)

Chinese Proverb
Good metal is not used for nails; Good men do not become soldiers

---

JME 440 Stroke 11 Rad 85

SEI; KIYOI, KIYORAKA, PURE, CLEAR.
THE BLUE, GREEN 青 WATER 氵 IS PURE, CLEAR 清.

WATER R 85 — PURE, CLEAR — BLUE, GREEN J 36 — FINE WEATHER, TO CLEAR, BE DISPELLED J 265

N2605
ch'ing 1
M1171
qīn

clear
pure
lucid

Renascence Edna St. Vincent Millay
While overhead the sky grows clear
And blue again after the storm?

*Illustrated on facing page

439 X

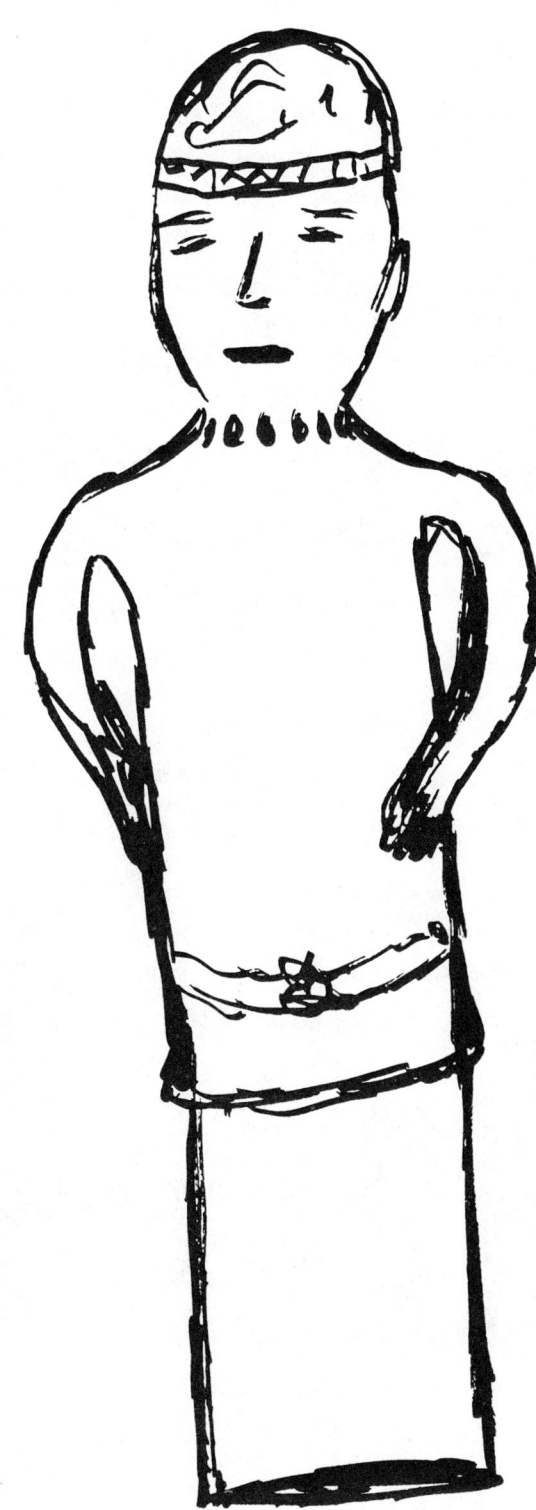

JAPANESE FUNERARY
HANIWA POTTERY
SOLDIER HAS VERY
NAILLIKE FORM

SEI, (ZEI); IKIOI, FORCE, VIGOR, POWER, INFLUENCE.

FORCE, VIGOR, POWER, INFLUENCE 勢 IS IN THE DIVISION 儿 OF LANDS UPON LANDS 坴 WHICH ARE FIEFS OF STRENGTH, POWER 力 ROUND, CIRCULAR 丸 (FROM THE CENTER). THE CENTRAL POWER OF IEYASU OR WM. THE CONQUEROR WAS HELD THUS.

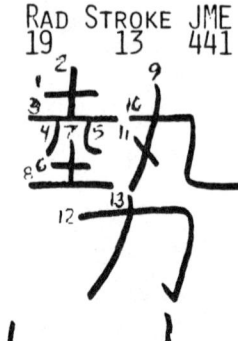

RAD 19 STROKE 13 JME 441

N735
shih4
M5799
shì
power
influence
authority
strength
aspect

陸 LAND J 529

坴 (LANDS UPON LANDS; FIEFS)

勢 FORCE, VIGOR, POWER, INFLUENCE

力 STRENGTH, POWER R 19

丸 ROUND, CIRCULAR N 155

九 NINE J 9

JŌ, SEI, SHIZUKANA, PEACE, QUIET, INACTIVITY; SHIZUMARU, TO BECOME QUIET; SHIZUMERU, TO MAKE CALM, TO SOOTHE.

THE QUARREL, DISPUTE 争 IS MADE CALM, SOOTHED, BECOMES QUIET, SILENT, PEACEFUL 青争 LIKE THE BLUE AND GREEN 青 (OF NATURE) OR WHAT IS UNRIPE, INEXPERIENCED 青.

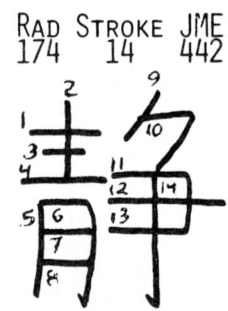

RAD 174 STROKE 14 JME 442

N5077
ching4
M1154
jìn
quiet
peaceful

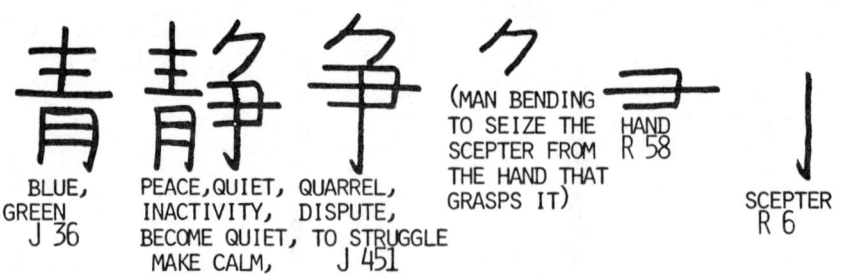

青 BLUE, GREEN J 36

静 PEACE, QUIET, INACTIVITY, BECOME QUIET, MAKE CALM, TO SOOTHE

争 QUARREL, DISPUTE, TO STRUGGLE J 451

⺈ (MAN BENDING TO SEIZE THE SCEPTER FROM THE HAND THAT GRASPS IT)

彐 HAND R 58

亅 SCEPTER R 6

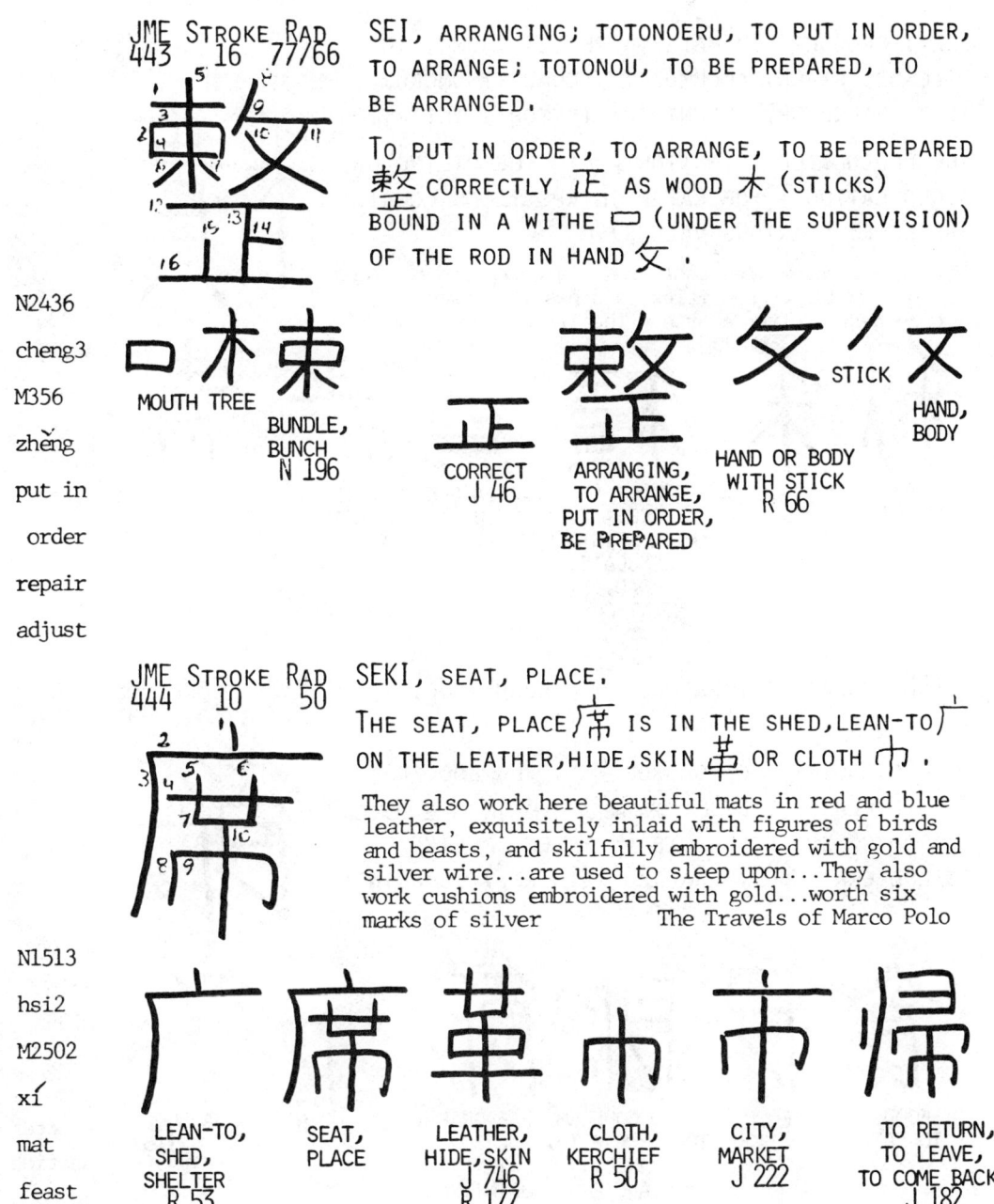

N2436
cheng3
M356
zhěng
put in
 order
repair
adjust

JME 443 Stroke 16 Rad 77/66

SEI, ARRANGING; TOTONOERU, TO PUT IN ORDER, TO ARRANGE; TOTONOU, TO BE PREPARED, TO BE ARRANGED.

TO PUT IN ORDER, TO ARRANGE, TO BE PREPARED 整 CORRECTLY 正 AS WOOD 木 (STICKS) BOUND IN A WITHE 口 (UNDER THE SUPERVISION) OF THE ROD IN HAND 攵.

口 MOUTH 木 TREE 束 BUNDLE, BUNCH N 196
正 CORRECT J 46
整 ARRANGING, TO ARRANGE, PUT IN ORDER, BE PREPARED
攵 / 又 STICK
HAND OR BODY WITH STICK R 66
HAND, BODY

N1513
hsi2
M2502
xí
mat
feast

JME 444 Stroke 10 Rad 50

SEKI, SEAT, PLACE.

THE SEAT, PLACE 席 IS IN THE SHED, LEAN-TO 广 ON THE LEATHER, HIDE, SKIN 革 OR CLOTH 巾.

They also work here beautiful mats in red and blue leather, exquisitely inlaid with figures of birds and beasts, and skilfully embroidered with gold and silver wire...are used to sleep upon...They also work cushions embroidered with gold...worth six marks of silver   The Travels of Marco Polo

广 LEAN-TO, SHED, SHELTER R 53
席 SEAT, PLACE
革 LEATHER, HIDE, SKIN J 746 R 177
巾 CLOTH, KERCHIEF R 50
市 CITY, MARKET J 222
帰 TO RETURN, TO LEAVE, TO COME BACK J 182

445

SEKI, PRODUCT (IN MATH), ACREAGE; TSUMU, TO PILE UP, STACK, ACCUMULATE, LOAD; TSUMORU, TO BE PILED UP, AMOUNT TO; TSUMORI, INTENTION.

RAD 115 STROKE 16 JME 445

THE PRODUCT OR INTENTION 積 IS THE PILING UP, ACCUMULATION 積 OF LAYERS, HEAPS 圭 AS COWRIE SHELLS 貝 (VARIOUS VALUES).

When the emperor sees that grain is cheap and abundant he buys up large quantities, and has it stored...his people never suffer dearth. The Travels of Marco Polo

N3306
chi 1
M500
jī
amass
store

秋 禾 積 貝 圭 青

AUTUMN J 89   GRAIN, RICE R 115   PRODUCT (MATH), ACREAGE, PILE UP, STACK, ACCUMULATE, LOAD, INTENTION   SEA SHELL, J 169   LAYERS, HEAPS   BLUE, GREEN J 36

SETSU, PARAGRAPH, SEASON, TIME; FUSHI, JOINT, KNOT, TUNE.

RAD 118 STROKE 13 JME 446

JOINTS, KNOTS 節 OF BAMBOO ⺮. BAMBOO ⺮ (FLUTE PLAYS) TUNE 節 BY PARAGRAPHS 節 IN TIME, SEASON 節. BAMBOO ⺮ SPROUTS, ROOTS 𠃍 EATEN 食 LIKE BOILED GRAIN 食. RAD 26 (TO RT.) IS JOINT 卩.

食 皀 即 節 卩 ⺮

FOOD, TO EAT J 253   GOOD R 138   TO CONFORM, TO AGREE WITH, NAMELY, TO TAKE ROOT N 3886   PARAGRAPH, SEASON, TIME, JOINT, KNOT, TUNE   JOINT R 26 RT. SIDE   BAMBOO R 118

N3402
chieh2
M795
jié
verse
chapter
section
joint
knot

JME	Stroke	Rad
447	15	120

SEN, LINE, TRACK, ROUTE, WIRE.
THE LINE, TRACK, ROUTE, WIRE 線 IS LIKE A THREAD 糸 OF WHITE 白 WATER 水 FROM A SPRING 泉.

The Bait   John Donne
Of golden sands, and crystal brooks,
With silken lines, and silver hooks.

N3580
hsien4
M2723
xiàn

thread
cotton
wire

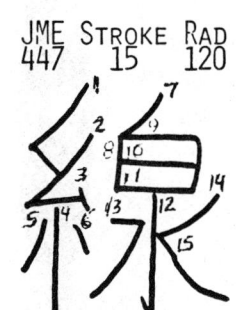
PICTURE OF COCOONS & THREADS

THREADS, STRINGS
J 83

LINE, TRACK, ROUTE, WIRE

SPRING, FOUNTAIN
N 3099

WATER
R 85

白
WHITE
J 37

JME	Stroke	Rad
448*	13	62

SEN, WAR, BATTLE, GAME, MATCH; TATAKAI, WAR, FIGHT, BATTLE, GAME, MATCH; TATAKAU, WAGE WAR, TO FIGHT, TO ENGAGE.

WAR, BATTLE, GAME, MATCH, TO FIGHT, TO ENGAGE IS A SPEAR 戈 (LA CROSSE, HOCKEY, POLO STICK) AND AN OBSERVATION POST 甲 OR SINGLE-WHEELED (DUG-IN) CHARIOT 車 OR OBSERVATION POST 甲 WHICH SEND APPLAUSE OR WARNINGS ヽゝ.

N1810
chan4
M147
chàn

to fight
to war
to contest

車
WHEEL, VEHICLE, CHARIOT
J 88

単
SINGLE
J 671

戦
WAR, BATTLE, GAME, MATCH, WAGE WAR, TO FIGHT

戈
SPEAR
R 62

弋
DART
R 56

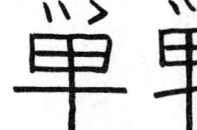
HAND HAND

Lastlie stode warre in glittering armes yclad,
With visage grim sterne lokes and blacklie hued;
In his right hand a naked sword he had
That to the hilt was all with blood imbrued.

A Vision of Warre
Thomas Sackville

*Illustrated on following page

448 X

SEN; ERABU, TO CHOOSE, TO SELECT.

TO CHOOSE, TO SELECT 選 IS TO STOP AND GO 辶 TURNING ONESELF 己 TO CHOOSE, TO SELECT 選, FROM THE BOTH 共 (OR WHAT IS) TOGETHER 共.

RAD STROKE JME
162   15   449

選

N4744
hsuan3
M2898
xuǎn
select
choose
elect
choice

辶 選 己 共 港

STOP & GO TO CHOOSE, TURN, CYCLE, TOGETHER, HARBOR
R 162   TO SELECT   I, MYSELF,   BOTH   J 397
                       ONESELF   J 376   (GOODS UNLOAD
                       J 777   FOR CHOICE &
                       ZODIAC SNAKE   SELECTION)
                       R 49

ZEN, NEN, (YES, BUT, HOWEVER).

YES, BUT, HOWEVER 然 (IS THE HUNGRY FAMILY'S RESPONSE TO COOKING) THE DOG'S 犬 BODY 夕 ON THE FIRE 灬. DOGS WERE COMMON FARE IN THE NORTH AM. PLAINS, CHINA, CENTRAL AM., ETC.

RAD STROKE JME
86   12   450

然

...we purchased all the dogs we could,
the fish being out of season
    Journals of the Lewis and Clark Expedition

夕 然 犬 灬 黑

BODY, MOON YES, BUT,   DOG   FIRE   BLACK
J 12   HOWEVER   J 66   R 86   J 80

N2770
jan2
M3072
rán
yes
certainly
really
still
but
although

A foreign diplomat gave Chinese statesman Li Hung-chang (1823-1901) a dog for a pet. Some time later, he asked Li what Li thought of the dog. "Yes, delicious," answered Li.

Two hundred dogs were cooked for a Hawaiian feast in 1820   Rev. Wm. Ellis

451

JME 451　STROKE 6　RAD 87

SŌ; ARASOI, DISPUTE, QUARREL, CONFLICT, CONTEST; ARASOU, TO SISPUTE, TO ARGUE, TO COMPETE.

DISPUTE, QUARREL, CONFLICT, TO ARGUE, TO COMPETE 争 IS A HAND ⇒ GRASPING A STICK, BATON, SCEPTER ｜ AS A MAN BENDS OVER ク IN THE CONFLICT, CONTEST, QUARREL, DISPUTE 争 FOR IT.

N186 cheng 1
M365 zhēng
contend
strive

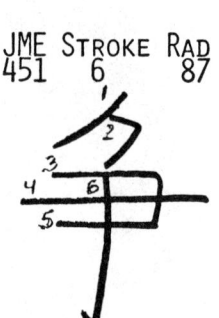

魚　　ク　　　　争　　　　　｜　　　　ヨ　　静
FISH　(MAN BEND-　DISPUTE,　　STICK, BARB,　HAND　SILENT,
J 190　ING OVER)　QUARREL,　NAIL SHAFT　R 58　QUIET,
　　　　　　　　CONFLICT,　R 6　　　　　　　PEACEFUL
　　　　　　　　TO DISPUTE,　　　　　　　　J 442
　　　　　　　　TO ARGUE,
　　　　　　　　TO COMPETE

JME 452　STROKE 9　RAD 109

SŌ, ASPECT, PHASE, PHYSIOGNOMY; SHŌ, MINISTER OF STATE; AI, MUTUAL, EACH OTHER.

TREE 木 AND EYE 目 ARE (LIKE) EACH OTHER, MUTUAL 相 IN HAVING AN ASPECT, PHASE, PHYSIOGNOMY 相. THE MINISTER OF STATE 相 IS (IMPOSING) LIKE A TREE 木 IN HIS EYE 目.

N2241 hsiang 4
M2562 xiàng
xiāng
mutual

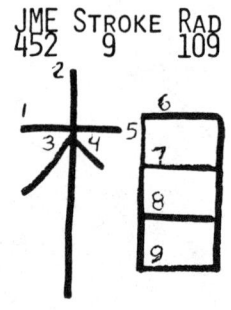

木　　　相　　　　　　目　　頁
TREE,　ASPECT, PHASE,　EYE　HEAD
WOOD　PHYSIOGNOMY,　R 109　R 181
J 15　MINISTER-OF-
　　　STATE,
　　　EACH OTHER

SOKU; HAYAI, SPEEDY, PROMPT, QUICK.

Speedy, prompt, quick 速 is stopping and going 辶 with the bundled wood 束 (bound 囗 wood 木). The fasces of the Roman Empire and of Fascist Italy as symbols for travel priority & speed.

Rad 162 Stroke 10 JME 453*

N4700
su4
M5505
sù
hurried
quickly
to urge

辶	速	束	木	囗	整
STOP & GO R 162	SPEEDY, PROMPT QUICK	BUNDLE, BUNCH N 196	TREE, WOOD J 15	MOUTH, EMBRASURE R 30	PUT IN ORDER, GET READY J 443

SOKU, (SON); IKI, BREATH.

The rubbing of noses 自 (as among Eskimos in greetings) between hearts, minds, spirits 心 in exchange of breath 息 (symbol of life itself).

Rad 132 Stroke 10 JME 454

Epipsychidion   Percy Bysshe Shelley
Our breath shall intermix, our bosoms bound,
And our veins beat together; and our lips
With other eloquence than words, eclipse
The soul that burns between them...

N3844
hsi2
M2495
xī
breath
vapor
to sigh

PICTORAL NOSE, (RHINE AS RHINECTOMY)

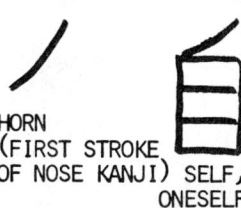
HORN (FIRST STROKE OF NOSE KANJI) | SELF, ONESELF, PERSON (ANCIENT KANJI FOR NOSE)

BREATH | SPIRIT, MIND, HEART J 95

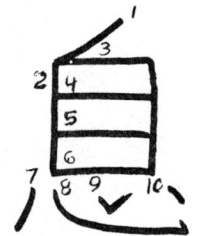
PICTOGRAPH OF HEART

Book of the Courtier   Baldassare Castiglione
...although the mouth is part of the body, the words that interpret the soul come from it so he delights in joining his mouth with that of a beloved woman in a kiss.

*Illustrated on following page

453 X

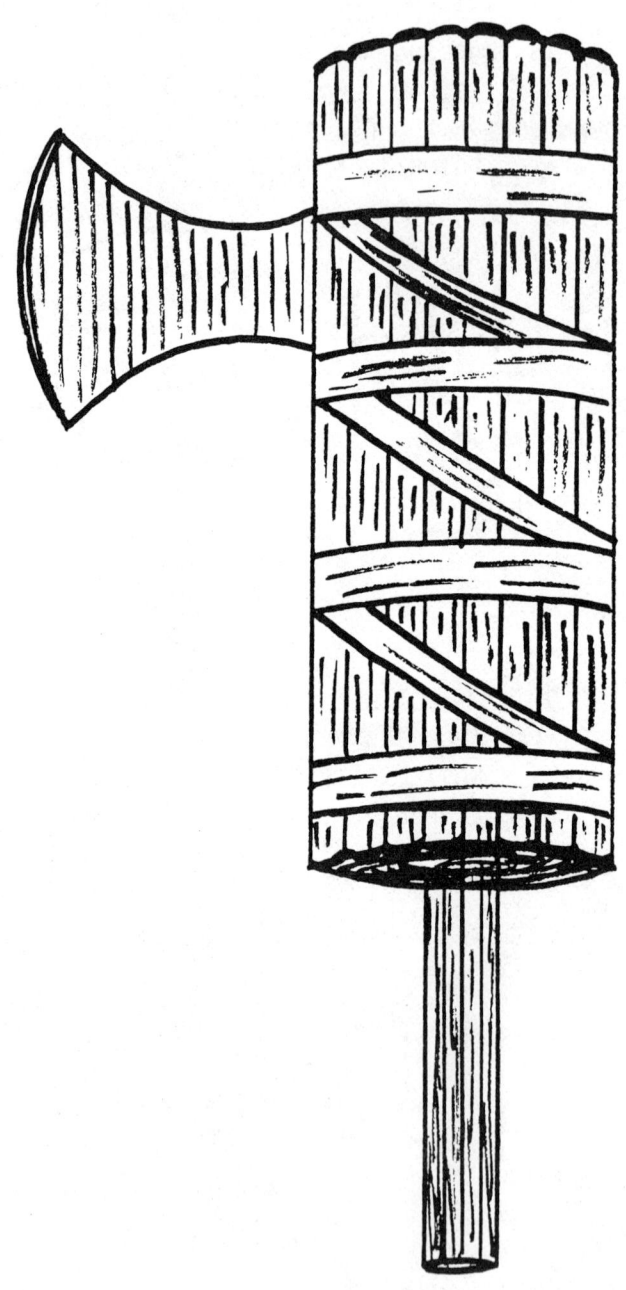

	JME	Stroke	Rad
	455	11	71

族

ZOKU, FAMILY, TRIBE, CLAN, RELATIVES.

The family, tribe, clan, relatives 方矢 (move together as nomads) in direction 方 like man's 𠂉 arrow 矢. (Volk: people & cloud).

Wolken meine Kinder, wandern gehen
Wollt ihr? Fahret wohl! Auf Wiedersehen!
Clouds, my children, do you want to wander off?
Farewell! Goodbye!
          Der Gesang des Meeres   Conrad Meyer

N2090
tsu2
M6830
zú

clan
tribe
class
family

方	族	矢	𠂉	𠆢
DIRECTION, WAY, PERSON J 138	FAMILY, TRIBE, CLAN, RELATIVES	ARROW R 111	PERSON, MAN R 9	PICTORAL PERSON STRIDING

	JME	Stroke	Rad
	456	13	120

続

ZOKU, CONTINUATION, SECOND SERIES; TSUZUKU, TO CONTINUE, TO FOLLOW IV; TSUZUKERU, TO CONTINUE TV; TSUZUKI, CONTINUITY.

A sale, selling 売 by a person 士 at a desk 冖 continues, follows, has continuation, a second series 続.

N3544
hsu4
M2865
xù

connect
join on
add to

糸	続	売	士	冖	読
THREADS, STRINGS R 120	CONTINUATION, 2ND SERIES, TO CONTINUE, TO FOLLOW, CONTINUITY	SALE, TO SELL J 301	MAN, FIGURE, SAMURAI J 410	DESK	TO READ J 123

457

SOTSU, SOLDIER, PRIVATE; SOSSURU, TO DIE.
PICTOGRAPH AS OF A RACK OF ARMS 卒, THE SOLDIER, PRIVATE 卒 WHO DIES 卒 AND IS A HEAD 亠 WITH DECORATIONS 人人 AND STANDS ON A SINGLE STEM ｜ READY TO BAR 一 WITH HIS ARMS.

RAD 8 STROKE 8 JME 457

亠 DIRECTION 人人 MEN, CORPSES 彳 STEP, WALK, FOLLOW 化 PICTORAL

卒 SOLDIER, PRIVATE, TO DIE
早 EARLY J104
草 GRASS J106
華 FLOWER, BLOSSOM N3995
準 TO RULE, IMITATE, STANDARD J637
単 SINGLE J671

N294 tsu2
M6827 zú
servant to die

The Charge of the Light Brigade   Lord Tennyson
Theirs not to reason why, theirs but to do and die;
Into the valley of death rode the six hundred.

The green grass, all that remains of the warrior's dream. Jpn. Proverb

SON, DESCENDANTS; MAGO, GRANDCHILD.
DESCENDANTS, GRANDCHILDREN 孫 ARE CHILDREN 子 IN THE SYSTEM, FAMILY LINE 系 WITH A HORN ノ (FOR CATTLE BLOODLINES & SELECTIVE BREEDING) AND THREAD 糸 FOR THE LINES 系 (OF DESCENT).

RAD 39 STROKE 10 JME 458

子 CHILD J31
孫 DESCENDANTS, GRANDCHILD
系 SYSTEM, FAMILY LINE J765
牛 COW, BULL, OX J62
糸 THREADS, STRINGS J83
係 CHARGE, DUTY, IN CHARGE OF, TO AFFECT, TO CONCERN J385

N1273 sun1
M5541 sūn
grandson posterity

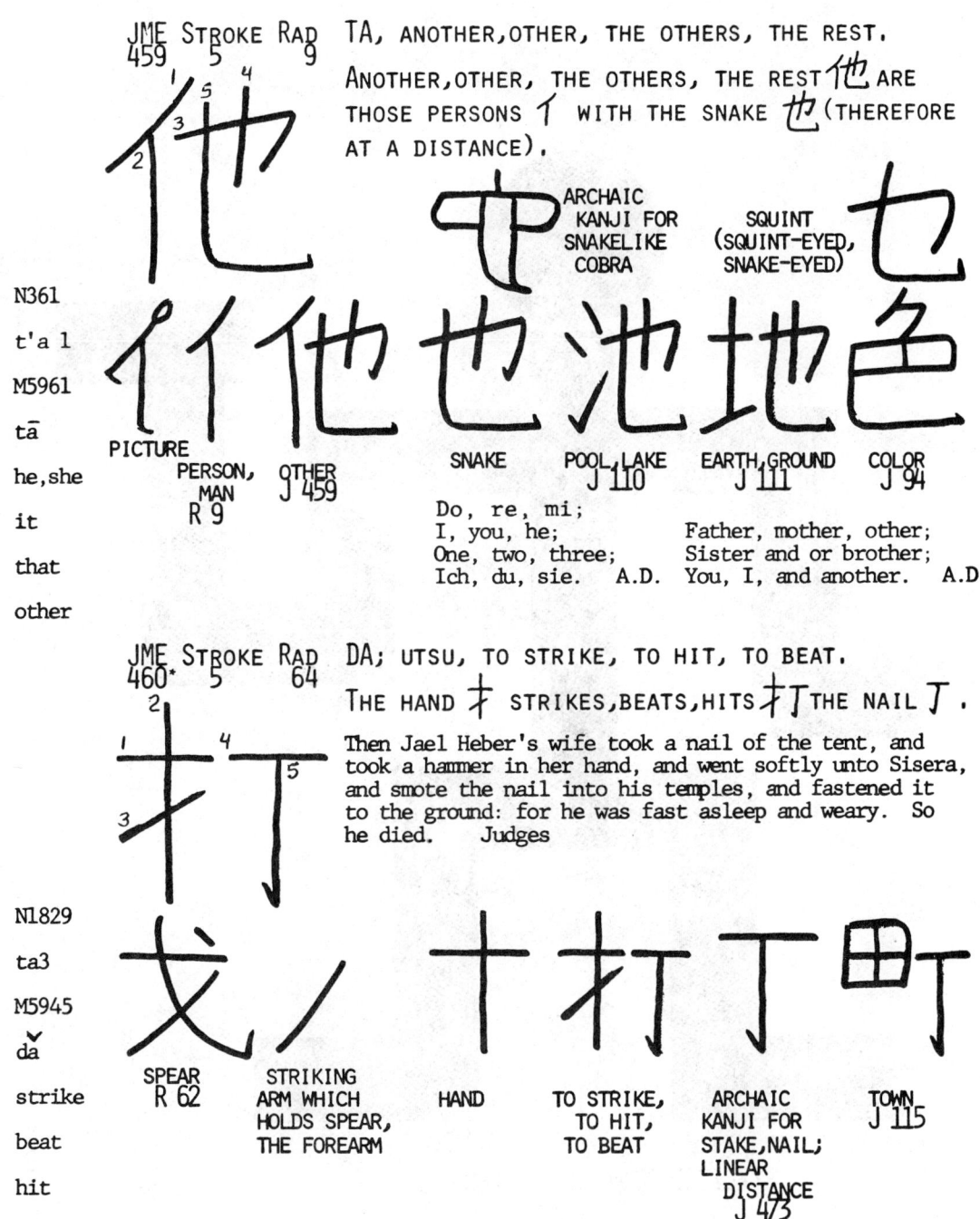

460X

STYLIZED HAWAIIAN PETROGLYPH

TAI, THE OPPOSITE, ANTONYM; TAI SURU, TO FACE TO CONFRONT; TSUI, PAIR, COUPLE.

CLASSIC SENTENCES IN ESSAYS, COMPOSITIONS 文 WERE MEASURED, CONTROLLED 寸 (AS IN THE LITERARY EXAMINATION STYLE OR GREEK AND HEBREW LITERATURE) BY PAIRING 对寸 SO THEY FACED OR CONFRONTED 对 (AS ON WALL SCROLLS).

RAD 67 STROKE 7 JME 461

N2067 tui4 M6562 duì opposite oppose to face

文	文	对	寸	寺	寸
PICTURE	ESSAY, COMPOSITION J 134	OPPOSITE, TO FACE, TO CONFRONT, PAIR, COUPLE	INCH, PULSE, "CONTROL" R 41	TEMPLE J 228	HAND

Psalms
Bless the Lord, O my soul: And all that is within me, bless His holy name.

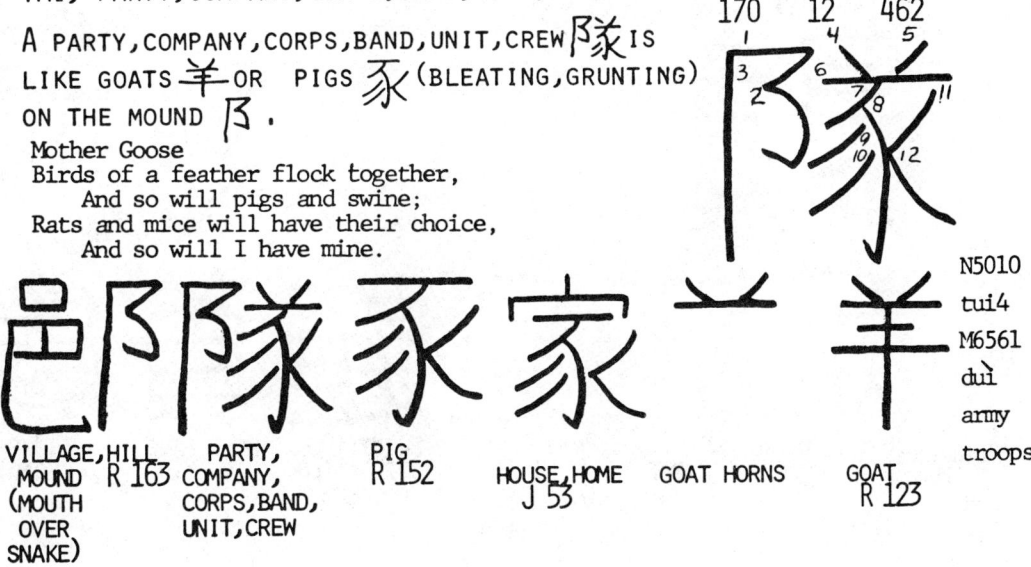

TAI, PARTY, COMPANY, CORPS, BAND, UNIT, CREW.

A PARTY, COMPANY, CORPS, BAND, UNIT, CREW 隊 IS LIKE GOATS 羊 OR PIGS 豕 (BLEATING, GRUNTING) ON THE MOUND 阝.

Mother Goose
Birds of a feather flock together,
  And so will pigs and swine;
Rats and mice will have their choice,
  And so will I have mine.

RAD 170 STROKE 12 JME 462

N5010 tui4 M6561 duì army troops

邑 阝	隊	豕	家		羊
VILLAGE, HILL, MOUND (MOUTH OVER SNAKE) R 163	PARTY, COMPANY, CORPS, BAND, UNIT, CREW	PIG R 152	HOUSE, HOME J 53	GOAT HORNS	GOAT R 123

(The Hawaiian demigod Kamapuaa took the form of a pig or a man).
(Man was known in Polynesia as long-pig for cannibal feasts).

463

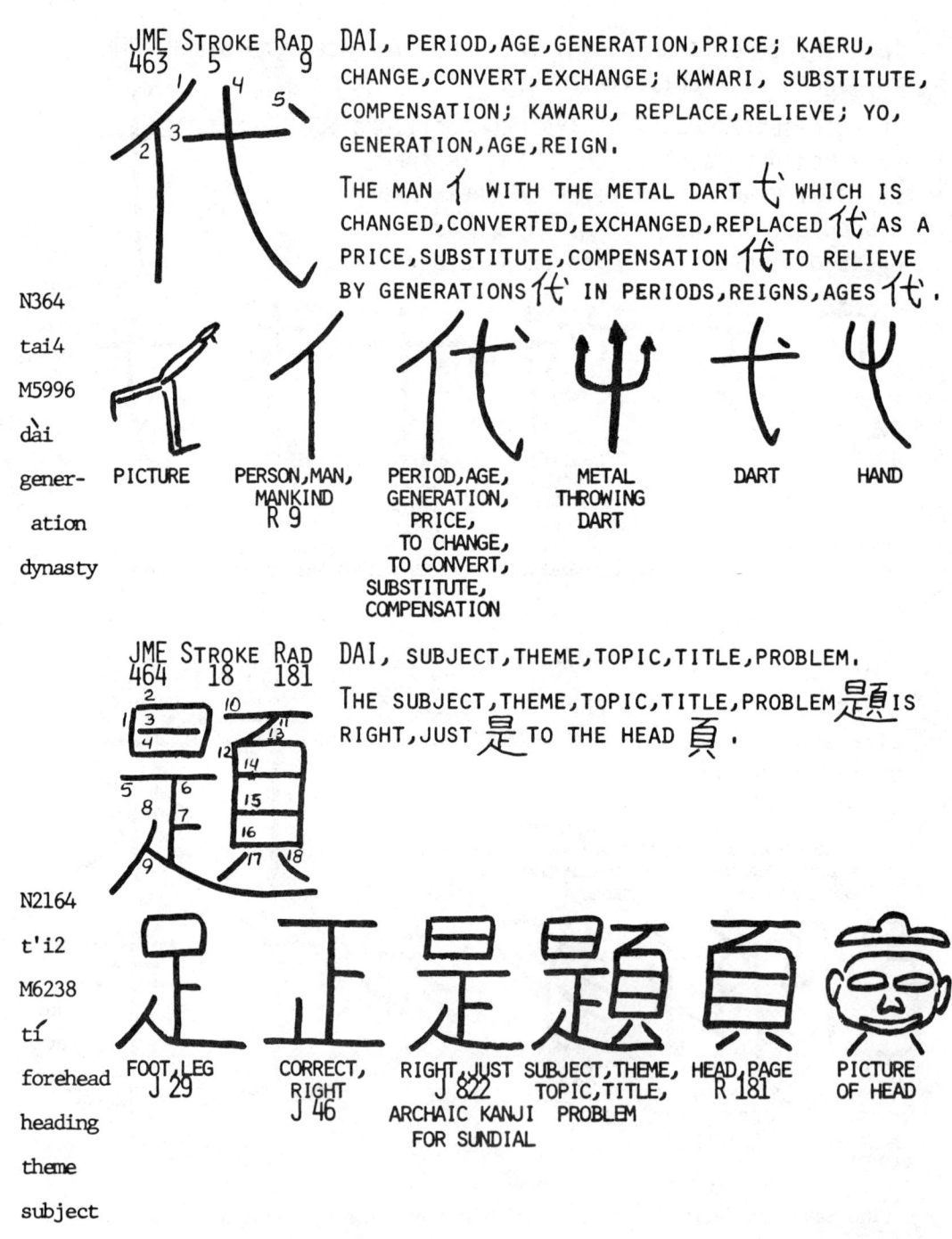

JME 463 · Stroke 5 · Rad 9

DAI, PERIOD, AGE, GENERATION, PRICE; KAERU, CHANGE, CONVERT, EXCHANGE; KAWARI, SUBSTITUTE, COMPENSATION; KAWARU, REPLACE, RELIEVE; YO, GENERATION, AGE, REIGN.

THE MAN 亻 WITH THE METAL DART 弋 WHICH IS CHANGED, CONVERTED, EXCHANGED, REPLACED 代 AS A PRICE, SUBSTITUTE, COMPENSATION 代 TO RELIEVE BY GENERATIONS 代 IN PERIODS, REIGNS, AGES 代.

N364 tai4
M5996 dài
gener-
 ation
dynasty

PICTURE | PERSON, MAN, MANKIND R 9 | PERIOD, AGE, GENERATION, PRICE, TO CHANGE, TO CONVERT, SUBSTITUTE, COMPENSATION | METAL THROWING DART | DART | HAND

JME 464 · Stroke 18 · Rad 181

DAI, SUBJECT, THEME, TOPIC, TITLE, PROBLEM.

THE SUBJECT, THEME, TOPIC, TITLE, PROBLEM 題 IS RIGHT, JUST 是 TO THE HEAD 頁.

N2164 t'i2
M6238 tí
forehead
heading
theme
subject

FOOT, LEG J 29 | CORRECT, RIGHT J 46 | RIGHT, JUST J 822 ARCHAIC KANJI FOR SUNDIAL | SUBJECT, THEME, TOPIC, TITLE, PROBLEM | HEAD, PAGE R 181 | PICTURE OF HEAD

TATSU; TASSURU, TO REACH, TO ARRIVE AT, TO ATTAIN, TO ACCOMPLISH.

TO REACH, TO ARRIVE AT, TO ATTAIN, TO ACCOMPLISH 達 IS GOING AND PAUSING 辶 OF THE GOAT 羊 ON THE EARTH 土 (AS UP & DOWN CLIFFS).

RAD 162 STROKE 12 JME 465

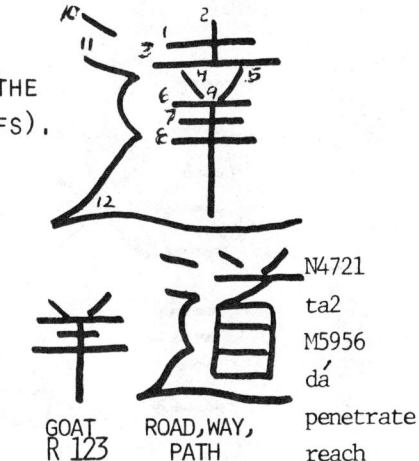

N4721
ta2
M5956
dá
penetrate
reach

辵	辶	達	土	羊	道
TO STOP & GO R 162	TO STOP & GO R 162 ABBRE.	TO REACH, TO ARRIVE AT, TO ATTAIN, ACCOMPLISH	SOIL, EARTH R 32	GOAT R 123	ROAD, WAY, PATH J 122

TAN, (SHORTNESS, BREVITY, DEFECT); MIJIKAI, SHORT, BRIEF.

SHORT, DEFECTIVE 短 ARE THE ARROWS 矢 USED IN THE VASE 豆 GAME. (TO SCORE, THE SHORT ARROWS ARE THROWN INTO THE OPENINGS OF THE VASE).

RAD 111 STROKE 12 JME 466

短

N3172
tuan3
M6542
duǎn
short
deficient

知	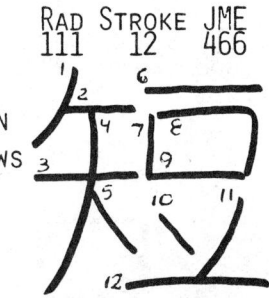	矢	短	豆	頭
TO KNOW J 122	PICTURE OF VASE TARGET	ARROW R 111	SHORT	BEANS, PEAS, VASE, URN R 151	BRAIN, HEAD, TOP J 294

467

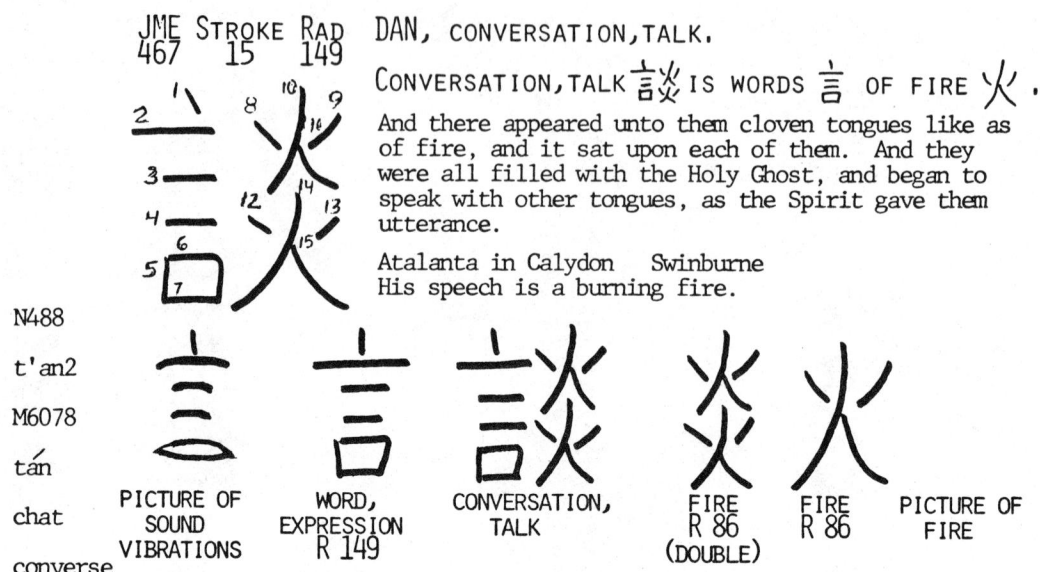

DAN, CONVERSATION, TALK.

CONVERSATION, TALK 談 IS WORDS 言 OF FIRE 火.

And there appeared unto them cloven tongues like as of fire, and it sat upon each of them. And they were all filled with the Holy Ghost, and began to speak with other tongues, as the Spirit gave them utterance.

Atalanta in Calydon   Swinburne
His speech is a burning fire.

N488
t'an2
M6078
tán
chat
converse

PICTURE OF SOUND VIBRATIONS | WORD, EXPRESSION R 149 | CONVERSATION, TALK | FIRE R 86 (DOUBLE) | FIRE R 86 | PICTURE OF FIRE

Out of his mouth go burning lamps, and sparks of fire leap out.   Job

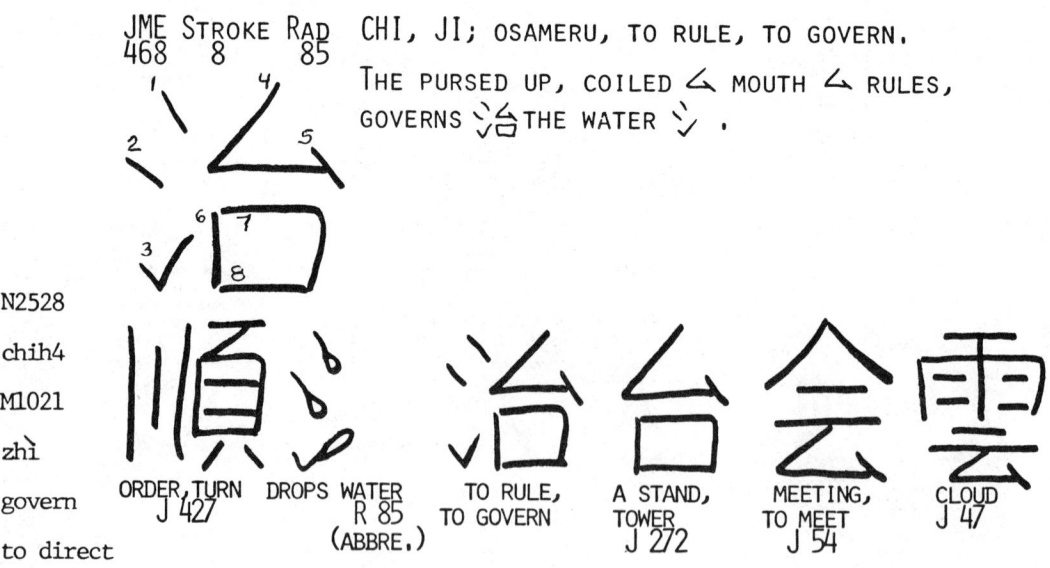

CHI, JI; OSAMERU, TO RULE, TO GOVERN.

THE PURSED UP, COILED 厶 MOUTH 厶 RULES, GOVERNS 治 THE WATER 氵.

N2528
chih4
M1021
zhì
govern
to direct

ORDER, TURN J 427 | DROPS WATER R 85 (ABBRE.) | TO RULE, TO GOVERN | A STAND, TOWER J 272 | MEETING, TO MEET J 54 | CLOUD J 47

CHI; OKU, TO PUT, TO PLACE, TO SET.
TEN 十 PAIRS OF EYES 目 AS WITH A SQUARE ∟
PUT, PLACE, SET 置 A NET ⎕.

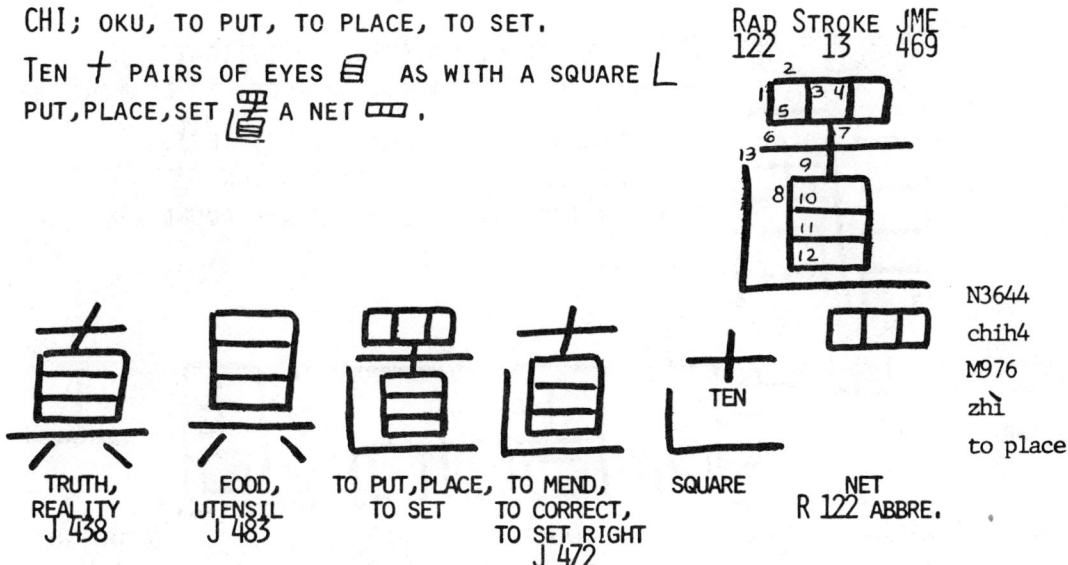

RAD 122   STROKE 13   JME 469

N3644
chih4
M976
zhì
to place

TRUTH, REALITY J 438

FOOD, UTENSIL J 483

TO PUT, PLACE, TO SET

TO MEND, TO CORRECT, TO SET RIGHT J 472

SQUARE
R 122

NET ABBRE.

TEN

CHŌ, (NOTEBOOK, REGISTER, CURTAIN).
NOTEBOOK, REGISTER, CURTAIN 帳 IS THE LONG 長
CLOTH 巾 OF THE HEAD, CHIEF 長 USED FOR THAT.

RAD 50   STROKE 11   JME 470

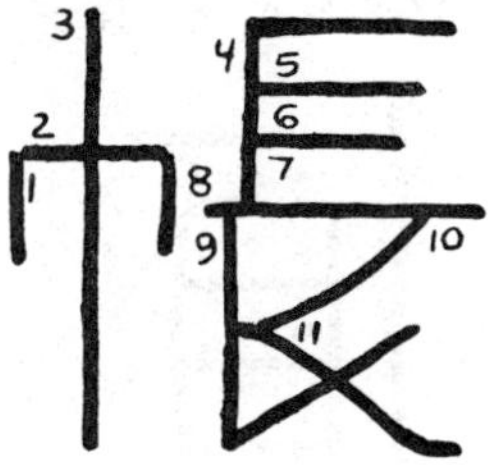

N1478
chang4
M197
zhàng
curtain
screen
scroll

CITY, MARKET J 222

CLOTH, KERCHIEF R 50

NOTEBOOK, REGISTER, CURTAIN

LONG, CHIEF, HEAD, ORGANIZATION J 116

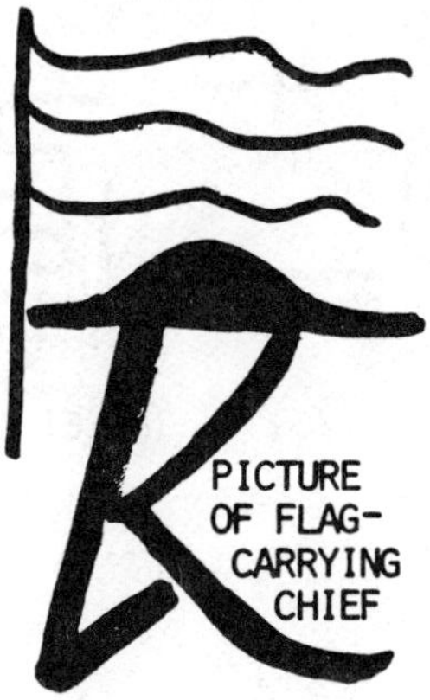

PICTURE OF FLAG-CARRYING CHIEF

471

JME 471 **Stroke** 15 **Rad** 149

CHŌ, TUNE, TONE; **CHOZURU**, INVESTIGATE, SCRUTINIZE; **SHIRABERU**, TO TEST, TO EXAMINE.

One investigates, scrutinizes, tests, examines 調 the words, expressions 言 and the tune or tone 調 going round and round 周.

N4392
t'iao2
M6298
diào
tiáo

tune
investigate
inspect

言 WORD, SPEECH, EXPRESSION J 392

調 INVESTIGATE, SCRUTINIZE, TO TEST, TO EXAMINE

周 TO GO ROUND, CIRCUMFERENCE J 632

回 TURN, ROTATION, ROLL, A TURN

週 WEEK J 242

土 EARTH, SOIL J 32

JME 472* **Stroke** 8 **Rad** 109

CHOKU, JIKI; **NAOSU**, TO MEND, TO REPAIR, TO REFORM, TO CORRECT.

Ten 十 pairs of eyes 目 with a square ∟ mend, repair, reform, correct 直.

Thou shalt me fynde as just as is a squyre...
— Geoffrey Chaucer

N775
chih2
M1006
zhí

straight
upright
perpendicular

∟ SQUARE

十 TEN

直 TO MEND, TO CORRECT, TO SET RIGHT

目 EYE R 109

置 TO PUT, PLACE J 469

真 TRUTH, REALITY J 438

県 PREFECTURE J 203 (THE HEAD HANGING AT THE CITY GATE REFORMS & CORRECTS)

*Illustrated on facing page

472X

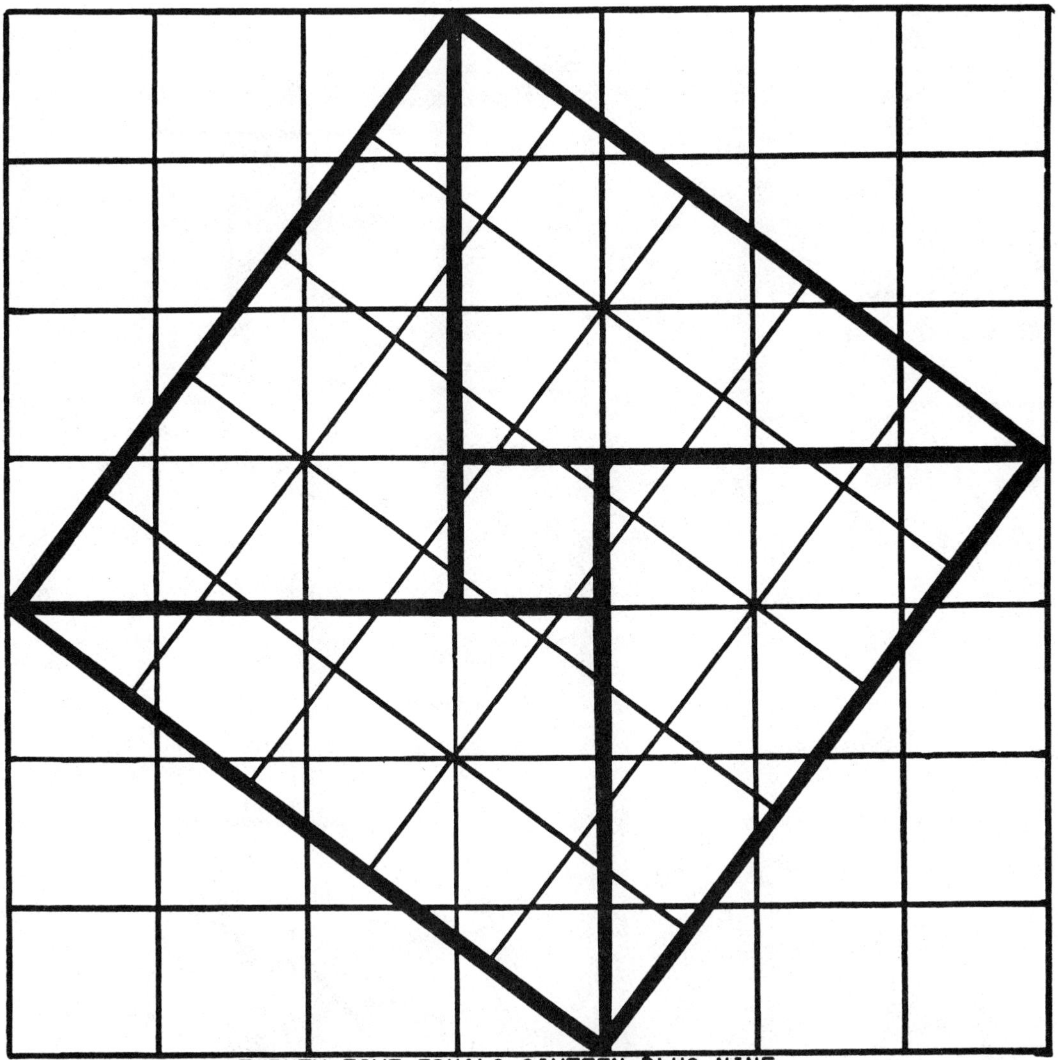

TWENTY-FIVE EQUALS SIXTEEN PLUS NINE

The Pythagorean Theorem (the square of the hypotenuse equals the squares of the legs of a right-angled triangle) proven diagramatically in the <u>Chou Pei Suan Ching.</u> The right angle, important in trignometric measurement, is appropriated in kanji.

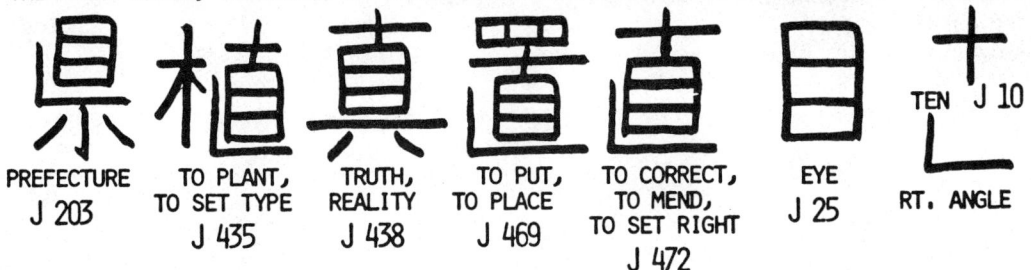

県 — PREFECTURE J 203
植 — TO PLANT, TO SET TYPE J 435
真 — TRUTH, REALITY J 438
置 — TO PUT, TO PLACE J 469
直 — TO CORRECT, TO MEND, TO SET RIGHT J 472
目 — EYE J 25
十 — TEN J 10
ᄂ — RT. ANGLE

473

TEI, "D", FOURTH; CHŌ, COUNTER FOR GUNS AND TOOLS; -CHO, (CITY) BLOCK, LEAF (OF PAPER).

THE ARCHAIC NAIL 丁 OR HEADED ─ BARB 亅 IS NOW A COUNTER 丁 FOR GUNS OR TOOLS (USUALLY OF METAL AND THE SAME SHAPE). THE SURVEY STAKE 丁 (AS A MEASURER NOW APPLIES) TO A (CITY) BLOCK 丁 & A LEAF 丁 (OF PAPER). AS A STELLAR CALENDAR SIGN 丁 NOW MEANS "D"

RAD 1 STROKE 2 JME 473

N2 ting 1 M6381 dīng person male adult

TO BECOME 成 J 439
TO STRIKE, TO HIT, BEAT 打 J 460
HOOK, BARB 亅 R 6
ARCHAIC NAIL, GUN COUNTER, TOOL COUNTER, FOURTH, CITY BLOCK, LEAF (OF PAPER) 丁
HEAD / SHAFT — FIRST / SECOND / THIRD / FOURTH
TOWN 町 J 115

TEI, JŌ; SADAMARU, TO BE DECIDED, BE SETTLED IV; SADAMERU, TO DECIDE, TO ESTABLISH, TO DETERMINE, TO FIX TV.

THE FOOT 足 STOPS 止 & THE NAIL, STAKE 丁 IS FIXED 定 TO DECIDE, SETTLE, ESTABLISH 定 THE ROOF 宀 RIGHTLY, CORRECTLY 正.

RAD 40 STROKE 8 JME 474

N1296 tìng4 M6393 dìng to fix decide

TOP, ON, ABOVE, GO UP, RISE 上 J 20
TO STOP 止 J 220
CORRECT, RIGHT 正 J 46
FOOT, LEG 足 J 29
FIX, DECIDE, ESTABLISH 定
ROOF 宀 J 40

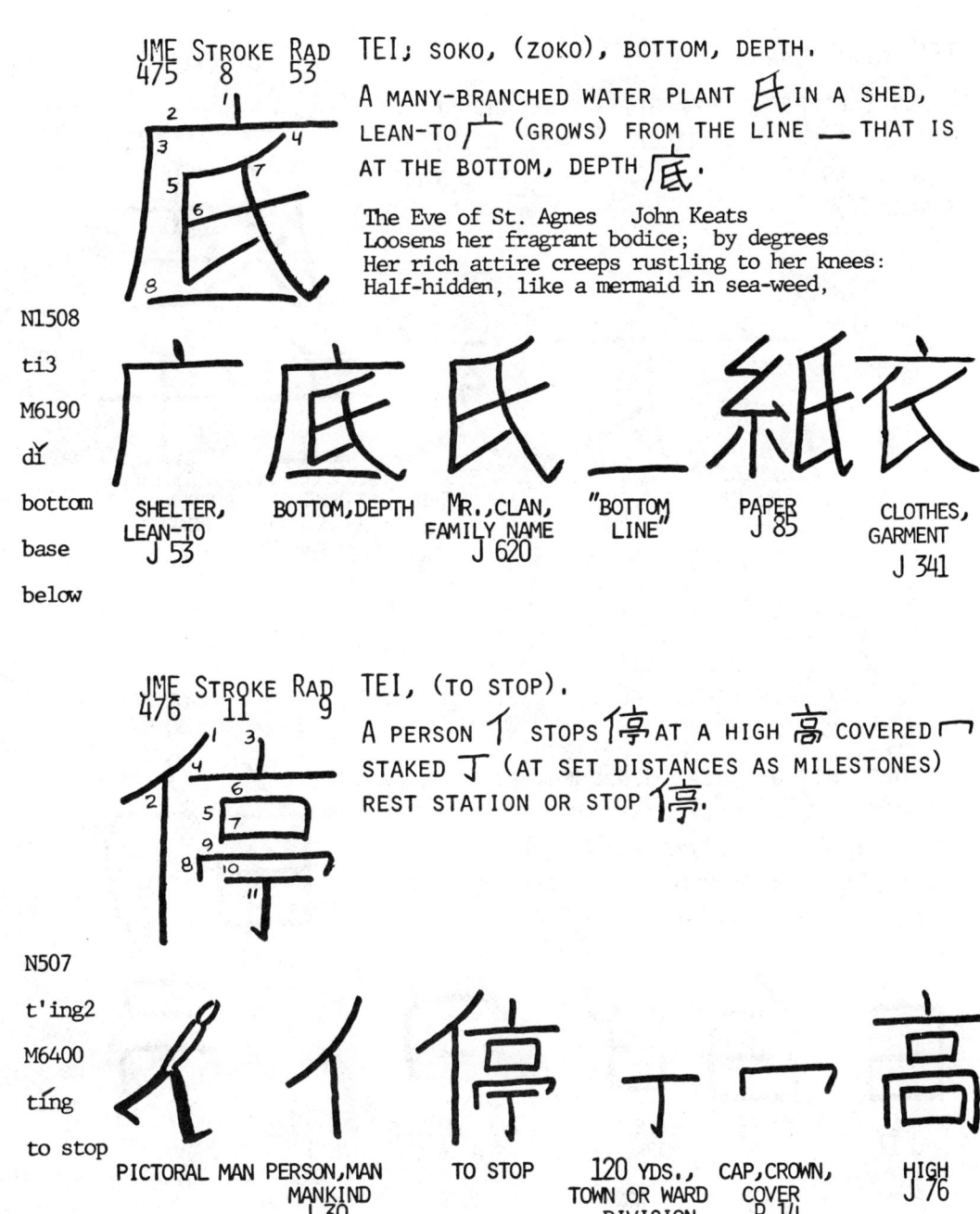

475

JME 475 Stroke 8 Rad 53

TEI; SOKO, (ZOKO), BOTTOM, DEPTH.

A MANY-BRANCHED WATER PLANT 氏 IN A SHED, LEAN-TO 广 (GROWS) FROM THE LINE ＿ THAT IS AT THE BOTTOM, DEPTH 底.

The Eve of St. Agnes   John Keats
Loosens her fragrant bodice; by degrees
Her rich attire creeps rustling to her knees:
Half-hidden, like a mermaid in sea-weed,

N1508
ti3
M6190
dǐ
bottom
base
below

广 SHELTER, LEAN-TO J 53
底 BOTTOM, DEPTH
氏 MR., CLAN, FAMILY NAME J 620
＿ "BOTTOM LINE"
紙 PAPER J 85
衣 CLOTHES, GARMENT J 341

JME 476 Stroke 11 Rad 9

TEI, (TO STOP).

A PERSON 亻 STOPS 停 AT A HIGH 高 COVERED 冖 STAKED 丁 (AT SET DISTANCES AS MILESTONES) REST STATION OR STOP 停.

N507
t'ing2
M6400
tíng
to stop

PICTORAL MAN
亻 PERSON, MAN MANKIND J 30
停 TO STOP
丁 120 YDS., TOWN OR WARD DIVISION
冖 CAP, CROWN, COVER R 14
高 HIGH J 76

477

TEI; NIWA, GARDEN.

UNDER THE SHED, LEAN-TO 广 (GREENHOUSE), A MAN 壬 IS CARRYING LOADS 二 AT THE ENDS OF A POLE 丨 AS HE TAKES LONG STEPS 廴 TO THE GARDEN 庭.

RAD 53　STROKE 10　JME 477

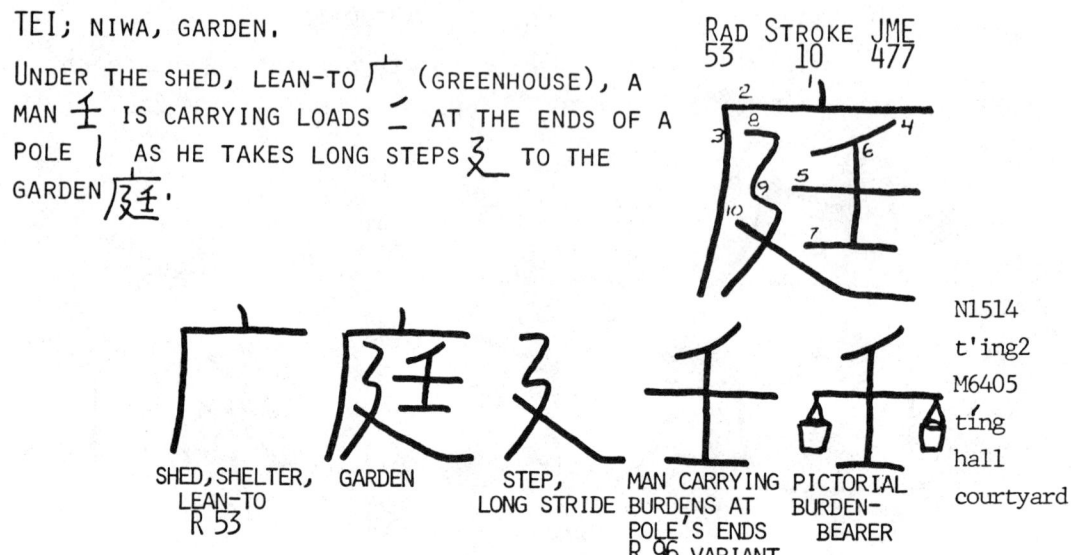

N1514 t'ing2
M6405 tíng
hall
courtyard

広 SHED, SHELTER, LEAN-TO R 53

庭 GARDEN

廴 STEP, LONG STRIDE

壬 MAN CARRYING BURDENS AT POLE'S ENDS R 96 VARIANT

乕 PICTORIAL BURDEN-BEARER

478

TEKI, (LIKE, SIMILAR); -TEKI, ADJECTIVE ENDING; MATO, MARK, TARGET.

RAD 106　STROKE 8　JME 478

THE OLD UNIT OF AREA (0.355 SQ. FT.) OR OF CAPACITY 勺 (.125 GI.) WAS LIKE, SIMILAR 的 TO THE WHITE 白 TARGET, MARK 白勺. THE MARK OR TARGET BEING HIT OR MISSED CAUSES ADJECTIVES.

To hit the bird in the eye.　English Proverb

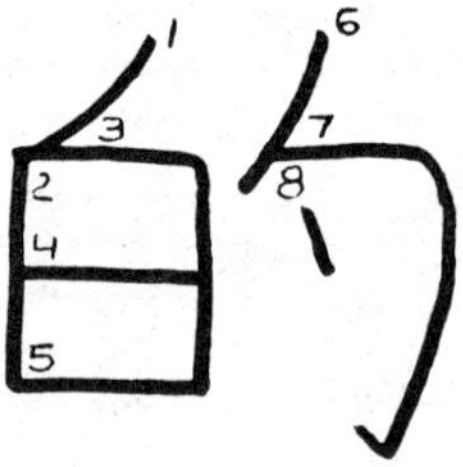

N3097 ti4
M6213 de
bull's-eye
clear
evident
possessive

日 SUN J 11

白 WHITE J 37

的 LIKE, SIMILAR, MARK, TARGET

勺 OLD UNIT OF AREA OR OF CAPACITY (0.152 GI.) (0.355 SQ.FT.)

白 WHITE J 37

勺 DIP, LADLE N 740

丶 DOT R 3 (LADLE'S EXTENDED POWERS) IRRIGATE

弓 BOW R 57

烏 CROW, ROOK M 7166

鳥 BIRD J 117

Romeo and Juliet　William Shakespear
MERCUTIO. Alas, poor Romeo, he is already dead! stabbed with a white woman's black eye: shot through the heart with a love-song; the very pin of his heart cleft with that blind bow-boy's butt-shaft.

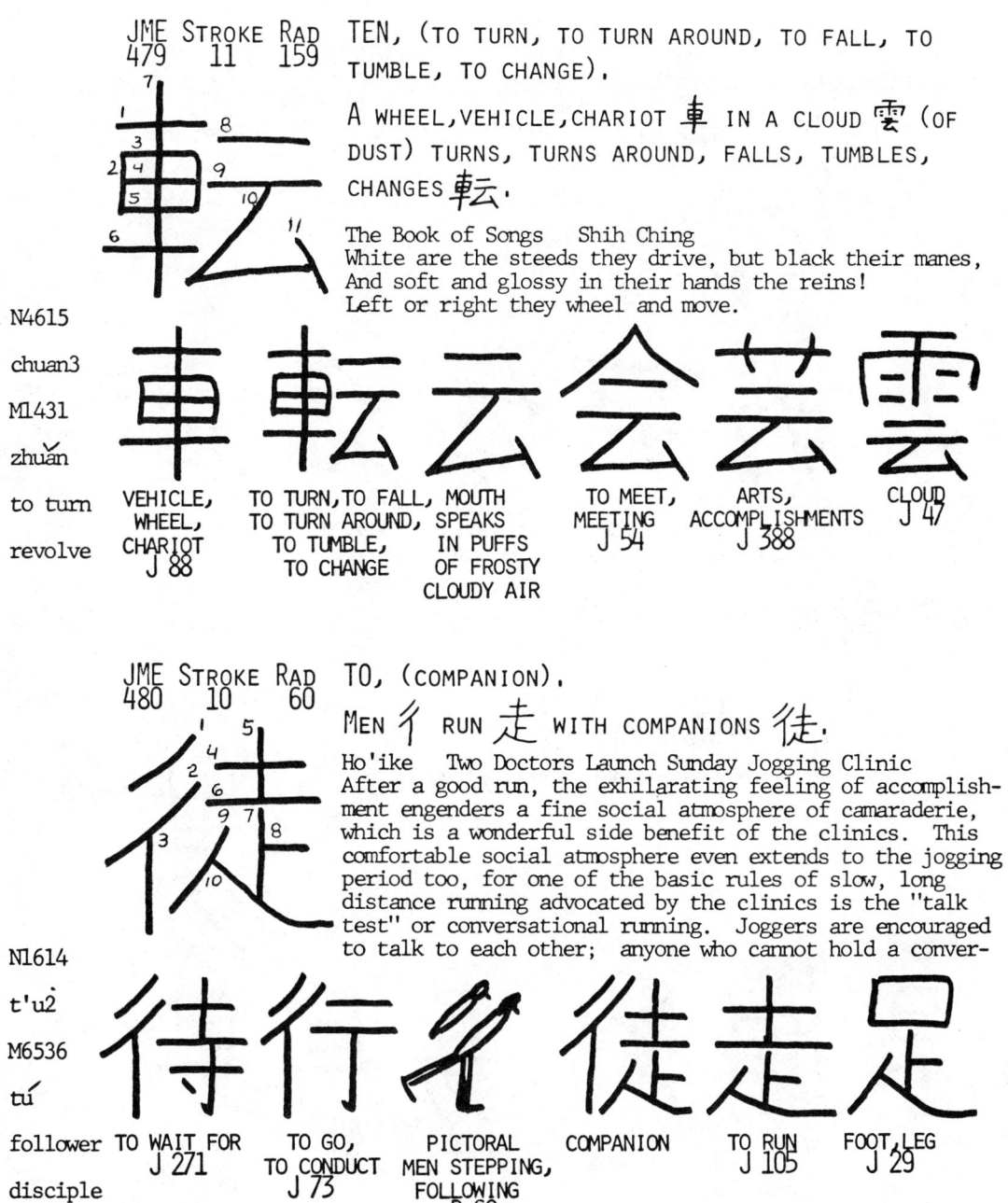

JME 479 Stroke 11 Rad 159

TEN, (TO TURN, TO TURN AROUND, TO FALL, TO TUMBLE, TO CHANGE).

A WHEEL, VEHICLE, CHARIOT 車 IN A CLOUD 雲 (OF DUST) TURNS, TURNS AROUND, FALLS, TUMBLES, CHANGES 転.

The Book of Songs   Shih Ching
White are the steeds they drive, but black their manes,
And soft and glossy in their hands the reins!
Left or right they wheel and move.

N4615 chuan3
M1431 zhuǎn
to turn
revolve

車 VEHICLE, WHEEL, CHARIOT J88
転 TO TURN, TO FALL, TO TURN AROUND, TO TUMBLE, TO CHANGE
云 MOUTH SPEAKS IN PUFFS OF FROSTY CLOUDY AIR
会 TO MEET, MEETING J54
芸 ARTS, ACCOMPLISHMENTS J388
雲 CLOUD J47

JME 480 Stroke 10 Rad 60

TO, (COMPANION).

MEN 彳 RUN 走 WITH COMPANIONS 徒.

Ho'ike   Two Doctors Launch Sunday Jogging Clinic
After a good run, the exhilarating feeling of accomplishment engenders a fine social atmosphere of camaraderie, which is a wonderful side benefit of the clinics. This comfortable social atmosphere even extends to the jogging period too, for one of the basic rules of slow, long distance running advocated by the clinics is the "talk test" or conversational running. Joggers are encouraged to talk to each other; anyone who cannot hold a conver-

N1614 t'u2
M6536 tú
follower
disciple

待 TO WAIT FOR J271
行 TO GO, TO CONDUCT J73
彳 PICTORAL MEN STEPPING, FOLLOWING R60
徒 COMPANION
走 TO RUN J105
足 FOOT, LEG J29

sation while jogging is running too fast for his physical condition.
                                                                    Tommy Kono

481

DO; TSUTOMERU, TO EXERT ONESELF, TO TRY HARD; RAD 19 STROKE 7 JME 481
TSUTOMETE, AS MUCH AS POSSIBLE, DILIGENTLY.

THE SERVANT, FELLOW 奴 WITH STRENGTH 力 EXERTS HIMSELF, TRIES HARD 努 DILIGENTLY, AS MUCH AS POSSIBLE 努.

努

N717
nu3
M4755
nǔ
exert
strive

力	努	奴	女	又
PICTURE OF STRENGTH	STRENGTH, POWER J 148	TO EXERT ONESELF, TO TRY HARD, AS MUCH AS POSSIBLE, DILIGENTLY	MANSERVANT, FELLOW, GUY N 1186	WOMAN, GIRL, FEMALE R 38	HAND R 29

TŌ; YU, HOT WATER.

FLUID 氵 HOT WATER 湯 IS WARM 温 LIKE THE FLAT — PLACE 場 WHERE CHAMELEONS 易 SUN 日

RAD 85 STROKE 12 JME 482

湯

N2633
t'ang 1
M6101
tāng
hot water

温	場	氵	湯	旦	易
WARM J 162	PLACE J 252	DROPS WATER	HOT WATER R 85	MORNING, DAWN, N 2098	EASY, DIVINATION J 545 (CHAMELEON)

483

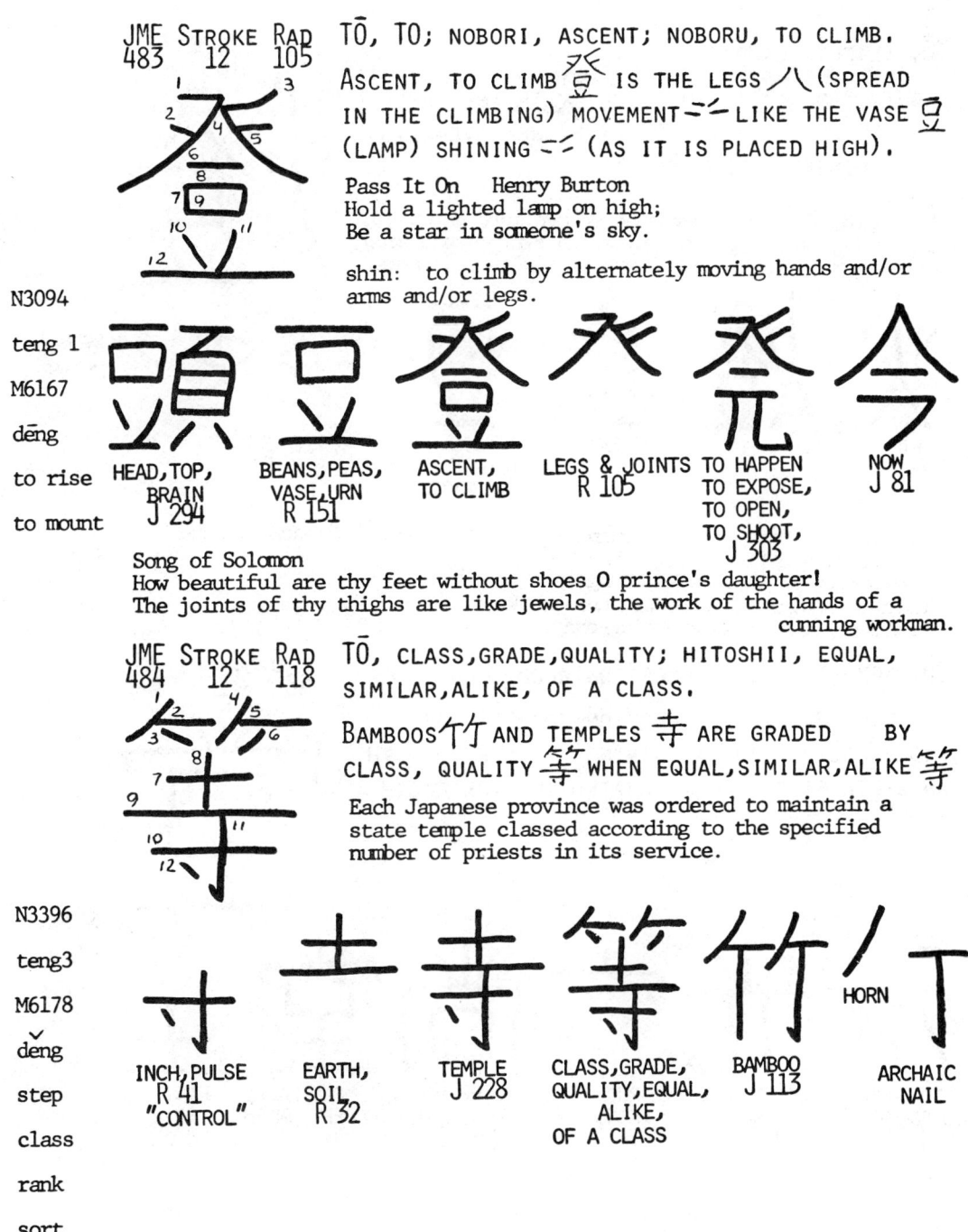

JME 483 Stroke 12 Rad 105

TŌ, TO; NOBORI, ASCENT; NOBORU, TO CLIMB.
ASCENT, TO CLIMB 登 IS THE LEGS 癶 (SPREAD IN THE CLIMBING) MOVEMENT ニ LIKE THE VASE 豆 (LAMP) SHINING ニ (AS IT IS PLACED HIGH).

Pass It On   Henry Burton
Hold a lighted lamp on high;
Be a star in someone's sky.

shin: to climb by alternately moving hands and/or arms and/or legs.

N3094
teng 1
M6167
dēng
to rise
to mount

HEAD, TOP, BRAIN   J 294
BEANS, PEAS, VASE, URN   R 151
ASCENT, TO CLIMB
LEGS & JOINTS   R 105
TO HAPPEN, TO EXPOSE, TO OPEN, TO SHOOT, J 303
NOW   J 81

Song of Solomon
How beautiful are thy feet without shoes O prince's daughter!
The joints of thy thighs are like jewels, the work of the hands of a cunning workman.

JME 484 Stroke 12 Rad 118

TŌ, CLASS, GRADE, QUALITY; HITOSHII, EQUAL, SIMILAR, ALIKE, OF A CLASS.
BAMBOOS 竹 AND TEMPLES 寺 ARE GRADED BY CLASS, QUALITY 等 WHEN EQUAL, SIMILAR, ALIKE 等

Each Japanese province was ordered to maintain a state temple classed according to the specified number of priests in its service.

N3396
teng3
M6178
děng
step
class
rank
sort
to wait

INCH, PULSE R 41 "CONTROL"
EARTH, SOIL   R 32
TEMPLE   J 228
CLASS, GRADE, QUALITY, EQUAL, ALIKE, OF A CLASS
BAMBOO   J 113
HORN
ARCHAIC NAIL

485

TŌ, (LIGHT, LAMP).

LIGHT, LAMP 燈 IS THE FIRE 火 IN THE LAMP-VASE 豆 WHICH SHINES 癶 LIKE THE MOVEMENTS OF A CLIMBER'S LEGS 癶.

Judges
And he divided the three hundred men into three companies, and he put a trumpet in every man's hand, with empty pitchers, and lamps within the pitchers.

RAD 86 STROKE 16 JME 485

N2800
teng 1
M6169
dēng
lamp
lantern

火	燈	登	豆	癶
FIRE J 13	LIGHT, LAMP	ASCENT, TO CLIMB	PEAS, BEANS (ARCHAIC KANJI FOR VASE)	LEG JOINTS R 105

The Drama at Home, or An Evening With Puff   James Robinson Planche
Ching-a-ring-a-ring-ching! Feast of Lanterns!
What a crop of chopsticks, hongs and gongs!
Hundred thousand Chinese crinkum-crankums,
Hung among the bells and ding-dongs!

DŌ, TEMPLE, HALL, RECEPTION ROOM.

THE TEMPLE, HALL, RECEPTION ROOM 堂 HAS A RIDGE POLE 冖 AND A SHINING ⺌ ROOF 冖 WITH AN UPPER STOREY 口 (ELEVATED ON) THE EARTH 土.

RAD 86 STROKE 11 JME 486

N1365
t'ang2
M6107
táng
hall

示	光	宀	尚	堂	土
TO SHOW, TO POINT OUT J 622	LIGHT, RAY, TO SHINE J 72	ROOF R 40	TO RESPECT, TO ADMIRE N 1361	TEMPLE, HALL, RECEPTION RM.	EARTH, SOIL J 32

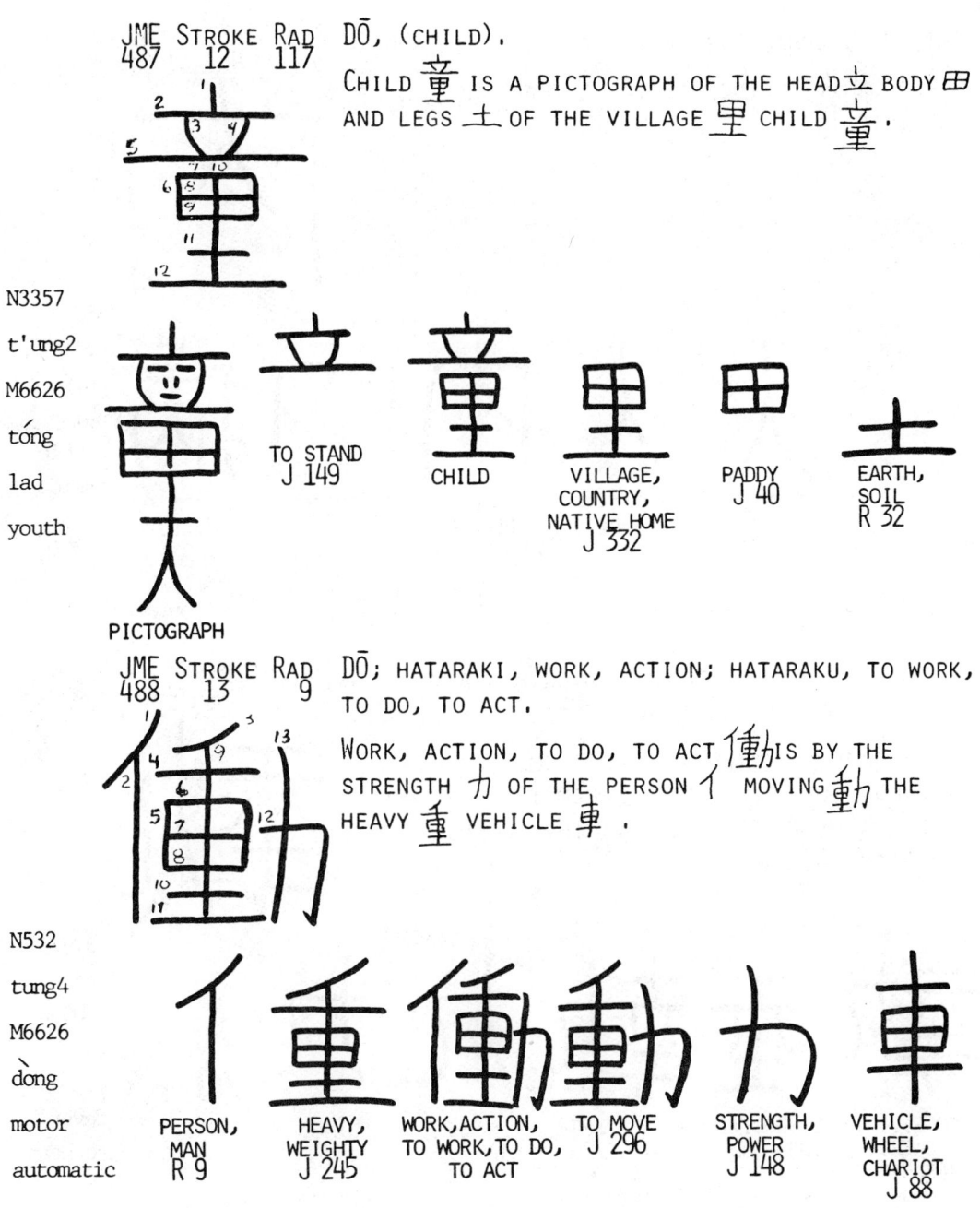

JME	Stroke	Rad
487	12	117

DŌ, (CHILD).

CHILD 童 IS A PICTOGRAPH OF THE HEAD 立 BODY 田 AND LEGS 土 OF THE VILLAGE 里 CHILD 童.

N3357
t'ung2
M6626
tóng
lad
youth

立 TO STAND J 149

童 CHILD

里 VILLAGE, COUNTRY, NATIVE HOME J 332

田 PADDY J 40

土 EARTH, SOIL R 32

PICTOGRAPH

JME	Stroke	Rad
488	13	9

DŌ; HATARAKI, WORK, ACTION; HATARAKU, TO WORK, TO DO, TO ACT.

WORK, ACTION, TO DO, TO ACT 働 IS BY THE STRENGTH 力 OF THE PERSON 亻 MOVING 動 THE HEAVY 重 VEHICLE 車.

N532
tung4
M6626
dòng
motor
automatic

亻 PERSON, MAN R 9

重 HEAVY, WEIGHTY J 245

働 WORK, ACTION, TO WORK, TO DO, TO ACT

動 TO MOVE J 296

力 STRENGTH, POWER J 148

車 VEHICLE, WHEEL, CHARIOT J 88

489

DAI, NAI; UCHI, INSIDE, INTERIOR, WITHIN, HOME.
A PERSON 人 INSIDE, WITHIN 内 THE SPACE 冂 OF
THE INTERIOR 内 OF A HOME 内.

RAD 2 STROKE 4 JME 489

N82
nei4
M4766
nèi
within
inside
inner
wife

入 人 内 冂 病
TO ENTER PERSON, MAN INSIDE, EMPTY SPACE SICK
J 125 MANKIND INTERIOR, R 13 J 310
 J 9 WITHIN, HOME

NETSU, HEAT, WARMTH, FEVER, FAD, ENTHUSIASM;
NESSURU, TO HEAT, MAKE HOT, BOIL; ATSUI, HOT.
HEAT, WARMTH, FEVER, FAD, ENTHUSIASM, TO HEAT,
MAKE HOT, TO BOIL, HOT 熱 FROM THE FIRE 灬
UNDER EARTH 土 SPLITTING 八 THE ROUND,
SPHERICAL 丸 EARTH 土

RAD 86 STROKE 15 JME 490

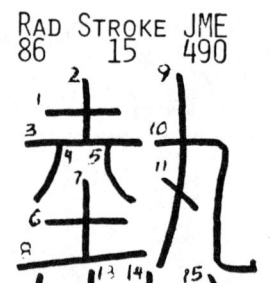

N2797
je4
M3095
rè
hot
fever
to heat

埶 垚 熱 丸 九 灬
FORCE, VIGOR, LAND DIVID- HEAT, WARMTH, ROUND, NINE FIRE
POWER, ING LAND FEVER, FAD, CIRCULAR J 9 R 86
INFLUENCE   ENTHUSIASM, N 155
J 441   TO HEAT, BOIL

The Egyptians believe that fire is a living animal which eats whatever it
reaches, and dies after eating its food. (So four legs).   Herodotus

491

NŌ, FARMING.

FARMING 農 MELODIOUSLY TWISTS, BENDS 曲 (THE EARTH) INTO DRAGON 辰 LIKE FURROWS & FORMS, AS IN CONTOUR PLOUGHING.

The Book of Songs — James Legge
The toilers come to clear the ground,
Where grass and brushwood thick abound,
Where plowshare never yet was found.
In thousands now they gather there;
The roots from out the soil they tear:--
Now they begin with patient care
The southern acres to prepare.
The soil is broken by the share.
They sow the various grains; each ear
With mystic life will soon appear,
When the young plants their heads uprear.

N4658 nung2 M4768 nóng farm farmer agri-culture

曲 MELODY, TO BEND, TO TURN, TO TWIST
農 FARMING
辰 ZODIAC DRAGON R 161 (HE IS A DRAGON RAMPANT)
長 HEAD, CHIEF, LONG J 116
衣 CLOTHES, ROBES J 341

HAN, ANTITHESIS, OPPOSED TO; TAN, UNIT OF MEASURE FOR LAND AND CLOTH.

THE (ROCK-THROWING MOUNTAINEER'S) HAND 又 ON THE CLIFF 厂 IS THE ANTITHESIS, OPPOSED TO 反 (THE CARAVAN OF MERCHANTS) WHICH MEASURES LAND AND CLOTH 反.

The Shroud of Turin in which Christ's body is reputed to have been wrapped after his death has a negative image as of a body wrapped after crucifixion.

N817 fan3 M1781 fǎn contrary to rebel

厂 CLIFF R 27
反 ANTITHESIS, OPPOSED TO, MEASURE FOR LAND & CLOTH
又 HAND R 29
坂 SLOPE, HILL J 304 (OPP. OF FLAT EARTH)
板 BOARD (WOOD) J 305 (OPP. OF TREE)

493

HI; TOBU, TO FLY.

TO FLY 飛 IS THE BEAK ´ & BREAST ｜, BODY & TAIL ｜ OF A FEATHERED ∴ AND WINGED 乙 (BIRD) FLYING 飛. PAIRED NINES 邜 VERIFY THE EFFECT OF ROTATING OR BEATING WINGS.

RAD 183 STROKE 9 JME 493

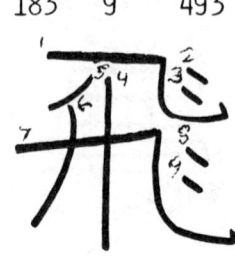

Volador is a sportive ceremonial festival of ancient Mexico. Men tied to ropes leap from a rotary platform mounted on a high pole and circle through the air to the ground as the ropes unwind.

N5152
fei 1
M1850
fēi
to fly
quick

佳 亻 BEAK BREAST   飛   邜   乙   ∴

SHORT-TAILED BIRD R. 172   TO FLY   (TURNING AS OF A PAIR OF NINES) PAIRED WINGS PINFEATHERS

羽   弱
NINE J 9   WINGS N 3673   WEAK J 236

HI; KANASHII, SAD.

AT FAULT, WRONG, NON-, UN- 非 IS A TABOO OR POISONOUS PLANT 非 PICTOGRAPH. NOTE LATERAL SHOOTS 三三. THE HEART, MIND 心 AT FAULT, WRONG, NON-, UN- 非 IS SAD 悲.

RAD 175 STROKE 12 JME 494

Romances sans paroles   Paul Verlaine
Il pleure dans mon coeur
Comme il pleut sur la ville.

N5082
pei 1
M4992
bēi
sorry
sad
lament

心   悲   非   韭
HEART, MIND, SPIRIT J 95   SAD   NOT, IS NOT R 175 FAULT, WRONG, NON-, UN- J 698   ONIONS, LEEKS, SCALLIONS R 179

The Taming of the Shrew   Wm. Shakespear
And if the boy have not a woman's gift
To rain a shower of commanded tears,
An onion will do well for such a shift.

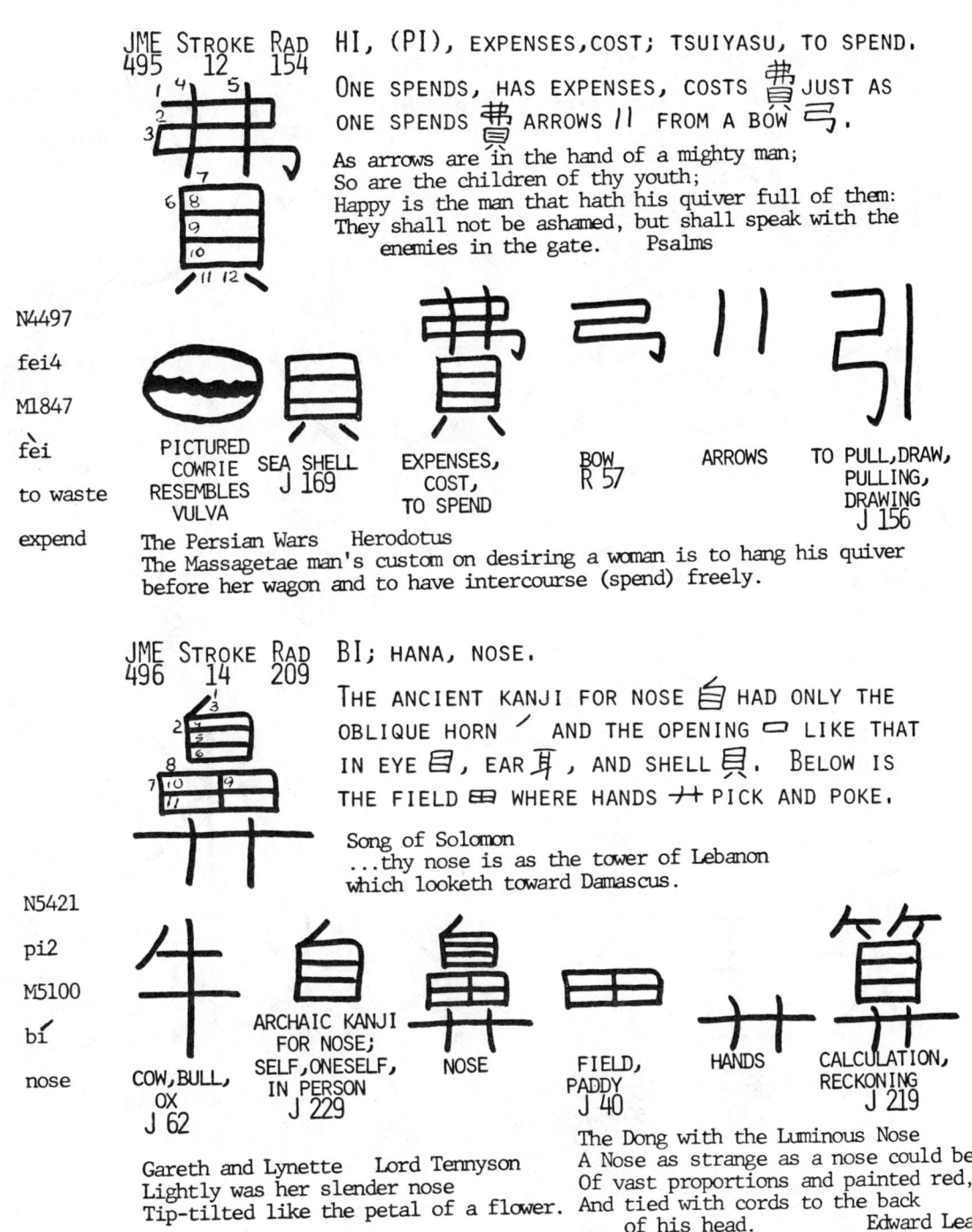

495

JME 495 STROKE 12 RAD 154

HI, (PI), EXPENSES, COST; TSUIYASU, TO SPEND.

One spends, has expenses, costs 費 just as one spends 費 arrows 川 from a bow 弓.

As arrows are in the hand of a mighty man;
So are the children of thy youth;
Happy is the man that hath his quiver full of them:
They shall not be ashamed, but shall speak with the enemies in the gate. Psalms

N4497
fei4
M1847
fèi
to waste
expend

- PICTURED COWRIE RESEMBLES VULVA
- SEA SHELL J 169
- EXPENSES, COST, TO SPEND
- BOW R 57
- ARROWS
- TO PULL, DRAW, PULLING, DRAWING J 156

The Persian Wars   Herodotus
The Massagetae man's custom on desiring a woman is to hang his quiver before her wagon and to have intercourse (spend) freely.

JME 496 STROKE 14 RAD 209

BI; HANA, NOSE.

The ancient kanji for nose 自 had only the oblique horn ノ and the opening 口 like that in eye 目, ear 耳, and shell 貝. Below is the field 田 where hands 廾 pick and poke.

Song of Solomon
...thy nose is as the tower of Lebanon
which looketh toward Damascus.

N5421
pi2
M5100
bí
nose

- COW, BULL, OX J 62
- ARCHAIC KANJI FOR NOSE; SELF, ONESELF, IN PERSON J 229
- NOSE
- FIELD, PADDY J 40
- HANDS
- CALCULATION, RECKONING J 219

Gareth and Lynette   Lord Tennyson
Lightly was her slender nose
Tip-tilted like the petal of a flower.

The Dong with the Luminous Nose
A Nose as strange as a nose could be!
Of vast proportions and painted red,
And tied with cords to the back
    of his head.   Edward Lear

497

HITSU; KANARAZU, CERTAINLY, INVARIABLY.

THE WEAPON ╱ INTO THE HEART ⌣ CERTAINLY, INVARIABLY ⌣ (KILLS).

Lord Thomas and Fair Annet
The bride she drew a long bodkin
Frae out her gay headgear,
And strake Fair Annet unto the heart
That word spak nevir mair.

RAD 3   STROKE 5   JME 497

N129
pi4
M5109
bì
certainly
must
will

| ARCHAIC KANJI FOR HEART | HEART, MIND, SPIRIT J 95 | HEART | CERTAINLY, INVARIABLY | WEAPON STRIKES |

And Rechab and Bannah came thither into the midst of the house, as though they would have fetched wheat; and they smote Ishbosheth under the fifth rib. II Samuel

HYŌ; KŌRI, ICE.

WATER 水 EXTENDED INTO TIME AND SPACE BY A DOT ` IS ICE 氷. AS THE ETERNAL EXPANSE OF POLAR ICE.

He casteth forth his ice like morsels: who can stand before his cold?   Psalms

When icicles hang by the wall. Winter. Wm. Shakespear
    And Dick the shepherd blows his nail,

RAD 3   STROKE 5   JME 498*

N131
ping 1
M5283
bīng
ice

| DOG J 66 | JADE, BALL, JEWEL J 64 | DOT R 4 (EXT. OF THE SCOPE, POWER, ETC.) | ICE | WATER R 85 | BARBED HOOK, NAIL BODY R 6 |

The Rime of the Ancient Mariner   Samuel Taylor Coleridge
And ice, mast-high, came floating by   It crack'd and growl'd,
    As green as emerald;   and roar'd and howl'd
The ice was here, the ice was there,   Like noises in a swound!
The ice was all around:

Illustrated on facing page

498 X

This Japanese dress design represents the forming of ice on ponds in the cold evenings. The blossoms are the plum flowers which bloom early and may fall on the ice in China's Yangtze River delta provinces. The plum, the pine, and the bamboo are the Three Friends of Winter since they withstand the cold, the snow, and the ice.

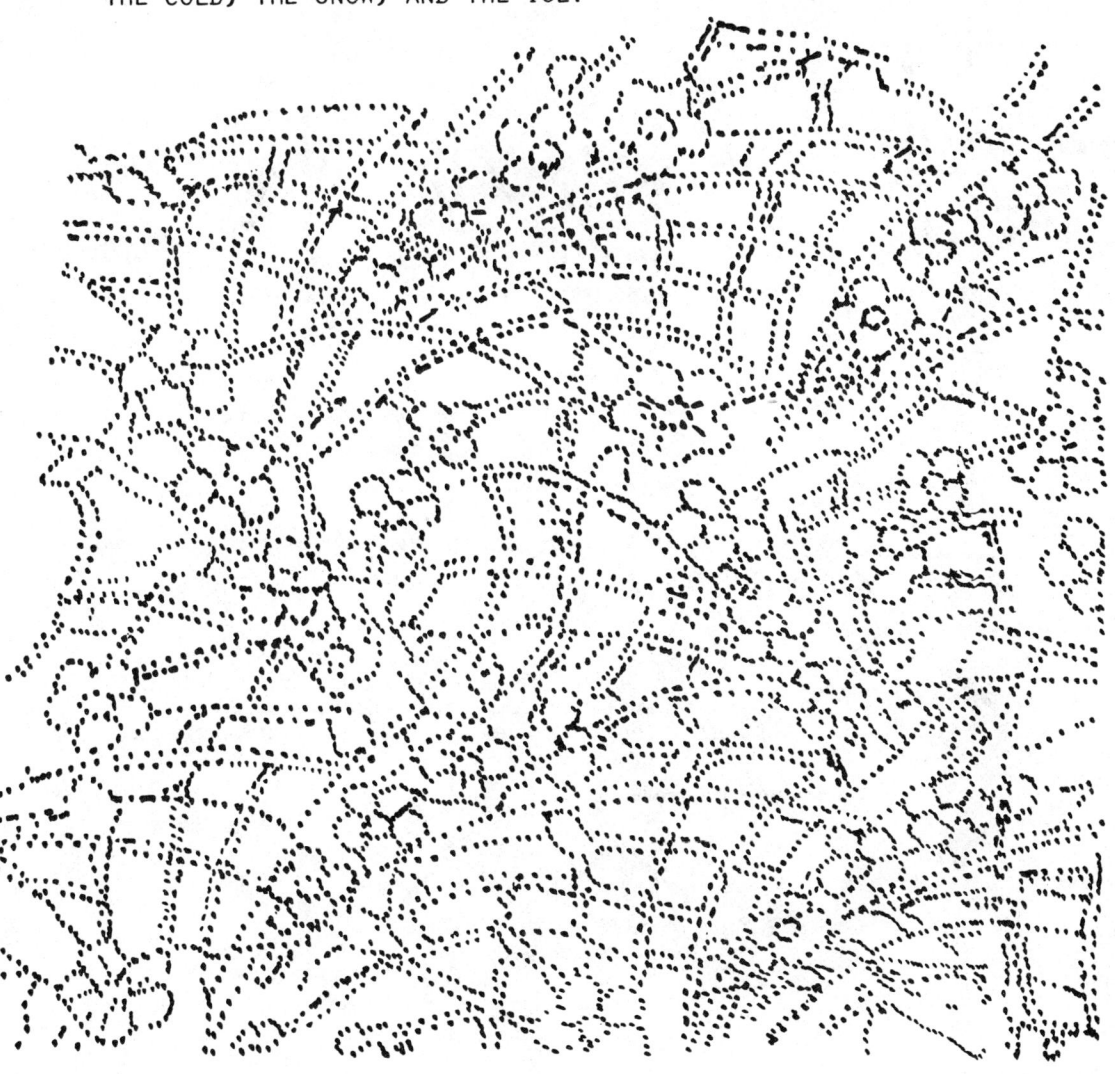

499

JME 499 | Stroke 9 | Rad 115

BYŌ, ONE SECOND (AS OF TIME, LATITUDE, DEGREE). A GRAIN 禾 SO SMALL 小 AS TO BE CARRIED ノ REPRESENTS A SECOND 秒 OF TIME, LATITUDE, DEGREE. ANCIENT PEOPLES MEASURED WITH BEANS AND GRAINS.

N3271
miao3
M4479
miǎo
minute
second

PRODUCT (MATH), INTENTION, PILE UP, LOAD, ACCUMULATE
J 445

GRAIN, ONE SECOND
RICE
R 115

LITTLE, FEW, SCARCE
J 93

LITTLE, SMALL
J 24

JME 500 | Stroke 4 | Rad 1

FU, NEGATION, DIS-, IN-, ILL-, MAL-, UN-. UN- 不 HIT BIRDS GO IN THREE DIRECTIONS FROM THE HORIZONTAL 一. NEGATIVE ORNITHOMANTIC RESPONSE AND UNSUCCESSFUL HUNTING.

The Greeks, Romans, Arabs, and other peoples believed in the flight of birds as an augury or foretelling of good or evil to come. The prediction could depend on whether the birds flew towards the right or the left. Left is traditionally the evil, sinister, or negative.

N17
pu4
M5379
bù
not

HORIZONTAL

NEGATION, DIS-, IN-, ILL-, MAL-, UN-

3 DIRECTIONS OF LINES

3 DIRECTIONS SHOWN BY ARROWS

FU, (PU), (FŪ), HUSBAND, MAN; OTTO, HUSBAND. RAD 4 STROKE 4 JME 501*

BIG 大 MAN 人 WITH THE PIN 一 (OF ADULTHOOD IN HIS TOPKNOT) IS A HUSBAND, MAN 夫.

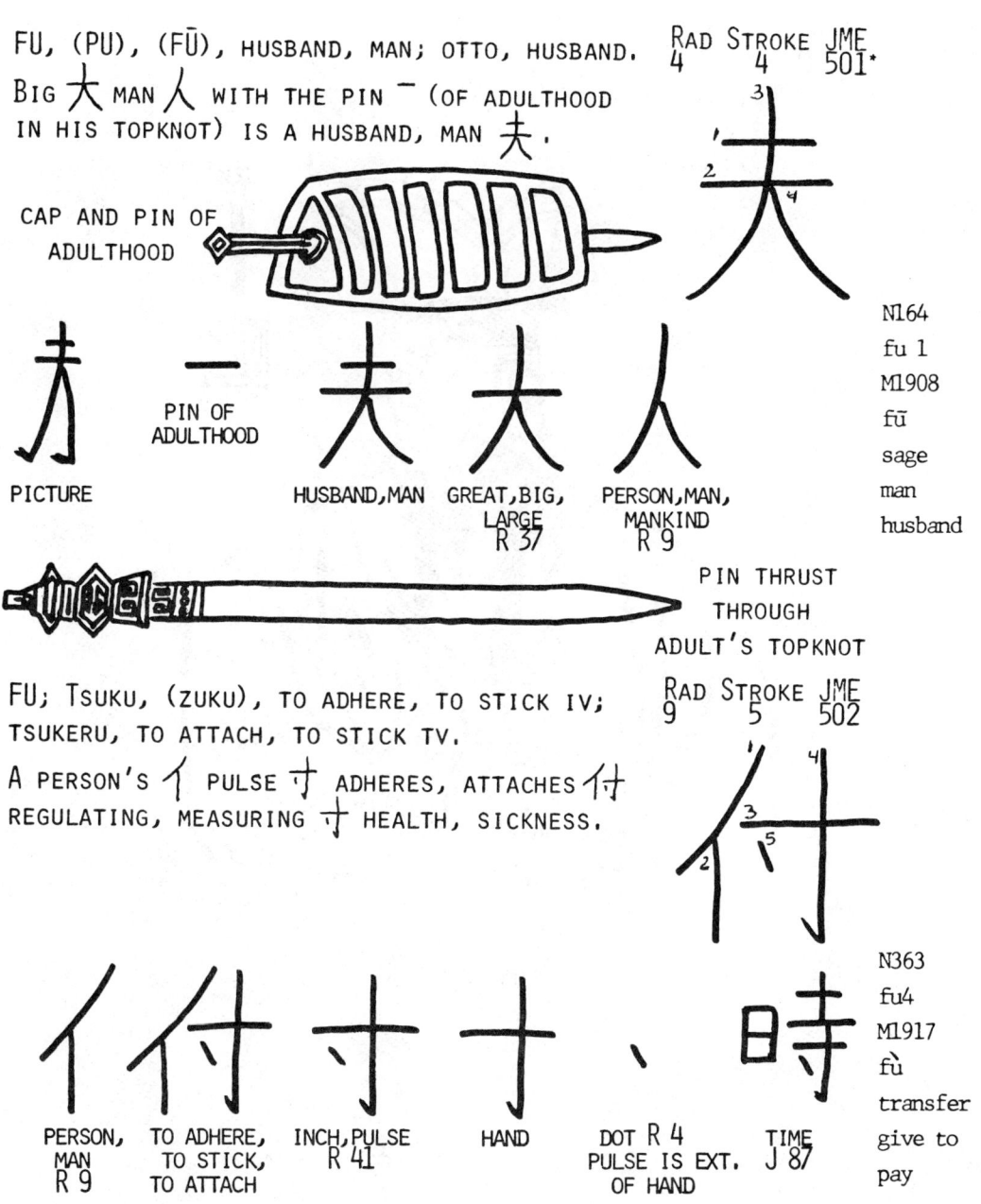

CAP AND PIN OF ADULTHOOD

PICTURE — 夫

一 PIN OF ADULTHOOD

夫 HUSBAND, MAN

大 GREAT, BIG, LARGE R 37

人 PERSON, MAN, MANKIND R 9

N164
fu 1
M1908
fū
sage
man
husband

PIN THRUST THROUGH ADULT'S TOPKNOT

FU; TSUKU, (ZUKU), TO ADHERE, TO STICK IV; TSUKERU, TO ATTACH, TO STICK TV. RAD 9 STROKE 5 JME 502

A PERSON'S 亻 PULSE 寸 ADHERES, ATTACHES 付 REGULATING, MEASURING 寸 HEALTH, SICKNESS.

亻 PERSON, MAN R 9

付 TO ADHERE, TO STICK, TO ATTACH

寸 INCH, PULSE R 41

寸 HAND

丶 DOT R 4 PULSE IS EXT. OF HAND

時 TIME J 87

N363
fu4
M1917
fù
transfer
give to
pay

*Illustrated on following page

501 X

CONFUCIUS
(PINNED)

503

503 — FU, urban prefecture, government office.

JME 503 · Stroke 8 · Rad 53

N1507 · fu3 · M1928 · fǔ · prefecture

The urban prefecture, government office is the shed, lean-to 广 where men 亻 attach, adhere 付 and measure, control 寸.

厂	广	府	付	亻	寸
CLIFF R 27	SHELTER, LEAN-TO R 53	URBAN PREFECTURE, GOV'T OFFICE	TO ADHERE, TO ATTACH J 502	PERSON, MAN J 9	INCH, PULSE R 41 (TO MEASURE, TO CONTROL)

504 — BU, department, bureau, copy, part, set.

JME 504 · Stroke 11 · Rad 163

N4767 · pu4 · M5376 · bù · class, section, sort

The department, bureau, copy, part, set 部 (is authoritative) in the city 阝 & stands over 立 (interrupts or shuts) one's mouth 口.

音	口	立	部	阝	邑
SOUND J 50	MOUTH R 30	TO STAND R 117	DEPT., BUREAU, COPY, PART, SET	MOUND, HILL, VILLAGE R 163	MOUND, HILL, VILLAGE R 163

505

FUKU, DRESS, CLOTHES, SUIT.
DRESS, CLOTHES, SUIT 服 ARE THE BODY'S 月 SEAL, SIGN 卩 (HELD BY A CLASP OR BROOCH) AS BY THE RIGHT HAND 又.

RAD 74 STROKE 8 JME 505

N3741
fu2
M1999
fú
clothes
to wear

月 服 卩 又
BODY, MOON   CLOTHES,   SEAL   HAND
J 12   DRESS, SUIT   R 26   R 29

FUKU, FORTUNE, BLESSING, LUCK, WEALTH.
FORTUNE, BLESSING, LUCK, WEALTH 福 COMES WITH UNITY AS OF ONE 一 MOUTH 口 (IN THE OPERATION) OF THE FIELDS, PADDIES 田 AS SHOWN, INFORMED 礻 (BY THE GODS 神).

Babylonian ziggurats and Mayan flat-topped pyramidal temples doubled as astronomical observatories for the reception of divine advice to the politically unified irrigated areas controlled from their cities.

RAD 113 STROKE 13 JME 506*

N3256
fu2
M1978
fú
happiness
prosperity
fortune

示   礻   福   畐
TO SHOW,   TO SHOW,   FORTUNE,   TO FILL,
TO INFORM,   TO INFORM   BLESSINGS,   A ROLL OF
TO POINT OUT   R 113 ABBRE.   LUCK,   CLOTH
R 113   WEALTH   M 1975

*Illustrated on facing page

506 X

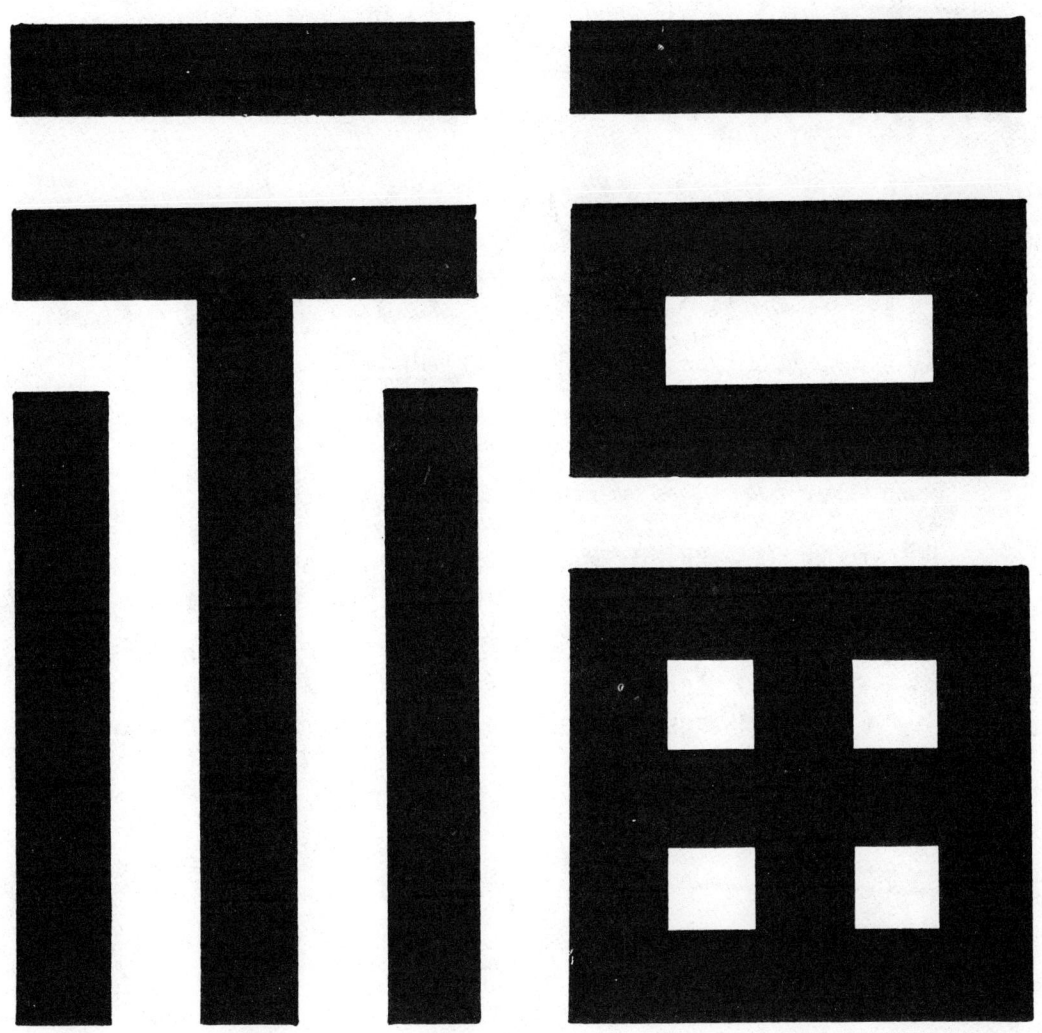

507

JME 507 **Stroke** 10 **Rad** 119

FUN; KONA, KO, POWDER, FLOUR, MEAL.

POWDER, FLOUR, MEAL 粉 IS RICE 米 DIVIDED 分 (OR PULVERIZED).

Sinngedichte   Friedrich von Logan
Though God's mills grind slowly,
He grinds exceeding small;
Patiently, exactly, He stands and grinds us all.   A.D.

We shall yet grind the Gods in their own mills.   A.D.

N3469
fen3
M1858
fěn
powder

十	米	粉	分	八	刀
TEN J 10	RICE J 135	POWDER, FLOUR, MEAL	TO PART, SHARE, TO DIVIDE, TO SEPARATE J 133	EIGHT, TO DIVIDE J 8; R 12	KNIFE, SWORD R 18

The Laboratory   Robert Browning
Grind away, moisten and mash up thy paste,
Pound at thy powder, --I am not in haste!

JME 508 **Stroke** 7 **Rad** 18

BETSU; ANOTHER, DIFFERENT, PARTICULAR, SEPARATE; WAKERU, SPLIT, BE DIVIDED, PART WITH.

THE BENT-OVER 勹 (SERVER) 另 WITH A KNIFE 刂 SPLITS, DIVIDES, PARTS WITH 別 (PORTIONS) FOR THE ANOTHER, DIFFERENT, PARTICULAR, SEPARATE 別 MOUTHS 口.

N674
pieh2
M5208
bié
separate
part
distin-
guish

召	另	別	刂	刀	刀
TO CALL, TO SEND FOR, TO WEAR J 668	(SERVER)	ANOTHER, DIFFERENT, PARTICULAR, SEPARATE	KNIFE, SWORD R 18	PICTURE OF SWORD	KNIFE, SWORD R 18

HEN, STRANGE, CHANGE, ACCIDENT; KAWARU, TO CHANGE, TO VARY, TO BE DIFFERENT.

THE BODY OR HAND 又 WITH A KNIFE, HORN ノ (AS A WEAPON) (ENCOUNTERS) A RED, FIERY 赤 PRINT 亦 OR SHAPE 亦.

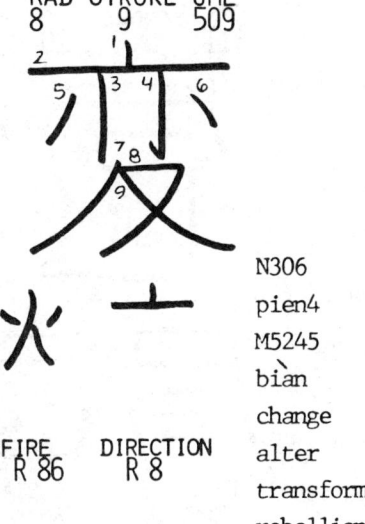

Rad Stroke JME
8   9   509

N306
pien4
M5245
biàn
change
alter
transform
rebellion

赤 RED J 35

文 COMPOSITION, ESSAY, SENTENCE J 134

変 STRANGE, CHANGE, ACCIDENT, TO CHANGE, VARY, BE DIFFERENT

又 BODY OR HAND WITH KNIFE OR HORN

火 FIRE R 86

DIRECTION R 8

BEN, CONVENIENCE, BODILY WASTE; BIN, MAIL.
CONVENIENCE, BODILY WASTE, MAIL 便 IS A PICTOGRAPH OF THE PERSON イ HATTED 一 WALKING 入 TO A FILLED, FILLABLE BOX 曰.

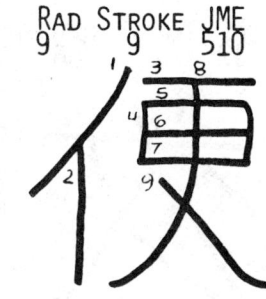

Rad Stroke JME
9   9   510

N450
pien4
M5224
biàn
conveneint
defecate
urinate

イ PERSON, MAN R 9

便 CONVENIENCE, BODILY WASTE, MAIL

更 TO CHANGE, TO RENEW, TO REFORM N 42

使 TO USE J 224

史 ANNALS, HISTORY, J 411

曰 TOILET SEAT, MAILBOX

511

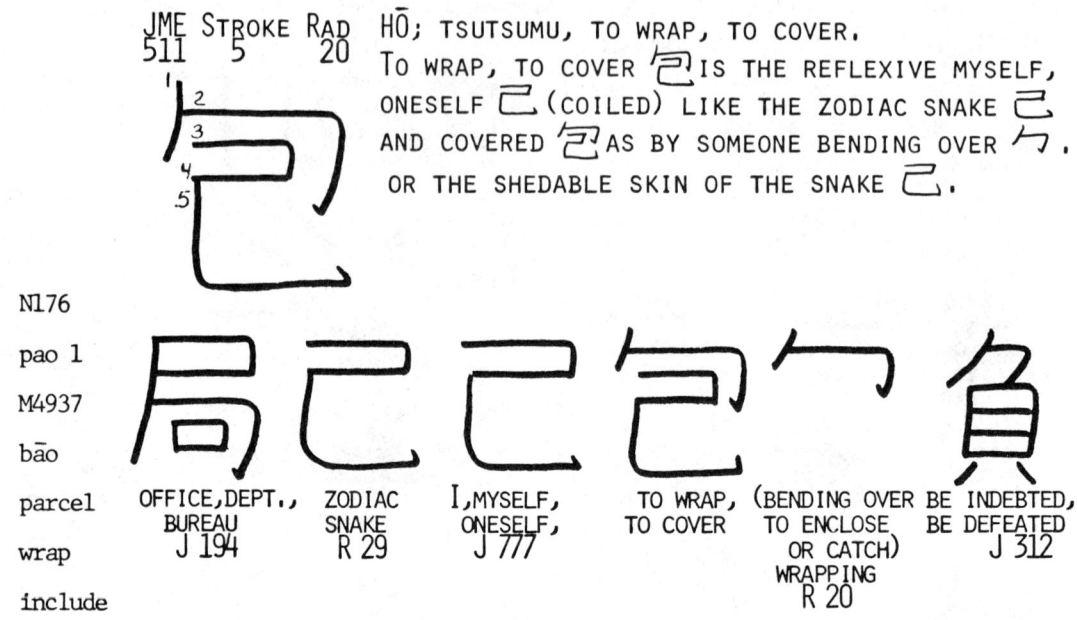

JME 511 Stroke 5 Rad 20

HŌ; TSUTSUMU, TO WRAP, TO COVER.
TO WRAP, TO COVER 包 IS THE REFLEXIVE MYSELF, ONESELF 己 (COILED) LIKE THE ZODIAC SNAKE 己 AND COVERED 包 AS BY SOMEONE BENDING OVER 勹, OR THE SHEDABLE SKIN OF THE SNAKE 己.

N176
pao 1
M4937
bāo
parcel
wrap
include

局	己	己	包	勹	負
OFFICE, DEPT., BUREAU	ZODIAC SNAKE	I, MYSELF, ONESELF	TO WRAP, TO COVER	(BENDING OVER TO ENCLOSE OR CATCH) WRAPPING	BE INDEBTED, BE DEFEATED
J 194	R 29	J 777		R 20	J 312

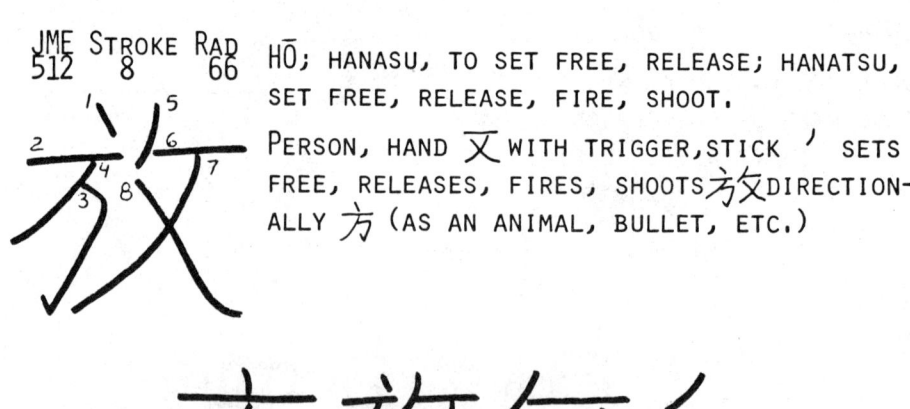

JME 512 Stroke 8 Rad 66

HŌ; HANASU, TO SET FREE, RELEASE; HANATSU, SET FREE, RELEASE, FIRE, SHOOT.
PERSON, HAND 又 WITH TRIGGER, STICK ノ SETS FREE, RELEASES, FIRES, SHOOTS 放 DIRECTIONALLY 方 (AS AN ANIMAL, BULLET, ETC.)

N2084
fàng4
M1807
fang
loosen
to free
let go

方	放	攵
DIRECTION, WAY, SIDE	TO SET FREE, TO RELEASE, TO FIRE, SHOOT	HAND WITH STICK, STICK
J 138		R 66

HŌ, (PŌ), LAW, DOCTRINE, REASON, METHOD.

THE LAW, DOCTRINE, REASON, METHOD 法 FOR WATER 氵 (DISTRIBUTION) ON THE LAND 土 IS (TO HOLD IT) AS IN A MOUTH ㄙ OR CLOUD 雲.

Riparian Law
Riparum usus publicus est jure gentium
Public use of banks is by the law of nations
   sicut ipsius fluminus.
      the same as that of the river itself.

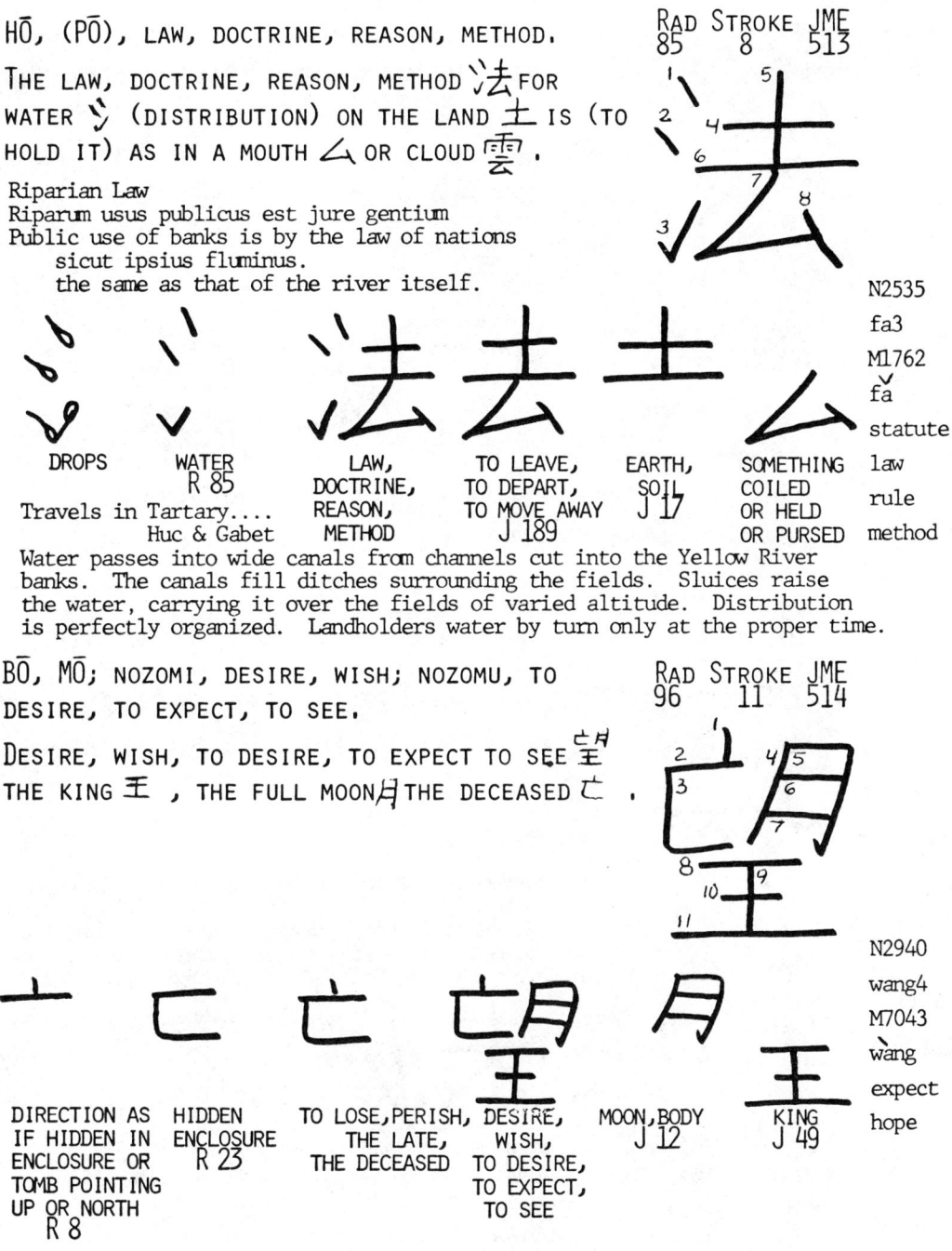

| DROPS | WATER R 85 | LAW, DOCTRINE, REASON, METHOD | TO LEAVE, TO DEPART, TO MOVE AWAY J 189 | EARTH, SOIL J 17 | SOMETHING COILED OR HELD OR PURSED |

N2535
fa3
M1762
fǎ
statute
law
rule
method

Travels in Tartary....
           Huc & Gabet
Water passes into wide canals from channels cut into the Yellow River banks. The canals fill ditches surrounding the fields. Sluices raise the water, carrying it over the fields of varied altitude. Distribution is perfectly organized. Landholders water by turn only at the proper time.

BŌ, MŌ; NOZOMI, DESIRE, WISH; NOZOMU, TO DESIRE, TO EXPECT, TO SEE.

DESIRE, WISH, TO DESIRE, TO EXPECT TO SEE 望 THE KING 王, THE FULL MOON 月 THE DECEASED 亡.

| ㅗ | 亡 | 亡 | 望 | 月 | 王 |

N2940
wang4
M7043
wàng
expect
hope

DIRECTION AS IF HIDDEN IN ENCLOSURE OR TOMB POINTING UP OR NORTH
R 8

HIDDEN ENCLOSURE R 23

TO LOSE, PERISH, THE LATE, THE DECEASED

DESIRE, WISH, TO DESIRE, TO EXPECT, TO SEE

MOON, BODY
J 12

KING
J 49

515

JME 515 Stroke 5 Rad 4

MATSU; SUE, END, FUTURE, YOUNGEST CHILD, TRIFLE; URE, NEW SHOOTS, NEW GROWTH (OF A TREE).

NEW SHOOTS, NEW GROWTH 末 OF A TREE 木 ARE THE END, FUTURE 末 LIKE THE YOUNGEST CHILD 末 A TRIFLE 末 (COMPARED TO OLDER SIBLINGS).

N177
mo4
M4546
mò

PICTURE OF NEW SHOOTS

末 END, FUTURE, YNGST. CHILD, TRIFLE, NEW SHOOTS, NEW GROWTH

木 TREE, WOOD J 15

妹 YNGR. SISTER

JME 516 Stroke 8 Rad 30

MI; AJI, TASTE, RELISH, EXPERIENCE.

THE TASTE, RELISH, EXPERIENCE 口味 OF THE MOUTH, APERTURE 口 OF THE YOUNGER SISTER 妹 TRADITIONALLY LOANED TO THE ALIEN TRAVELLER BY THE HOSPITABLE KIRGHIZ TRIBESMAN.

> Their custom is...when travelers come, the old women take their unmarried daughters or other girls related to them, and go to the strangers...and make over the young women...and the travelers do their pleasure.
> Concerning the Province of Tibet   The Travels of Marco Polo

N913
wei4
M7115
wèi

口 APERTURE, MOUTH, OPENING R 30

味 TASTE, RELISH, EXPERIENCE

未 ZODIAC SHEEP, NEVER, YET, TILL NOW, UN- J 872

妹 YNGR. SISTER J 319

末 END, FUTURE, YNGST. CHILD, NEW SHOOTS, NEW GROWTH TRIFLE J 515

There was a young gaucho named Pedro
Who said, "Frigging is one thing I do know;
A maiden is fine And a sheep is divine,
But a llama is Numero Uno."

Othello
Wm. Shakespear
An old black ram
Is tupping your white ewe.

MIYAKU, PULSE, HOPE, BLOOD VESSEL, VEIN (OF ORE).

The body's 月 blood vessels 脈, the streams from the cliff 厂 pulse 脈 with hope 脈 as blood vessels 脈 or veins of ore 脈 (as they spread like rippling clothes).

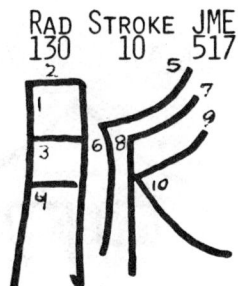

RAD 130 STROKE 10 JME 517

N3764 mei4
M4382 mài
pulse
veins
arteries

月	脈	厂	镸	衤	衣
BODY, MOON J 12	PULSE, HOPE, BLOOD VESSEL VEIN OF ORE	CLIFF R 27	CLOTHING (EFFECT OF VEINS, RIPPLES, ROOTS)	CLOTHES R 145 ABBRE.	CLOTHES R 145; J 341

MIN; TAMI, PEOPLE, SUBJECTS.

People, subjects 民 are a clan 氏 with a mouth 口 (showing politico-economic unity in consumption, etc.) Nomadic people 民 drift like floating water plants in bottom, depths 底

The country now called Hellas was not properly settled in ancient times. The people were migratory and easily left their homes when overwhelmed numerically.
                                         Thucydides

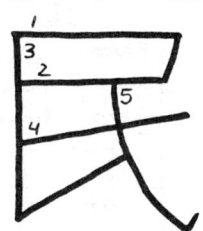

RAD 85 STROKE 5 JME 518

N25 min2
M4508 mín
the people

紙	底	氏	民	口
PAPER J 85	BOTTOM, DEPTHS J 475	FAMILY, CLAN, MR. J 620	PEOPLE, SUBJECTS J 518	MOUTH J 27

If I may be regarded in some true sense as the head of this great and widespread family, sharing its life and sustained by its affection, this will be a long and full reward for the loyal and sometimes anxious labours of my reign.   Christmas Greeting   King George V

Volk is folk and Volk is clouds. Both wander.

519

JME 519* Stroke 8 Rad 30

MEI, ORDER, COMMAND; MYO, INOCHI, LIFE.

ORDERS, COMMANDS 命 ARE BY THE MOUTH 口 AND THE SEAL 卩 IN THE TIGHT, CONSTRICTED 亼 NOW, PRESENT 今. ORDERS, COMMANDS 命 LIKE CHILDBIRTH 㝍 ARE LIFE 命.

One rich in virtue is like a baby. It has a strong grip although its bones are weak and its sinews are soft. The baby has potency although it does not yet understand the joining of male and female. It can cry all day without becoming hoarse. The baby's harmony is perfect and its understanding is enlightened. Thus it retains its wholeness and its vitality.
— Tao Te Ching

N430
ming4
M4537
mìng
command
decree
fate, destiny
life

今 — NOW, THE PRESENT — J 81
亼 — (TIGHT, JOINED AS MOTHER'S LEGS & NEONATE)
合 — TO FIT, TO BE TOGETHER — J 77
命 — ORDER, COMMAND, LIFE
口 — MOUTH — R 30
卩 — SEAL — R 26

JME 520 Stroke 11 Rad 30

MON; TOU, TO ASK, TO QUESTION, TO CARE, TO ACCUSE.

THE MOUTH 口 WITHIN THE GATES 門 ASKS, CARES, QUESTIONS, ACCUSES 問.

Job 41:14
Who can open the doors of his face?
his teeth are terrible round about.

N4944
wen4
M7141
wèn
ask
inquire
to sentence

日日 — PICTURE AS OF BAR DOORS
門 — GATE — J 143
問 — TO ASK, CARE, TO QUESTION, TO ACCUSE
間 — INTERVAL, SPACE, DISTANCE, ROOM
開 — TO OPEN — J 171
戶 — DOOR — J 69

*Illustrated on facing page

521

YAKU; KUSURI, MEDICINE, CHEMICALS.

MEDICINE, CHEMICALS 藥 ARE THE HERBS, GRASS 艹 FOR MUSIC, COMFORT, EASE, PLEASURE 樂. THE STAND, TREE 木 HOLDS THE DRUM 白 WHICH VIBRATES 幺幺 WHEN STRUCK BY THE STICK ノ AND PRODUCES THE MUSIC 樂 JOINED BY THE GRASS 艹.

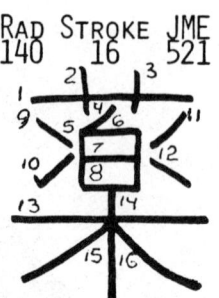

RAD 140   STROKE 16   JME 521

N4074
yao4
M7501
yào
drugs
medicine

樂	幺幺	白	藥	(drum)	木
MUSIC, EASE, COMFORT, PLEASANT J 331	(VIBRATORY SOUNDS OF THE DRUM)	WHITE J 37	MEDICINE, CHEMICALS	(PICTURE OF DRUM ON STAND)	TREE, WOOD J 15

GRASS R 140

Herodotus describes the Scythian use of hemp. Ancient Scythian bronzes found in the Altai Mountains still contain hemp seeds. The hemp was steamed and the vapors inhaled.

YU; ABURA, OIL.

OIL 油 IS THE FLUID 氵 FROM WHAT HAS REASON, SIGNIFICANCE 由, THE TORTOISE SHELL 甲 USED FOR DIVINATION SINCE SHANG DYNASTY TIMES.

The Encantadas   Herman Melville
...a French whaler...bound beyond the Enchanted Isles proposed...to procure tortoise oil a fluid which for its great purity and delicacy is held in high esteem wherever known; and it is well known all along this part of the Pacific coast.

RAD 85   STROKE 8   JME 522

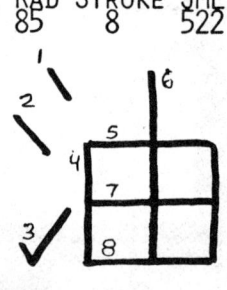

N2534
yu2
M7515
yóu
oil
fat
grease

氵	油	由	(tortoise)	甲
WATER R 85	OIL J 522	REASON, SIGNIFICANCE J 325	PICTURE OF TORTOISE FOR DIVINATION (UNDER VIEW OF PLASTRON)	TORTOISE SHELL, ARMOR, GRADE A, BACK OF HAND N 92

JME 523 STROKE 9 RAD 19

YŪ, U; ARU, TO EXIST, TO HAVE, TO MEASURE, TO HAVE EXPERIENCE, TO CONSIST OF.

TO EXIST, TO HAVE, TO MEASURE, TO HAVE EXPERIENCE, TO CONSIST OF 有 IS THE BODY OF THE GRUB, THE MEAT, THE MOONLIKE BODY 月 IN ONE'S HAND ナ.

N3727
yu3
M7533
yǒu
have
exist
to be

ARCHAIC HAND | HAND | TO EXIST, HAVE, TO MEASURE, TO OWN, POSSESS | BODY, MOON, GRUB J 12 | BODY J 255 | (PREGNANT BODY)

The white crescent moon closely resembles the insect grubs or larvae eaten as delicacies in many parts of the world. In Australia's Arnhem Land these grubs are eaten raw as a vital protein source. Greeks and Romans ate the grubs of the large Coccus beetle.

JME 524* STROKE 9 RAD 19

YŪ; ISAMASHII, BRAVE.

BRAVE 勇 IS THE MAN, MALE 男 WHO EXPENDS, POURS OUT マ (HIS GUTS, ENERGY ETC.)

Abdul the Bulbul Amir
The sons of the prophet are brave men and bold,
And quite unaccustomed to fear,
But the bravest by far in the ranks of the Shah
Was Abdul the Bulbul Amir.

N726
yung3
M7571
yǒng
brave
daring
courage

ZODIAC TIGER | MAN, MALE J 109 | BRAVE | (POURED OUT, EXPENDED; OPP. OF ㄙ) | BUSINESS, TO USE J 146 | (COILED UP, HELD) PRIVATE, SECRET, SELFISH

I take the world to be but as a stage,
Where net-maskt men do play their personage.
    Divine Weekes and Workes   Guillaume de Salluste

FALSTAFF (rising up) Embowelled? If thou embowel me today, I'll give thee leave to powder me and eat me tomorrow. 'Sblood,....
        Henry the Fourth   Wm. Shakespeare

*Illustrated on following page

524 X

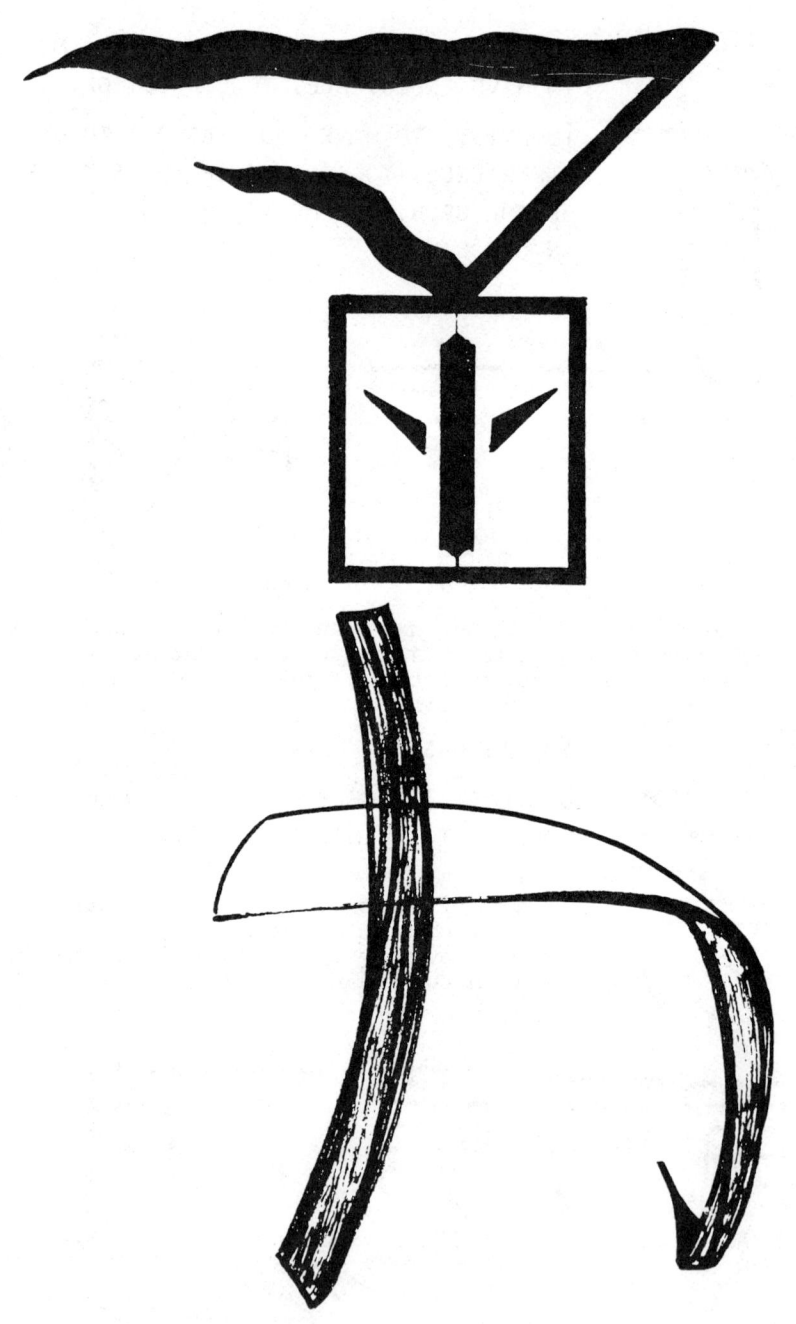

YO, (PREVIOUS). I, MYSELF.

THE PREVIOUS 予 (WEAPON) LIKE A STAKE, SPIKE 丁 WITH EXPENDED マ (HURLING EFFORT) EVOLVED INTO A HALBERD 矛 WITH A PROJECTING ARM ノ.

RAD 6 STROKE 4 JME 525

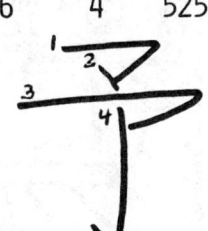

N271
yu2
M7601
yù
I
me
to grant
confer

野 FIELD, PLAIN J 323   矛 HALBERD (ADDED STROKE FOR ARM OR THROWING DEVICE)   マ (POURED OUT, EXPENDED)   予 PREVIOUS, I, MYSELF   丁 (ARCHAIC NAIL, STAKE, SPIKE) 120 YDS., DIVISION OF A WARD OR TOWN   PICTURES OF HALBERDS

YŌ, OCEAN, FOREIGN, WESTERN.

THE OCEAN 洋 IS WATER 氵 WITH SHEEP 羊 BACKED WAVES. WHAT IS FOREIGN, WESTERN 洋 IS FROM THE OCEAN. THE FOREIGN, WESTERN ODOR THAT INCITES CHINESE DOGS AND ENRAGES BUFFALO IS SIMILAR TO THE AROMA OF THE MALE GOAT 羊 WHICH SPRAYS 氵 ITS OWN URINE ON ITS BODY BY FIRST MOUTHING IT. RESEMBLES WESTERN WOOL & SWEAT.

RAD 85 STROKE 9 JME 526

N2550
yang2
M7252
yáng
ocean
foreign

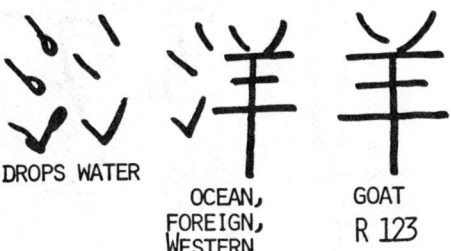

DROPS WATER   OCEAN, FOREIGN, WESTERN   GOAT R 123

The Wreck of the Hesperus   Longfellow
She struck where the white and fleecy waves Looked soft as carded wool;
But the cruel rocks, they gored her side Like the horns of an angry bull.

527

JME 527 **Stroke** 12 **Rad** 170

YŌ, (YANG PRINCIPLE, POSITIVE, MALE, HEAVEN, DAYTIME, TOP).

THE YANG PRINCIPLE, POSITIVE, MALE, HEAVEN, DAYTIME, TOP 陽 IS REPRESENTED BY THE SUN 日 AND BEAMS 勿 ON A MOUND 阝 AND THE CHAMELEON 易 WHICH LIVES IN THE FIRE & LOVES THE SUN.

She lived on the shady side of the mountain
And he lived on the sunny side of the hill.

N5012
yang2
M7265
yáng

clear
bright
sun, heat
upper

阝	陽	日	旦	易	勿
MOUND R 170	YANG, POSITIVE, MALE, HEAVEN, TOP, DAYTIME	SUN	DAWN, MORNING N 2098	EASY, DIVINATION J 545 (CHAMELEON)	SUNBEAMS FROM ABOVE

Brahma — Emerson
Far or forgot to me is near;   The vanquished gods to me appear;
Shadow and sunlight are the same;   And one to me are shame and fame.

JME 528* **Stroke** 7 **Rad** 18

RI, ADVANTAGE, PROFIT, GAIN, INTEREST.

ADVANTAGE, PROFIT, GAIN, INTEREST 利 IS THE KNIFE 刂 (CUTTING) THE GRAIN 禾.

Chinky Chinky Chinaman sitting on a fence:
Trying to make a dollar out of fifteen cents.
            Foreign Folklore in Oppressed China A.D.

"Chinks" was a generally used term for money in England of the seventeenth century and can be found in Romeo and Juliet. Probably onomatopeic in origin.

N3264
li4
M3867
lì

profit
gain
advantage

	禾	利	刂		刀
PICTURED RICE	RICE, GRAIN R 115	ADVANTAGE, PROFIT, GAIN, INTEREST	SWORD, KNIFE R 18	PICTURED KNIFE	KNIFE, SWORD R 18

*Illustrated on facing page

528X

529

RIKU, LAND.

LAND 陸 IS EARTH, SOIL 土 DIVIDED ハ INTO EARTH, SOIL 土 WITH MOUNDS 阝 (FOR DEFENSE).

Feudalism: Its Frankish Birth and English Development
By a process called "subinfeudation," lands were granted in parcels to other men by those who received them from the king or otherwise, and by these lower landholders to others again.   Wm. Stubbs

(Terpen mounds in Friesland used for refuge & defense)

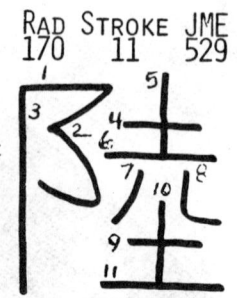

RAD 170 STROKE 11 JME 529

N5005
lu4
M4191
lù
dry land

熱	阝	坴	ハ	勢
HEAT, FEVER, CRAZE, ZEAL J 490	MOUND R 170	LAND	EARTH, SOIL (DOUBLED) J 32	TO DIVIDE	FORCE, VIGOR, POWER, INFLUENCE J 441

Two Kopjes   Rudyard Kipling (kopjes: strategic mounds in the Boer War).
Then scorn not the African kopje,   The wholly unoccupied kopje,
The kopje that smiles in the heat,   The home of Cornelius and Piet.

RYŌ; II, YOI, GOOD, PLEASING, LOVELY, FINE, RIGHT, SUITABLE.

GOOD, PLEASING, LOVELY, FINE, RIGHT, SUITABLE 良 ARE THE WHITE 白 RIPPLES, BRANCHES, ROOTS 艮.

RAD 138 STROKE 7 JME 530

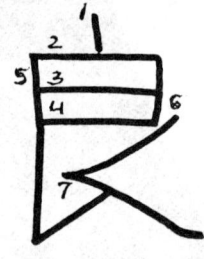

N3885
liang2
M3941
liáng
good
excellent
peaceful
virtuous

食	白	良	艮	銀	娘
FOOD, TO EAT J 253	WHITE J 37	GOOD, FINE, PLEASING, SUITABLE	RIPPLES, BRANCHES, ROOTS	SILVER J 196	DGHTR., GIRL, YNG. WOMAN N 1225

531

JME 531 **Stroke** 10 **Rad** 119

RYŌ, (CHARGE, MATERIALS).
IN CHARGE 料 OF THE DIPPING 斗 OF THE RICE 米,
THUS IN CHARGE 料 OF THE MATERIALS 料.

N3468
liao4
M3959
liào
materials
ingredients

米	米	料	斗	斗	科
PICTURED GRAINS SUPERIMPOSED ON TEN	RICE, AMERICA J 135	IN CHARGE OF, MATERIALS	UNIT OF CAPACITY, A MEASURE N 2073	DIPPER OF SEVEN STARS	COURSE, BRANCH J 164

JME 532 **Stroke** 14 **Rad** 120

RYOKU, ROKU; MIDORI, GREEN.
GREEN 緑 IS THE STRINGY 糸 (ALGAED) WATER 氺
OF THE BOAR'S ヨ (LAIR).

N3564
lu4
M4197
lǜ
green

緑	氺	水	氺	氺
	WATER (VARIANT FORM)	WATER R 85	FLOWING STREAM	WATER OR BOAR SPLASHES

糸	緑	ヨ	当	球
PICTURED COCOONS & FILAMENTS	THREADS, STRINGS R 120	GREEN	BOAR'S HEAD R 58	TO WIN, HIT, BE EQUAL TO J 290	SPHERE, GLOBE J 188

King Lear Wm. Shakespear
The green mantle of the standing pool.

The Book of Songs   James Legge
Five boars collect where grow
    the rushes rank and strong;
He only sends one arrow all the five
    among. Oh! the Tsou Yü is he!

533

RIN; WA, RING, CIRCLE, WHEEL.

THE RING, CIRCLE, WHEEL 輪 IS ABOUT THE HUB, CHILDBIRTH ORIFICE 亼 (AS IN NOW, PRESENT 今), THE BENT, TWISTED, TWINING 曲 (CIRCUMFERENCE) OF THE RING, CIRCLE, WHEEL 輪, THE RINGING, CIRCLING, WHEELING 輪 CARRIAGES, WAGONS 車 OF AFRIKAANERS' LAAGER OR CONESTOGA CIRCLE.
Leather, shrinking as it dried, or iron, contracting as it cooled, were used for wheel rims of chariots.

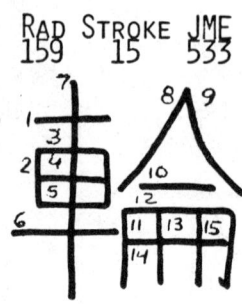

RAD 159 STROKE 15 JME 533

N4630
lun2
M4254
lún
revolve
a wheel

転 TURN AROUND, TO CHANGE, TO FALL J 479

車 WHEEK, VEHICLE J 88

輪 RING, CIRCLE, WHEEL
Afrikaander Wain

亼 TIGHT, CLOSE (LEGS & NEONATE HEAD)
A.D.

冊 COUNTER FOR BOOKS & MAGAZINES N 88

曲 MELODY, TO BEND, TO TWIST J 381

Beleaguered laager, Boer waagen train;   Malayan kris, Vauban's pointed star;
Alberich's ring: Teuton world to gain; Viennese kreis, Turkic scimitar.

RUI, KIND, VARIETY, CLASS, GENUS.

KIND, VARIETY, CLASS, GENUS 類 INCLUDES POLISHED BUT UNCOOKED RICE 米, HUMAN HEAD 頁 AND SOMETHING LARGE 大.

Bird, beast, or fish? Animal, mineral, or vegetable?

All: the tall, the fat, and the small.

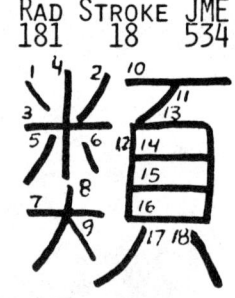

RAD 181 STROKE 18 JME 534

N5138
lei4
M4244
lèi
class
species
kind

犬 DOG J 66

大 BIG, LARGE, GREAT R 37

米 POLISHED & UNCOOKED RICE R 119

類 KIND, VARIETY, CLASS, GENUS

頁 HEAD R 181

PICTURED HEAD

L'Envoi   Rudyard Kipling
There be triple ways to take, of the eagle and the snake,
Or the way of a man with a maid;
But the sweetest way to me is a ship's upon the sea
In the heel of the North East Trade.

535

JME 535 Stroke 7 Rad 15

REI, COLD, COOL; HIERU, BECOME COLD, FEEL CHILLY; HIYASU, TO COOL, REFRIGERATE; TSUMETAI, COLD.

COLD, COOL, TO COOL DOWN, FEEL CHILLY, TO REFRIGERATE 冷 (IS THE SENSATION) OF THE ICINESS 冫 OF A PROCLAMATION, LAW, ORDER 令.

Amenenhet I of the Twelfth Dynasty
Be cold toward all underlings;
People obey him who terrorizes them.

N642
leng3
M3844
lěng
cold
indifferent

命 ORDER, COMMAND J 519
合 JOINED, TIGHT
冫 ICE R 15
冷 COLD, COOL, COOL DOWN, FEEL CHILLY, REFRIGERATE
令 PROCLAMATION, LAW, ORDER J 736
今 NOW, PRESENT J 81

(The iciness of law. proclamation from the now of childbirth scene)

Half sunk, a shattered visage lies, whose frown,
And wrinkled lip, and sneer of cold command,
Tell that its sculptor well those passions read. Ozymandias Shelley

JME 536 Stroke 14 Rad 27

REKI, (CONTINUATION, PASSING OF TIME).

THE CONTINUATION, PASSING OF TIME 歷 WHILE STOPPING 止 AT THE FORESTS 林 AND CLIFFS 厂.

A few feet are like a thousand miles;
The cliffs gleam with cinnabar and indigo hues;
An embroidery dazzling with brilliant colors;
The far-off trees are a verdant green
Beyond the Yangtze River narrows of Ching Men.
                                        Li Tai-po

N835
li4
M3931
lì
calculate
calendar

厈 PICTURED CLIFFS
厂 CLIFF R 27
歷 CONTINUATION, PASSING OF TIME J 150
林 WOODS
止 TO STOP J 220
PICTURED STOPPED LEG

537

RETSU, ROW, RANK, FILE, COLUMN, LINE.

A ROW, RANK, FILE, LINE, COLUMN 列 OF CORPSES 歹 WITH A KNIFE 刂 (FOR CUTTING RUMP ROASTS).

In Flanders Fields
In Flanders Fields the poppies grow
Between the crosses, row on row,
That mark their place....

RAD 78 STROKE 6 JME 537

N2438
lieh4
M3984
liè
arrange
file
rank
series

月	死	ONE J1 夕	歹	列	刂
BODY J 12	TO DIE, DEATH J 223	EVERY J 98 (SINKING MOON)	DEATH R 78	ROW, LINE	SWORD, KNIFE R 18

REN, A REAM, GROUP, SET, PARTY, COMPANY, SERIES COUNTER; -REN, SUFFIX FOR GROUP; TSURANARU, TO RANGE, STAND IN A ROW; TSURERU, TO TAKE ALONG; TSURE, COMPANION.

THE REAM, GROUP, SET, PARTY, COMPANY 連 RANGING, STANDING IN A ROW, COMPANIONS TAKING (EACH OTHER) ALONG 連 ARE CHARIOTS, VEHICLES, 車 STOPPING & GOING 辶 PANZERGRUPPEN.

the king of the north shall come at him like a whirlwind with chariots...
                                                            Daniel

RAD 162 STROKE 10 JME 538

N4702
lien2
M4009
lián
connect
join

辶	辶	連	車	十	日
STOP & GO R 162	STOP & GO R 162	A REAM, GROUP, SET, COMPANY, PARTY, COUNTER FOR SERIES, SUFFIX FOR GROUP,	WHEEL, VEHICLE, CHARIOT J 88	(WHEELS & AXLE)	SUN J 11 (CHASSIS & DRIVER)

Transportation of the merchandise across the Tartary deserts is by these small two-wheeled chariots. Oxen drawing them have a little iron nose-ring. A cord from this ring attaches the animal to the chariot in front of him. In this way, all the chariots from first to last are connected, and form a long uninterrupted line.
Huc & Gabet. Travels in Tartary...

539

JME 539 **Stroke** 14 **Rad** 120

REN; NERU, TO TRAIN, TO DRILL, TO SOFTEN, TO REFINE.

TRAINED, DRILLED, SOFTENED, REFINED 練 LIKE SILK, STRANDS 糸 FROM THE EASTERN 東 (CULTURED AREA OF CHINA).

N3565
lien4
M4020
liàn
to drill
select
to practice

| PICTURED COCOONS & THREADS | THREAD R 120 | TO TRAIN, DRILL, SOFTEN, REFINE | EAST J 121 | TREE J 15 | SUN J 11 |

JME 540 **Stroke** 13 **Rad** 157

RO, (ROAD, ROUTE, PATH); -JI, ROUTE, ROAD.

PERSON 各 WHOSE FOOT 足 STOPS 止 AS HE SITS 夂 ON A MILESTONE 口 ALONG THE ROAD, ROUTE, PATH 路

N4561
lu4
M4181
lù
road
path
way
journey

| TO STOP J 220 | FOOT, LEG J 29 | ROAD, ROUTE, PATH | EACH, EVERY J 568 | (PERSON & FAN) (CHAIR) MOUTH R 30 | (PICTURED) |

541

RŌ, AGING, OLD AGE, OLD MEN; OI, OLD AGE, THE AGED, OIRU, TO GROW OLD.

THE AGING, IN OLD AGE, OLD MEN, GROWN OLD 老 SIT SPOON OR MUMMY 匕 (FASHION) BURDENED ノ BY THE EARTH 土.

RAD 125 STROKE 6 JME 541

N3683 lao3
M3833 lǎo
old
aged

死 — DIE, DEATH J 223
匕 — SPOON, POINTER R 21 (AS MUMMY FACING NORTH)
老 — OLD AGE, OLD R 541
耂 — OLD MAN R 125
土 — EARTH, SOIL J 12
ノ — TUMPLINE (TO CARRY BURDENS)

Dulce et Decorum Est Wilfred Owen (WW I)
Bent double, like old beggars under sacks,
Knock-kneed, coughing like hags, we cursed through sludge...

RŌ, LABOR, TROUBLE, SERVICE.

LABOR, TROUBLE, SERVICE 労 IS THE STRENGTH 力 (THAT GAINS) THE CROWN 冖 WITH THE LAURELS 丷.

One Persian especially asked and was told that the Greeks celebrated the Olympic festival. When he inquired about the prize, the Arcadians described the Greek custom of giving a garland of olive leaves to the victors of the athletic contests and the chariot races. Tritantaechmes, son of Artabanus, shouted, "What kind of men do you bring us to war against, Mardonius, that compete only for honor?" Herodotus

RAD 19 STROKE 7 JME 542

N720 lao2
M3826 láo
to toil
suffer
weary

学 — LEARNING, SCIENCE, TO LEARN J 57
力 — STRENGTH, POWER J 148
労 — LABOR, TROUBLE, SERVICE
冖 — CROWN R 14
丷 — (LAURELS)
加 — PICTURED STRENGTH, POWER

JME	Stroke	Rad
543	16	167

ROKU, (TO RECORD).

TO RECORD 録 IN THE METALLIC 金 GREEN 緑 (PATINAED COPPER OR BRONZE)

Cartagena   Armando Solano
Poems of bronze, resonant and deathless, have told
                                    Cartagena's glory.

Engraved on my heart like a bronze inscription.
                                    (Chinese phrase)

N4879
lu4
M4200
lù
to record

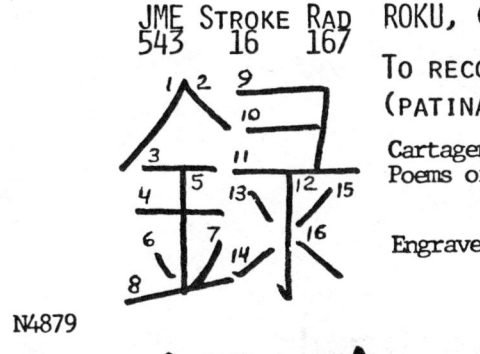

GREEN
J 532

METAL, MONEY
GOLD
R 167

TO RECORD

BOAR'S HEAD
R 58
(HIS TUSKS
CARVE)

(GREEN ALGAED)
WATER (OF
BOAR'S LAIR)

WATER
R 85

(Malachite, a green copper carbonate, for ages has been converted to a powder for pigment and to copper metal).

JME	Stroke	Rad
544	5	27

ATSU, (PRESSURE).

PRESSURE 圧 (VARIES) FROM THE CLIFF 厂 TO THE EARTH 土.

Blaise Pascal measured air pressure 圧 on the Puy de Dome 厂 and on the earth 土 in Paris.

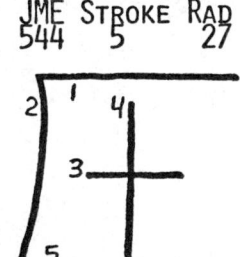

N818
ya 1
M7231
yā
press
oppress
crush

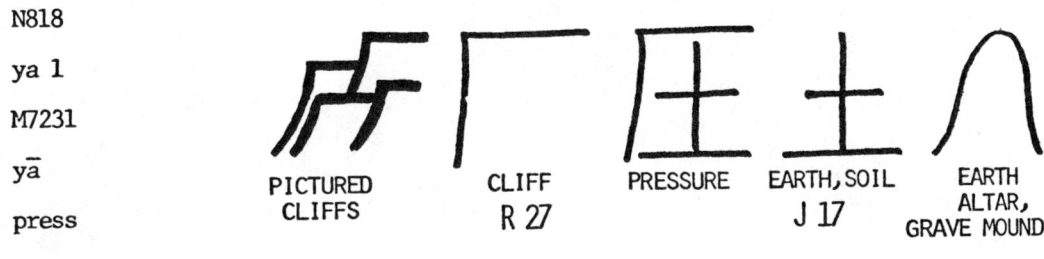

PICTURED
CLIFFS

CLIFF
R 27

PRESSURE

EARTH, SOIL
J 17

EARTH
ALTAR,
GRAVE MOUND

The 214 Radicals

Kanji Stroke Index

Alphabetical Japanese Word Index for JME Numbers

Katakana and Hiragana

THE 214 RADICALS

#	0	10	20	30	40	50
0	THE 214 RADICALS	10 儿 man, legs	20 勹 wrap, wrapping	3 STROKE 30 口 mouth, seat, aperture	40 宀 roof, crown	50 巾 cloth, width, kerchief
1	1 STROKE 1 一 one, unity	11 入 to enter	21 匕 spoon, pointer corpse	31 囗 enclosure, boundaries	41 寸 inch, rule, pulse, standard	51 干 shield, dry, weapon
2	2 丨 up or down movement	12 八 eight, to divide	22 匚 basket, vessel, enclosure	32 土 earth, soil	42 小 small, little	52 幺 cocoons, tiny thread (top) young (left)
3	3 丶 locus, point ext of time & space	13 冂 borders, empty space	23 匸 cover, conceal	33 士 gentleman, scholar, samurai	43 尢 crooked leg reasonable, weak	53 广 shelter, shed, lean-to
4	4 丿 support, horn, scyth	14 冖 cover, a cap	24 十 ten, perfect complete	34 夂 follow, end, walk, to go, hand & stick	44 尸 corpse, body	54 廴 long stride, stretch, lengthen
5	5 乙 tail of snake or dragon	15 冫 ice	25 卜 to divine, (plastron cracks)	35 夊 to walk, go	45 屮 sprout, plant, grass	55 廾 twenty legs, joined hands
6	6 亅 barb, hook, nail body	16 几 table, stool	26 卩 seal, joint	36 夕 evening, moon	46 山 mountain	56 弋 dart, ceremony
7	2 STROKE 7 二 two, duality heaven & earth	17 凵 open vessel	27 厂 cliff	37 大 large, big, man	47 巛 river, stream	57 弓 a bow
8	8 亠 head, cover, directional	18 刀 sword, knife	28 厶 cocoon, held, private	38 女 woman, girl, female	48 工 work, worker the square	58 彐 boarhead, pighead
9	9 人 person, man, human	19 力 strength, power, energy	29 又 again, also rt. hand	39 子 child, son, seed, mouse	49 己 self, snake, personal	59 彡 hair, hairshape

544

545

#		#		#		#		#		#	
60	彳 going men, to follow, short step	70	方 direction, side, square, person, way	80	毋 Do not! mother	90	爿 (as of tree) left side, left half	100	生 birth, life, grow	110	矛 spear, lance
4 STROKE 61	心 忄 㣺 heart, mind	71	无 旡 nothing, no, crooked heaven	81	比 to compare	91	片 (as of tree) left side, left half	101	用 to use, business	111	矢 arrow
62	戈 tasseled spear	72	日 sun, day	82	毛 hair, wool, fur, feather	92	牙 tusk, tooth	102	田 paddy, field	112	石 stone
63	戶 door, house, family	73	曰 say, speak	83	氏 clan, family	93	牛 cow, ox, bull	103	疋 足 animal ctr. cloth bolt	113	示 礻 to show, inform
64	扌 手 hand, arm	74	月 moon, month	84	气 vapor, steam air	94	犭 犬 dog, animal	104	疒 sickness, disease	114	禸 track, footprint, pawprint
65	支 branch, hold	75	木 tree, wood	85	水 氵 water	5 STROKE 95	玄 dark, black, mysterious	105	癶 to shin, move legs	115	禾 grain (growing)
66	攴 strike, rap	76	欠 exhale, lack, owe, yawn	86	灬 火 fire	96	玉 王 jewel, jade	106	白 white, clear	116	穴 hole, cave, (loess) pit
67	文 literature, writing, pattern	77	止 stop, halt	87	爫 爪 claw, hand hoof, talon	97	瓜 melon	107	皮 skin, hide, leather	117	立 to stand
68	斗 capacity unit, Big Dipper	78	歹 death, bad, evil, dried bones	88	父 father	98	瓦 tile, pottery	108	皿 dish, vessel	6 STROKE 118	竹 ⺮ bamboo
69	斤 ax, wt.unit or unit of value	79	殳 to strike, hit, lance	89	爻 to mix	99	甘 sweet	109	目 eye	119	米 rice (polished but uncooked)

546

#	120	130	140	150	160	170
0	120 糸 long thread, silk, string	130 朋 肉月 flesh, meat	140 艹 艹 grass	150 谷 valley	160 辛 bitter	170 阝阜 mound, hill (to left)
1	121 缶 water jar, earthenware	131 臣 retainer, subject, minister	141 虍 tiger	151 豆 bean, pea, vase	161 辰 dragon	171 隶 隷 to reach, (servant)
2	122 网 罒 net	132 自 oneself, nose, from	142 虫 insect, bug, worm	152 豕 pig, hog	162 辶 辶 go fast & stop sudden	172 隹 short-tailed bird
3	123 羊 sheep, goat	133 至 arrive	143 血 blood	153 豸 beast	163 邑 阝 city, village (to rt.)	173 雨 雨 rain
4	124 羽 羽 wings, feathers	134 臼 mortar	144 行 go, going	154 貝 shell, cowrie	164 酉 bird, sake	174 青 青 blue, green, unripe, inexperienced
5	125 耂 老 old, aged	135 舌 tongue	145 衤 衣 衷 clothing	155 赤 red	165 釆 distinguish beast claws	175 非 not, is not, negative
6	126 而 whiskers, and, but	136 舛 oppose, dancing legs	146 襾 西 west, a cover	156 走 to run	166 里 village, ri	176 面 face, front, mask, surface
7	127 耒 plow	137 舟 boat, ship	147 見 see, show	157 足 足 leg, foot	167 金 gold, metal, money	177 革 tanned hide, leather, skin, flay
8	128 耳 ear	138 艮 obstinate, hard, good	148 角 horn, corner	158 身 body	168 镸 長 long, headman, senior	178 韋 leather, to rebel
9	129 聿 brush pen	139 色 color	149 言 words, speaking	159 車 car, vehicle, carriage, chariot	169 門 gate, door	179 韭 leek, garlic onions

THE 214 RADICALS

	180	190	200	210
0	180 音 sound, noise voice, tone	190 髟 髟 long hair	200 麻 麻 hemp	210 齊 level, even, Mr. Saito
1	181 頁 head, page	191 鬥 to fight	12 STROKE 201 黃 黄 yellow	15 STROKE 211 齒 tooth
2	182 風 wind, custom fashion, style	192 鬯 fragrant herbs, sacrificial wine	202 黍 millet	16 STROKE 212 龍 dragon
3	183 飛 to fly	193 鬲 tripod, cauldron	203 黑 黒 black	213 龜 tortoise
4	184 食 food, to eat	194 鬼 demon, devil, ogre, spirit	204 黹 needlework, embroidery, sewing	17 STROKE 214 龠 flute, fife
5	185 首 neck, head	11 STROKE 195 魚 fish	13 STROKE 205 黽 frog, toad	
6	186 香 fragrance, perfume, incense	196 鳥 long-tailed bird	206 鼎 tripod, 3-leg kettle	
7	10 STROKE 187 馬 horse	197 鹵 salt, salt earth	207 鼓 drum	
8	188 骨 bone	198 鹿 deer	208 鼠 rat, mouse	
9	189 髙 高 high, tall	199 麥 wheat	14 STROKE 209 鼻 nose	

The 214 radicals are used to construct kanji or characters much as words are formed from letters of the alphabet or chemical compounds from elements and radicals. Some of the radicals are complicated, some are seldom used, some have more than one form. Sometimes those on the right affect the sound of the kanji, and those on the left have more to do with meaning. Learn the kanji as separate building blocks, and try to understand how and why they belong in the character or kanji. The radicals are the keys to the kanji. The radical may have different meanings, but the meanings may be related or belong to a single concept. Often the radical will give you the clue to the meaning of a new kanji. The radical for tree may be on the left in kanji for various kinds of trees. This is also true for the radical on the left meaning gold or money and the kanji for different kinds of metals. Just as the study of kanji will explain much of Chinese and Japanese culture, so will the study of Japanese and Chinese history, social life, furniture, and archeology explain the forming of the kanji.

KANJI STROKE INDEX: LOOK UP THE KANJI IN THIS BOOK BY THE NUMBER OF STROKES TO FIND THE J-NUMBER GIVING THE LOCATION.

1	十 10	女 32	五 5	午 207	支 621	火 13	付 502	半 129	失 418	正 46	皮 307
一 1	**3**	子 31	仁 820	友 145	収 631	父 131	代 463	去 189	写 419	母 137	目 25
2	三 3	小 24	今 81	反 492	文 134	牛 62	令 736	古 70	左 18	民 518	石 44
丁 473	上 20	山 38	仏 711	円 48	方 138	犬 66	以 342	句 592	市 222	氷 498	示 622
七 7	下 21	川 39	元 68	天 119	日 11	王 49	兄 199	可 744	布 706	永 550	礼 337
九 9	久 582	工 71	内 489	太 269	月 12	欠 597	冬 120	史 411	平 315	玉 64	立 149
二 2	千 101	己 777	公 210	夫 501	木 15	予 525	出 90	右 19	広 211	生 34	台 272
人 30	口 27	才 217	六 6	少 93	止 220	**5**	刊 750	司 412	必 497	用 146	旧 759
入 125	土 17	万 320	分 133	引 156	比 697	世 263	功 605	四 4	打 460	田 40	処 811
八 8	士 410	**4**	切 99	心 95	毛 142	主 237	加 356	圧 544	未 872	由 325	号 215
刀 289	夕 98	不 500	化 163	戸 69	氏 620	仕 221	包 511	外 56	末 515	申 254	弁 715
力 148	大 22	中 23	区 591	手 28	水 14	他 459	北 139	央 554	本 45	白 37	辺 713

549

KANJI STROKE INDEX: LOOK UP THE KANJI IN THIS BOOK BY THE NUMBER OF STROKES TO FIND THE J-NUMBER GIVING THE LOCATION.

6	再 788	在 613	曲 381	米 135	行 73	来 147	否 862	序 638	改 359	究 185	貝 169
灯 485	交 212	列 537	地 111	会 54	糸 83	衣 341	兇 801	告 398	延 743	材 403	系 765	売 301
	件 598	印 348	多 108	有 523	老 541	西 96	兵 712	囲 343	弟 282	条 817	声 97	赤 35
	任 688	各 568	字 86	次 227	考 74	弐 854	冷 535	図 261	形 200	求 583	臣 436	走 105
	休 61	合 77	守 421	死 223	耳 26	**7**	初 428	坂 304	役 324	決 202	良 530	足 29
	仮 559	同 295	安 153	妥 318	肉 297	似 625	判 860	均 590	志 623	汽 60	花 43	身
	伝 681	名 140	寺 228	気 59	自 229	位 344	別 508	壱 740	快 566	災 789	芽 358	車 88
	先 33	后 780	州 424	池 110	至 796	低 677	利 528	孝 781	応 556	状 818	芸 388	近 195
	光 72	向 213	年 126	争 451	舌 827	住 244	助 248	完 571	我 745	男 109	見 67	返 316
	全 267	回 168	式 417	当 290	色 94	何 51	努 481	対 461	技 579	町 115	角 173	医 345
	両 336	因 548	成 439	百 130	虫 114	作 82	労 542	局 194	投 291	社 234	言 392	里 332
	共 376	団 672	早 104	竹 113	血 389	体 270	君 198	希 575	折 651	私 797	谷 78	防 718

KANJI STROKE INDEX: LOOK UP THE KANJI IN THIS BOOK BY THE NUMBER OF STROKES TO FIND THE J-NUMBER GIVING THE LOCATION.

7 CONT.	制 823	和 338	官 364	忠 842	東 121	注 277	育 347	9	品 311	思 84	昼 279
余 728	刷 405	固 393	定 474	念 689	板 305	泳 352	舎 629	乗 251	単 671	急 186	査 611
麦 128	券 768	国 79	実 233	性 645	林 150	版 861	苦 197	係 385	型 595	拾 425	柱 278
8	効 782	夜 144	居 586	所 246	果 560	牧 720	英 353	便 510	客 184	持 231	栄 549
事 230	卒 457	妹 319	届 852	承 639	歩 136	物 313	表 309	俗 834	宣 829	指 226	洋 526
京 63	協 377	妻 790	岩 178	招 814	武 708	画 167	述 809	保 716	室 232	政 646	活 174
使 224	参 616	姉 413	岸 177	拝 858	妻 686	的 478	金 16	信 437	専 830	故 778	派 857
例 737	取 238	始 225	幸 395	拡 747	河 561	直 472	長 116	則 666	屋 161	星 264	海 55
供 760	受 240	委 346	底 475	放 512	油 522	知 112	門 143	前 102	度 288	春 91	浅 655
価 563	周 632	季 284	店 284	明 141	治 468	空 65	雨 42	勇 524	建 391	昨 404	炭 274
具 383	味 516	学 57	府 503	易 545	法 513	者 235	青 36	南 124	後 208	昭 249	独 687
典 680	命 519	完 805	往 555	服 505	波 298	肥 699	非 698	厚 606	待 271	是 822	界 170

KANJI STROKE INDEX: LOOK UP THE KANJI IN THIS BOOK BY THE NUMBER OF STROKES TO FIND THE J-NUMBER GIVING THE LOCATION.

9 CONT	秒 499	軍 593	飛 493	兼 769	差 399	料 531	流 334	純 810	財 793	馬 127	問 520
発 303	紀 578	迷 724	食 253	勉 317	師 624	旅 335	浴 732	紙 85	起 181	高 76	基 755
皇 783	約 726	追 280	首 239	原 205	席 444	時 87	消 429	素 658	通 281	党 848	堂 486
県 203	級 187	退 839	点 285	員 349	帯 669	書 92	特 685	耕 784	速 453	11	婦 707
相 452	美 308	送 268	10	夏 52	庫 206	校 75	留 733	能 691	造 662	停 476	宿 634
省 640	胃 546	逆 758	修 633	孫 458	庭 477	株 749	病 310	脈 517	連 538	健 599	寄 576
研 204	茶 275	重 245	俵 702	宮 374	弱 236	根 216	益 742	航 396	郡 384	側 667	帳 470
祖 657	草 106	限 601	倉 659	害 362	徒 480	格 569	真 438	荷 165	配 299	副 709	常 642
祝 635	要 729	面 322	個 603	家 53	従 808	安 340	破 692	蚕 617	酒 422	動 296	康 608
神 257	計 201	革 746	倍 694	容 730	恩 558	帰 182	称 815	討 849	陛 867	務 722	張 675
秋 89	変 509	音 50	候 607	展 847	息 454	残 409	粉 507	訓 764	院 350	唱 430	強 192
科 164	負 312	風 132	借 420	島 292	挙 375	殺 614	納 856	記 180	除 813	商 431	得 850

551

KANJI STROKE INDEX: LOOK UP THE KANJI IN THIS BOOK BY THE NUMBER OF STROKES TO FIND THE J-NUMBER GIVING THE LOCATION.

11 CONT.	望 514	産 408	経 596	貨 357	魚 190	報 717	景 386	港 397	税 826	着 276	買 300
情 643	械 360	略 879	習 426	責 649	鳥 117	場 252	晴 265	湖 394	程 846	落 330	貸 670
悪 152	欲 876	異 738	船 266	転 479	黄 214	富 864	暑 247	湯 482	童 487	葉 327	費 495
授 803	液 552	眼 754	菜 401	週 242	黒 80	寒 175	最 402	温 162	筆 701	象 806	貿 719
採 791	深 258	票 703	著 843	進 259	12	尊 838	朝 118	満 721	等 484	補 868	賀 565
接 652	混 787	祭 400	術 636	部 504	備 700	就 807	期 183	無 723	答 293	覚 363	軽 387
推 821	清 440	移 547	規 577	都 287	創 832	属 835	森 41	然 450	策 795	評 863	遊 326
教 191	済 792	章 432	視 798	釈 802	勝 250	復 710	植 435	焼 434	結 390	詞 799	運 157
救 584	率 878	第 273	設 653	野 323	勤 762	悲 494	極 382	営 741	絶 828	証 816	過 562
敗 693	現 602	細 218	許 587	陸 529	博 695	提 845	検 771	番 306	給 585	象 663	道 122
断 841	球 188	終 241	訳 874	険 770	善 831	散 407	減 775	登 483	統 682	貯 674	達 465
族 455	理 333	組 103	貧 705	雪 100	喜 370	敬 766	測 668	短 466	絵 172	貴 756	量 734

553

KANJI STROKE INDEX: LOOK UP THE KANJI IN THIS BOOK BY THE NUMBER OF STROKES TO FIND THE J-NUMBER GIVING THE LOCATION.

12 CONT.	13	損 837	節 446	話 151	預 875	様 328	綿 725	酸 618	鼻 496	執 490	賛 619
開 171	働 488	数 262	絹 772	誠 825	塩 354	歌 166	練 539	銀 196	15	確 570	輪 533
間 58	勢 441	新 256	続 456	豊 870	14	歴 536	総 661	銅 683	億 557	線 447	選 449
陽 527	勧 752	暗 154	罪 794	債 844	像 664	漁 588	聞 314	銭 656	器 372	編 714	遺 739
隊 462	園 159	業 380	置 469	資 800	境 761	演 553	製 648	関 365	導 684	蔵 833	養 731
階 361	墓 869	楽 331	群 594	路 540	増 665	疑 757	複 865	際 612	敵 678	課 564	16
集 243	幹 751	準 637	義 580	辞 626	察 406	種 423	認 855	雑 615	暴 871	調 471	奮 866
雲 47	想 660	漢 572	聖 824	農 491	徳 851	穀 786	語 209	需 804	標 704	談 467	憲 773
順 427	意 155	照 433	腸 676	遠 160	能 840	算 219	誤 779	静 442	横 355	論 881	敷 443
飲 351	愛 339	盟 873	解 567	鉄 283	慣 574	管 573	説 654	領 735	権 774	諸 812	橋 193
飯 696	感 176	禁 763	試 416	鉱 610	旗 371	精 647	読 123	駅 158	歓 753	賞 641	機 373
歯 414	戦 448	福 506	詩 415	電 286	構 785	緑 532	適 679	鳴 321	潔 767	質 628	燃 690

KANJI STROKE INDEX: LOOK UP THE KANJI IN THIS BOOK BY THE NUMBER OF STROKES TO FIND THE J-NUMBER GIVING THE LOCATION.

16 CONT.	17	題 464	20
積 445	厳 776	額 748	競 379
築 673	績 650	顔 179	議 581
興 589	講 609	類 534	護 604
薬 521	謝 630	験 600	
衛 551	18	19	
親 260	曜 329	識 627	
輸 727	織 644	鏡 378	
録 543	職 819	願 368	
頭 294	臨 880		
館 366	観 367		
燈 485	難 853		

ALPHABETICAL JAPANESE WORD INDEX FOR JME NUMBERS

(On readings are in capitals; kun readings in small letters).

abiru 浴 732	aratamaru 改 359	BAI 売 301	BUN 聞 314
abura 油 522	aratameru 改 359	BAI 倍 694	BUTSU 物 313
agaru 上 20	aratani 新 256	bakasu 化 163	BUTSU 仏 711
ageru 上 20	arawareru 現 602	bakeru 化 163	BYAKU 白 37
AI 愛 339	arawasu 現 602	BAKU 麦 128	BYŌ 病 310
aisuru 愛 339	arawasu 表 309	BAKU 暴 871	BYŌ 平 499
ai 相 452	arawasu 著 843	BAN 番 306	
aida 間 58	aru 有 523	BAN 万 320	cha 茶 275
aji 味 516	aruku 歩 136	BAN 判 860	chaku 着 276
aka 赤 35	asa 朝 118	BEI 米 135	CHI 池 110
akai 赤 35	asai 浅 655	BEN 勉 317	CHI 地 111
akarui 明 141	ashi 足 29	BEN 便 510	CHI 知 112
akeru 明 141	asobu 遊 326	BEN 弁 715	CHI 治 468
aki 秋 89	atai 価 563	BETSU 別 508	CHI 置 469
akinau 商 431	atama 頭 294	BI 美 308	chi 千 101
akiraka 明 141	atarashii 新 256	BI 鼻 496	chi 血 389
AKU 悪 152	ataru 当 290	BI 備 700	chichi 父 131
amari 余 728	ateru 当 290	BIN 便 510	chiisai 小 24
amaru 余 728	ATSU 圧 544	BIN 貧 705	chikai 近 195
amasu 余 728	atsui 暑 247 厚 606	BO 母 137	chikara 力 148
ame 雨 42	atsui 熱 490	BO 墓 869	CHIKU 竹 113
ame 天 119	atsumaru 集 243	BŌ 望 514	CHIKU 築 673
amu 編 714	atsumeru 集 243	BŌ 防 718	CHIN 賃 844
AN 行 73	au 会 54	BŌ 貿 719	chirasu 散 407
AN 安 153	au 合 77	BŌ 暴 871	chiru 散 407
AN 暗 154	ayamari 誤 779	BOKU 木 15	CHO 貯 674
AN 案 340	ayumu 歩 136	BOKU 牧 720	CHO 著 843
anjiru 案 340	aza 字 86	BU 分 133	CHŌ 町 115
ane 姉 413	azukaru 預 875	BU 歩 136	CHŌ 長 116
ani 兄 199	azukeru 預 875	BU 部 504	CHŌ 鳥 117
ao 青 36		BU 武 708	CHŌ 朝 118
aoi 青 36	BA 馬 127	BU 無 723	CHŌ 重 245
arasoi 争 451	ba 場 252	BUN 分 133	CHŌ 帳 470
arasou 争 451	BAI 買 300	BUN 文 134	CHŌ 調 471

CHŌ 調 471	DOKU 読 123	fude 筆 701	GE 下 21
CHŌ 張 675	DOKU 毒 686	fukai 深 258	GE 外 56
CHŌ 腸 676	DOKU 独 687	fukasa 深 258	GEI 芸 388
CHOKU 直 472		FUKU 服 505	GEN 元 68
CHŪ 中 23	E 会 54	FUKU 福 506	GEN 原 205
CHŪ 虫 114	E 絵 172	FUKU 副 709	GEN 言 392
CHŪ 注 277	EI 泳 352	FUKU 復 710	GEN 限 601
CHŪ 柱 278	EI 英 353	FUKU 複 865	GEN 現 602
CHŪ 昼 279	EI 栄 549	FUN 分 133	GEN 減 775
CHŪ 忠 842	EI 永 550	FUN 粉 507	GEN 厳 776
	EI 衛 551	FUN 奮 866	GETSU 月 12
DA 打 460	EI 営 741	fune 船 266	GI 技 579
DAI 大 22	EKI 駅 158	funa 船 266	GI 義 580
DAI 台 272	EKI 役 324	furui 古 70	GI 議 581
DAI 第 273	EKI 易 545	furuu 奮 866	GI 疑 757
DAI 弟 282	EKI 液 552	fusegu 防 718	GIN 銀 196
DAI 代 463	EKI 益 742	fushi 節 446	GO 五 5
DAI 題 464	ekisuru 益 742	futatabi 再 788	GO 期 183
DAI 内 489	EN 円 48	futoi 太 269	GO 午 207
DAN 男 109	EN 園 159	futoru 太 269	GO 後 208
DAN 談 467	EN 遠 160	fuyu 冬 120	GO 語 209
DAN 団 672	EN 塩 354		GO 護 604
DAN 断 841	EN 演 553	GA 画 167	GO 誤 779
-date 建 391	enzuru 演 553	GA 芽 358	GŌ 合 77
DEN 田 40	EN 延 743	GA 賀 565	GŌ 強 192
DEN 電 286	erabu 選 449	GA 我 745	GŌ 号 215
DEN 伝 681	eru 得 850	GAI 外 56	GO 業 380
deru 出 90		GAI 害 362	GOKU 極 382
DO 土 17	FU 父 131	GAKU 学 57	GON 言 392
DO 度 288	FU 負 312	GAKU 楽 331	GON 権 774
DO 努 481	FU 不 500 夫 501	GAKU 額 748	GON 厳 776
DŌ 道 122	FU 付 502	GAN 元 68	GU 具 383
DŌ 同 295	FU 府 503	GAN 岸 177	Gu 供 760
DŌ 動 296	FU 布 706	GAN 岩 178	GŪ 宮 374
DŌ 堂 486	FU 婦 707	GAN 顔 179	Gun 郡 384
DŌ 童 487	FU 富 864	GAN 願 368	GUN 軍 593
DŌ 働 488	FU 風 132	GAN 眼 754	GUN 群 594
DŌ 銅 683	FŪ 夫 501	-gata 形 200	GYAKU 逆 758
DŌ 導 684	FŪ 富 864	GATSU 月 12	gyakuni 逆 758

GYO 魚 190	hana 花 43	HI 飛 493	HO 保 716
GYO 漁 588	hana 鼻 496	HI 悲 494	HO 補 868
GYŌ 行 73	hanashi 話 151	HI 費 495	HŌ 方 138
GYO 形 200	hanasu 話 151	HI 比 697	HŌ 包 511
GYŌ 業 380	hara 原 205	HI 非 698	HŌ 放 512
GYOKU 玉 64	hare 晴 265	HI 肥 699	HŌ 法 513
GYŪ 牛 62	hareru 晴 265	HI 否 862	HŌ 報 517
	hari 張 675	hi 日 11	HŌ 豊 870
HA 波 298	haru 張 675	hi 火 13	hoka 外 56
HA 破 692	haru 春 91	hidari 左 18	HOKU 北 139
HA 派 857	hashi 橋 193	hieru 冷 535	hon 本 45
ha 葉 327	hashira 柱 278	hiyasu 冷 535	hoshi 星 264
ha 歯 414	hashiru 走 105	higashi 東 121	hosoi 細 218
habuku 省 640	hata 畑 302	hikari 光 72	hossuru 欲 876
HACHI 八 8	hatake 畑 302	hikaru 光 72	hotoke 仏 711
haha 母 137	hata 旗 371	hiki 引 k56	HYAKU 百 130
HAI 配 299	hata 機 373	hiku 引 156	HYŌ 表 309
HAI 敗 153	hataraki 働 488	hikiiru 率 878	HYŌ 氷 498
HAI 拝 858	hataraku 働 488	hikui 低 677	HYŌ 俵 702
hajimaru 始 225	hatasu 果 560	HIN 品 311H	HYŌ 票 703
hajimeru 始 225	hate 果 560	HIN 貧 705	HYŌ 標 704
hajime 初 428	HATSU 発 303	hiraku 開 171	HYŌ 評 863
haka 墓 869	hatsu 初 428	hiratai 平 315	hyōsuru 評 863
hakaru 計 201	haya 早 104	hirogaru 広 211	
hakaru 図 261	hayai 早 104	hirogeru 広 211	I 意 155
hakaru 測 668	hayai 速 453	hiroi 広 211	I 衣 341
hakaru 量 734	hayashi 林 150	hiromaru 広 211	I 以 342
hakobu 運 157	HEI 平 315	hiro(u) 拾 425	I 囲 343
HAKU 白 37	HEI 兵 712	hiru 昼 279	I 位 344
HAKU 博 695	HEI 陛 867	hisashii 久 582	I 医 345
HAN 半 129	HEN 返 316	hisashiku 久 582	I 委 346
HAN 坂 304	HEN 変 509	hitai 額 748	I 易 545 胃 546
HAN 板 305	HEN 辺 713	hito 人 30	I 異 738 移 547
HAN 反 492	HEN 編 714	hitoshii 等 484	I 遺 739
HAN 飯 696	herasu 減 775	hitotsu 一 1	ICHI 一 1
HAN 犯 859	heru 減 775	HITSU 必 497	ICHI 壱 740
HAN 判 860	heru 経 596	HITSU 筆 701	ichi 市 222
HAN 版 861	HI 皮 307	HO 歩 136	ichijirushii 著 843

ie 家 53		JŌ 定 474	KA 価 563 科 164
ike 池 110	JAKU 弱 236	JŌ 常 642	KA 課 564
iki 息 454	JI 耳 26	JŌ 情 643	KA 可 744
ikioi 勢 441	JI 字 86	JŌ 条 817	kabu 株 749
ikiru 生 34	JI 時 87	JŌ 状 818	kado 門 143
IKU 育 347	JI 地 111	JU 受 240	kaerimiru 省 640
iku 行 73	JI 次 227	JU 授 803	kaeru 帰 182
ima 今 81	JI 寺 228	JU 需 804	kaeru 変 509
imoto 妹 319	JI 自 229	JŪ 就 807	kaeshi 返 316
IN 音 50	JI 事 230	JŪ 十 10 拾 425	kaesu 返 316
IN 引 156	JI 持 231	JŪ 住 244	kagami 返 373
IN 印 348	JI 治 468	JŪ 重 245	kagiri 限 601
IN 員 349	JI 示 622	JŪ 従 808	kagiru 限 601
IN 因 548	JI 似 625	JUN 順 427	KAI 会 54 海 55
ina 否 862	JI 辞 626	JUN 準 637	KAI 回 168
inochi 命 519	jisuru 辞 626	JUN 純 810	KAI 界 170 開 171
ireru 入 125	JI 児 801	JUTSU 術 636	KAI 絵 172
iri 入 125	-ji 路 540	JUYSU 述 809	KAI 改 359
iro 色 94	JIKI 直 472		KAI 械 360
iru 居 586	JIN 人 30	KA 火 13	KAI 階 361
isagiyoi 潔 767	JIN 神 257	KA 下 21	KAI 快 566
isamashii 勇 524	JIN 臣 436	KA 花 43	KAI 解 567
ishi 石 44	JIN 仁 820	KA 何 51	kai 貝 169
isogu 急 186	JITSU 実 233 日 11	KA 夏 52	kaiko 蚕 617
ita 板 305	JO 女 32	KA 家 53	kakari 係 385
itaru 至 796	JO 助 248	KA 化 163	kakaru 係 385
ito 糸 83	JO 序 638	KA 荷 165	kakeru 欠 597
itonami 営 741	JO 除 813	KA 歌 166	kakomu 囲 343
itonamu 営 741	JŌ 上 20	KA 加 356	KAKU 画 167
itsutsu 五 5	JŌ 乗 251	KA 賀 357	KAKU 角 173
iu 言 392	JŌ 場 252	KA 仮 559	KAKU 客 184
iwa 岩 178	JŌ 星 264	KA 果 560	KAKU 覚 363
iwai 祝 635	JŌ 成 439	KA 河 561	KAKU 各 568
iwau 祝 635	JŌ 静 442	KA 過 562	KAKU 格 569

KAKU-kisou   KAKU-kisou

KAKU 確 570	karui 軽 387	KEI 競 379	KI 帰 182
KAKU 革 746	kasanaru 重 245	KEI 係 385	KI 期 183
KAKU 拡 747	kasaneru 重 245	KEI 景 386	KI 季 369
kaku 書 92	kashi 貸 670	KEI 軽 387	KI 喜 370
kaku 欠 597	kasu 貸 670	KEI 型 595	KI 旗 371
kamae 構 785	kata 方 138	KEI 経 596	KI 器 372
kamaeru 構 785	kata 型 595	KEI 境 761	KI 機 373
kami 上 20	katachi 形 200	KEI 系 765	KI 希 575
kami 紙 85	katai 固 393	KEI 敬 766	KI 寄 576
kami 神 257	katai 難 853	KEN 間 58	KI 規 577
KAN 間 58	katamaru 固 393	KEN 大 66	KI 紀 578
KAN 寒 175	katameru 固 393	KEN 見 67	KI 基 755
KAN 感 176	katana 刀 289	KEN 県 203	KI 貴 756
KAN 官 364	katari 語 209	KEN 研 204	KI 己 777
KAN 関 365	kataru 語 209	KEN 建 391	ki 木 15
KAN 館 366	katsu 勝 250 活 174	KEN 件 598	ki 生 34
KAN 観 367	kau 買 300	KEN 健 599	ki 黄 214
KAN 完 571	kawa 川 39	KEN 験 600	kieru 消 429
KAN 漢 572	kawa 皮 307	KEN 券 768	
─kan 漢 572	kawa 側 667	KEN 兼 769	kikoeru 聞 314
KAN 管 573	kawari 代 463	KEN 険 770	kiku 聞 314
KAN 慣 574	kawaru 代 463	KEN 検 771	kimaru 決 202
KAN 刊 750	kawaru 変 509	KEN 絹 772	kimeru 決 202
KAN 幹 751	kayou 通 281	KEN 憲 773	kimasu 来 147
KAN 勧 752	kaze 風 132	KEN 権 774	kimi 君 198
KAN 歓 753	kazoeru 数 262	kesu 消 429	KIN 金 16
kanarazu 必 497	kazu 数 262	KETSU 決 202	KIN 今 81
kanashii 悲 494	KE 家 53	KETSU 決 202	KIN 近 195
kane 金 16	KE 気 59	KETSU 血 389	KIN 均 590
kangae 考 74	KE 化 163	KETSU 結 390	KIN 勤 762
kangaeru 考 74	KE 景 386	KETSU 欠 597	KIN 禁 763
kaneru 兼 769	KE 仮 559	KETSU 潔 767	kinjiru 禁 763
kao 顔 179	ke 毛 142	kewashii 険 770	kinu 絹 772
kari 借 420	KEI 京 63	KI 気 59	kiru 切 99
kariru 借 420	KEI 兄 199	KI 汽 60	kiru 着 276
kari 仮 559	KEI 形 200	KI 記 180	kishi 岸 177
karu 軽 387	KEI 計 201	KI 起 181	kisou 競 379

kita-KYŪ

kita 北 139	KŌ 康 608	kotae 答 293	kusa 草 106
kiyoi 清 440	KŌ 講 609	kotaeru 答 293	kusuri 薬 521
kiyoraka 清 440	KŌ 鉱 610	koto 事 230	kuu 食 253
kizuku 築 673	KŌ 右 780	koto 言 392	kuwaeru 加 356
KO 戸 69	KŌ 孝 781	kotonaru 異 738	kuwawaru 加 356
KO 古 70	KŌ 効 782	kotowaru 断 841	KYAKU 客 184
KO 去 189	KŌ 皇 783	KU 九 9	KYO 去 189
KO 庫 206	KŌ 耕 784	KU 口 27	KYO 挙 375
KO 固 393	KŌ 橫 785	KU 工 71	KYO 居 586
KO 湖 394	koe 声 97	KU 苦 197	KYO 許 587
KO 個 603	koeru 肥 699	KU 宮 374	KYŌ 京 63
KO 己 777	koyasu 肥 699	KU 久 582	KYŌ 教 191
KO 故 778	koi 来 147	KU 区 591	KYŌ 強 192
ko 小 24	kokonotsu 九 9	KU 句 592	KYŌ 橋 193
ko 子 31	kokoro 心 95	KU 功 605	KYŌ 兄 199
ko 粉 507	kokoromi 試 416	KŪ 空 65	KYŌ 共 376
KŌ 口 27	kokoromiru 試 416	kubaru 配 299	KYŌ 協 377
KŌ 工 71	kokoroyoi 快 566	kubi 首 239	KYŌ 鏡 378
KŌ 光 72	kokorozashi 志 623	kuchi 口 27	KYŌ 競 379
KŌ 行 73	kokorozasu 志 623	kuda 管 573	KYŌ 興 589
KŌ 考 74	KOKU 石 44	kudaru 下 21	KYŌ 経 596
KŌ 校 75	KOKU 谷 78	kumi 組 103	KYŌ 供 760
KŌ 高 76	KOKU 国 79	kumu 組 103	KYŌ 境 761
KŌ 後 208	KOKU 黒 80	kumo 雲 47	KYOKU 局 194
KŌ 公 210	KOKU 告 398	KUN 君 198	KYOKU 曲 381
KŌ 広 211	KOKU 穀 786	KUN 訓 764	KYOKU 極 382
KŌ 交 212	komakai 細 218	kuni 国 79	KYŪ 九 9
KŌ 向 213	kome 米 135	kura 倉 659	KYŪ 休 61
KŌ 黄 214	KON 金 16	kura 蔵 833	KYŪ 究 185
KŌ 幸 395	KON 今 81	kuraberu 比 697	KYŪ 急 186
KŌ 航 396	KON 根 216	kurai 暗 154	KYŪ 級 187
KŌ 港 397	KON 混 787	kurai 位 344	KYŪ 球 188
KŌ 興 589	kona 粉 507	kuro 黒 80	KYŪ 宮 374
KŌ 功 605	kori 郡 384	kuroi 黒 80	KYŪ 久 582
KŌ 厚 606	kori 氷 498	kuru 来 147	KYŪ 求 583
KŌ 候 607	koromo 衣 341	kuruma 車 88	KYŪ 救 584
KŌ 侯 607	korosu 殺 614	kurushii 苦 197	KYŪ 給 585
		kusa 草 106	KYŪ 旧 759

ma 間 58
ma 真 438
machi 町 115
mae 前 102
magaru 曲 381
mageru 曲 381
mago 孫 458
MAI 米 135
MAI 毎 318
MAI 妹 319
mairu 参 616
majiru 交 212
majiwaru 交 212
majiru 混 787
makaseru 任 688
make 負 312
makeru 負 312
maki 牧 720
makoto 誠 825
mamo(ru) 守 421
MAN 万 320
MAN 満 721
manabu 学 57
manako 眼 754
maneku 招 814
masu 増 665
mato 的 478
MATSU 末 515
matsu 待 271
matsuri 祭 400
matsuru 祭 400
matsurigoto 政 646
mattaku 全 267
mawaru 回 168
mawasu 回 168
mayou 迷 724
mayowasu 迷 724

mazeru 混 787
mazushii 貧 705
me 目 25
me 芽 385
MEI 名 140
MEI 明 141
MEI 鳴 321
MEI 命 519
MEI 迷 724
MEI 盟 873
MEN 面 322
MEN 綿 725
meshi 飯 696
MI 味 516
MI 未 872
mi 三 3
mi 実 233
mi 身 255
michi 道 122
michibiki 導 684
michibiku 導 684
michiru 満 721
midori 緑 532
migi 右 19
mijikai 短 466
miki 幹 751
mimi 耳 26
MIN 民 518
minami 南 124
minato 港 397
minoru 実 233
miru 見 67
mise 店 284
mitomeru 認 855
mittsu 三 3
miya 宮 374
miyako 都 287
mizu 水 14

mizu 水 14
mizukara 自 229
mizuumi 湖 394
MŌ 毛 142
MŌ 望 514
mochi 持 231
motsu 持 231
mochiiru 用 146
moeru 燃 690
mōkeru 設 653
MOKU 木 15
MOKU 目 25
MON 文 134
MON 門 143
MON 問 520
mono 者 235
mono 物 313
mori 森 41
mosu 申 254
moto 下 21
moto 元 68
motome 求 583
motomeru 求 583
motoi 基 755
motozuku 基 755
MOTSU 物 313
mottomo 最 402
moyasu 燃 690
MU 武 708
MU 務 722
MU 無 723
mugi 麦 128
mukau 向 213
muku 向 213
mukui 報 717
mukuiru 報 717
mura 村 107

muragaru 群 594
mure 群 594
mureru 群 594
muro 室 232
mushi 虫 114
musubi 結 390
musubu 結 390
muttsu 六 6
MYAKU 脈 517
MYŌ 名 140
MYŌ 明 141
MYŌ 命 519

NA 納 856
na 名 140
na 菜 401
nagai 長 116
nagare 流 334
nagareru 流 334
nagasu 流 334
nageru 投 291
NAI 内 489
nai 無 723
nashi 無 723
naka 中 23
nakaba 半 129
naku 鳴 321
nama 生 34
nami 波 298
NAN 男 109
NAN 南 124
NAN 難 853
nanatsu 七 7
nani 何 51
nan 何 51
naosu 直 472
narau 習 426

nareru 慣 574	noboru 上 20	okiru 起 181	oyogu 泳 352
naru 成 439	nochi 後 208	okosu 起 181	
nasu 成 439	nokori 残 409	okonau 行 73	RAI 来 147
nasake 情 643	nokoru 残 409	okoru 興 589	RAKU 落 330
natsu 夏 52	nokosu 残 409	okosu 興 589	RAKU 楽 331
ne 音 50	nomu 飲 351	OKU 屋 161	REI 礼 337
ne 根 216	noru 乗 251	OKU 億 557	REI 冷 535
negai 願 368	noseru 乗 251	oku 置 469	REI 令 736
negau 願 368	nozoku 除 813	okuru 送 268	REI 例 737
NEN 年 126	nozomi 望 514	omo 面 322	REKI 歴 536
NEN 然 450	nozomu 望 514	omote 面 322	REN 連 538
NEN 念 689	nozomu 臨 880	omoi 重 245	REN 練 539
NEN 燃 690	nuno 布 706	omote 表 309	RETSU 列 537
neru 練 539	nushi 主 237	omou 思 84	RI 里 332
NETSU 熱 490	NYO 女 32	ON 音 50	RI 理 333
nessuru 熱 490	NYŪ 入 125	ON 遠 160	RI 利 528
NI 二 2		ON 恩 558	RIKI 力 148
NI 児 801	o 小 24	onaji 同 295	RIKU 陸 529
NI 弐 854	Ō 王 49	onna 女 32	RIN 林 150
ni 荷 165	Ō 黄 214	ono-ono 各 568	RIN 輪 533
NICHI 日 11	Ō 横 355	ori 織 644	RIN 臨 880
nigai 苦 197	Ō 央 554	oru 織 644	RITSU 立 149
NIKU 肉 297	Ō 往 555	oru 折 651	RITSU 律 877
NIN 人 30	Ō 応 556	osameru 治 468	RITSU 率 878
NIN 任 688	ōzuru 応 556	osameru 収 631	RO 路 540
NIN 認 855	Ō 皇 783	osameru 修 633	RŌ 老 541
niru 似 625	obi 帯 669	osameru 納 856	RŌ 労 542
nishi 西 96	obiru 帯 669	oshieru 教 191	ROKU 緑 532 六 6
niwa 庭 477	oboeru 覚 363	osu 推 821	ROKU 録 543
no 野 323	ochiru 落 330	oto 音 50	RON 論 881
NO 農 491	otosu 落 330	otoko 男 109	RU 流 334
NO 能 691	oeru 終 241	ototo 弟 282	RU 留 733
NO 納 856	ogamu 拝 858	otto 夫 501	RUI 類 534
nobasu 延 743	oginau 補 868	ou 追 280	RYAKU 略 879
nobe 延 743	oi 老 541	ou 負 312	ryakusuru 略 879
nobiru 延 743	oiru 老 541	owari 終 241	RYO 旅 335
noberu 述 809	oi 多 108	owaru 終 241	RYŌ 両 336
nobori 登 483	okasu 犯 859	oya 親 260	RYŌ 良 530
noboru 登 483	okii 大 22	oyake 公 210	RYŌ 料 531

SHIKI 色 94
SHIKI 式 417
SHIKI 識 627
SHIKI 織 644
shima 島 292
shimesu 示 622
shimo 下 21
SHIN 森 41
SHIN 心 95
SHIN 申 254
SHIN 身 255
SHIN 新 256
SHIN 神 257
SHIN 深 258
SHIN 進 259
SHIN 親 260
SHIN 臣 436
SHIN 信 437
shinzuru 信 437
SHIN 真 438
shina 品 311
shinu 死 223
shio 塩 354
shirabe 調 471
shiraberu 調 471
shiraseru 知 112
shiru 知 112
shirizokeru 退 839
shirizoku 退 839

shiro 白 37
shiroi 白 37
shirushi 印 348
shita 下 21
shita 舌 827
shitagau 従 808
shitashii 親 260
shitashimu 親 260
SHITSU 室 232
SHITSU 失 418 質 628
shizuka 静 442
shizumaru 静 422
shizumeru 静 442
SHO 書 92
SHO 所 246
SHO 暑 247
SHO 初 428
SHO 処 811
shosuru 処 811
SHO 諸 812
SHŌ 小 24
SHŌ 生 34
SHŌ 青 36
SHŌ 正 46
SHŌ 少 93
SHŌ 昭 249
SHŌ 勝 250
SHŌ 消 429
SHŌ 唱 430

SHŌ 商 431
SHŌ 章 432
SHŌ 照 433
SHŌ 焼 434
SHŌ 相 452
SHŌ 承 639
SHŌ 省 640
SHŌ 賞 641
SHŌ 性 645
SHŌ 政 646
SHŌ 精 647
SHŌ 象 663
SHŌ 招 814
SHŌ 称 815
shōsuru 称 815
SHŌ 証 816
SHOKU 色 94
SHOKU 食 253
SHOKU 植 435
SHOKU 織 644
SHOKU 職 819
SHU 手 28
SHU 主 237
SHU 取 238 首 239
SHU 守 421
SHU 酒 422
SHU 種 423
SHU 修 633
SHŪ 秋 89

SHŪ 終 241
SHŪ 週 242
SHŪ 集 243
SHŪ 州 424
SHŪ 拾 425
SHŪ 習 426
SHŪ 牧 631
SHŪ 周 632
SHŪ 修 633
SHŪ 宗 805
SHŪ 衆 806
SHŪ 就 807
SHUKU 宿 634
SHUKU 祝 635
SHUN 春 91
SHUTSU 出 90
SO 組 103
SO 祖 657
SO 素 658
SŌ 早 104
SŌ 走 105
SŌ 草 106
SŌ 送 268
SŌ 争 451
SŌ 相 452
SŌ 倉 659
SŌ 想 660
SŌ 総 661
SŌ 宗 805

SŌ 創 832	SU 素 658	tabi 旅 335	tane 種 423
sodateru 育 347	SŪ 数 262	tachi 立 149	tani 谷 78
soko 底 475	suberu 統 682	tadashii 正 46	tanoshii 楽 331
SOKU 足 29	sue 末 515	taeru 絶 828	tariru 足 29
SOKU 速 453	sugiru 過 562	tagayasu 耕 784	tashika 確 570
SOKU 息 454	sugosu 過 562	TAI 大 22	tashikameru 確 570
SOKU 則 666	SUI 水 14	TAI 太 269	tasukaru 助 248
SOKU 側 667	SUI 出 90	TAI 体 270	tasukeru 助 248
SOKU 測 668	SUI 推 821	TAI 待 271	tatakai 戦 448
SON 村 107	suke 助 248	TAI 台 272	tatakau 戦 448
SON 孫 458	sukoshi 少 93	TAI 対 461	tateru 達 391
SON 存 836	sukoyaka 健 599	TAI 隊 462	tatsu 達 391
SON 損 837	sukui 救 584	TAI 帯 669	TATSU 達 465
sonsuru 損 837	sukuu 救 584	TAI 貸 670	tatsu 立 149
SON 尊 838	sukunai 少 93	TAI 退 839	tatsu 断 841
sonae 備 700	sumasu 済 792	TAI 態 840	tattobu 尊 838
sonaeru 備 700	sumu 済 792		tattoi 尊 838
sonawaru 備 700	sumi 炭 274	taira 平 315	tawara 俵 702
sonaeru 供 760	sumu 住 244	takai 高 76	te 手 28
sono 園 159	suru 刷 405	take 竹 113	TEI 体 270
sora 空 65	susumeru 勧 752	tama 玉 64	TEI 弟 282
sosogu 注 277	susumu 進 259	tama 玉 64	TEI 丁 473
soto 外 56		tami 民 518	TEI 定 474
SOTSU 卒 457	TA 多 108	tamotsu 保 716	TEI 底 475
SOTSU 率 878	TA 太 269	TAN 炭 274	TEI 停 476
SU 子 31	TA 他 459	TAN 短 466	TEI 庭 477
SU 主 237	ta 田 40	TAN 反 492	TEI 低 677
SU 守 421	taberu 食 253	TAN 単 671	TEI 提 845

TEI 程 846	TŌ 湯 482	tome 供 760	tsuma 妻 790
TEKI 的 478	TŌ 等 484	tonaeru 唱 430	tsumetai 冷 535
TEKI 敵 678	YŌ 燈 485	tori 鳥 117	tsumi 罪 794
TEKI 適 679	TŌ 統 682	toru 取 238	tsumori 積 445
tekisuru 適 679	TŌ 覚 848	toru 採 791	tsumoru 積 445
TEN 天 119	TŌ 討 849	tōru 通 281	tsumu 積 445
TEN 店 284	TŌ 納 856	toshi 年 126	tsune 常 642
TEN 点 285	tō 十 10	totonoeru 整 443	tsuno 角 173
TEN 転 479	tobu 飛 493	totonou 整 443	tsuranaru 連 538
TEN 典 680	todokeru 届 852	tou 問 520	tsureru 連 538
TEN 展 847	todoku 届 852	TSU 都 287	tsutaeru 伝 681
tera 寺 228	toi 遠 160	TSŪ 通 281	tsutawaru 伝 681
terasu 照 433	toki 時 87	tsuchi 土 17	tsutome 努 722
teru 照 433	tokoro 所 246	tsugeru 告 398	tsutome 勤 762
TETSU 鉄 283	TOKU 読 123	tsugi 次 227	tsutomeru 努 481
TO 土 17	TOKU 特 685	tsugu 次 227	tsutsumu 包 511
TO 図 261	TOKU 得 850	TSUI 追 280	tsuyoi 強 192
TO 都 287	TOKU 徳 851	TSUI 対 461	tsuzukeru 続 456
TO 徒 480	toku 解 567	tsuiyasu 費 495	tsuzuki 続 456
TO 登 483	toku 説 654	tsukaeru 仕 221	tsuzuku 続 456
to 戸 69	tomaru 止 220	tsukau 使 224	U 右 19
TŌ 冬 120	tomeru 止 220	tsukeru 付 502	U 雨 42
TŌ 東 121	tome 止 220	tsuku 付 502	U 有 523
TŌ 刀 289 当 290	tomeru 留 733	tsuki 月 12	uchi 内 489
TŌ 投 291	tomi 富 864	tsuku 着 276	ue 上 20
TŌ 島 292	tomu 富 864	tsukuri 造 662	ueru 植 435
TŌ 答 293	tomo 友 145	tsukuru 造 662	ugoku 動 296
TŌ 頭 294	tomo 共 376	tsukuru 作 82	uji 氏 620

uke 受 240	WA 和 338	輪 533	yamai 病 310	YOKU 欲 876
ukeru 受 240	wakareru 分 133	yamu 病 310	yomu 読 123
uketamawaru 承 639	wakeru 分 133	yashinau 養 731	yon 四 4
uma 馬 127	wakareru 別 508	yashiro 社 234	yoru 夜 144
umareru 生 34	wake 訳 874	yasui 安 153	yoru 因 548
umu 生 34	ware 我 745	yasumu 休 61	yoru 寄 576
umi 海 55	warui 悪 152	yasumi 休 61	yoseru 寄 576
umu 産 408	wata 綿 725	yattsu 八 8	yorokobi 喜 370
UN 雲 47	watakushi 私 797	yawaragu 和 338	yorokobu 喜 370
UN 運 157	wazawai 災 789	YO 予 525	yoshi 由 325
uo 魚 190		YO 余 729	yottsu 四 4
uri 売 301		YO 預 875	yowai 弱 236
uru 売 301	YA 夜 144	yo 四 4	YŪ 由 325
ushi 牛 62	YA 野 323	yo 夜 144	YU 油 522
ushinau 失 418	ya 家 53	yo 世 263	YU 輸 727
ushiro 後 208	ya 屋 161	yo 代 463	yu 湯 482
uta 歌 166	yabure 破 692	YŌ 用 146	YŪ 右 19
utau 歌 166	yaburu 破 692	YŌ 葉 327	YŪ 友 145
utagai 疑 757	yabureru 敗 693	YŌ 様 328	YŪ 友 145
utagau 疑 757	yado 宿 634	YŌ 曜 329	YŪ 由 325
utsu 打 460	yadoru 宿 634	YŌ 洋 526	YŪ 遊 326
utsu 討 849	YAKU 役 324	YŌ 陽 527	YŪ 有 523
utsukushii 美 308	YAKU 薬 521	YŌ 要 729	YŪ 勇 524
utsuru 移 547	YAKU 約 726	yōsuru 要 729	yū 夕 98
utsuru 移 547	YAKU 訳 874	YŌ 容 730	yubi 指 226
utsusu 写 419	yakusuru 訳 874	YŌ 養 731	YUI 遺 739
utsuwa 器 372	yaku 焼 434	yoi 良 530	yuki 雪 100
uyamau 敬 766	yakeru 焼 434	yoko 横 355	yuku 行 73
WA 話 151	yama 山 38	YOKU 浴 732	yurushi 許 587

yurusu 許 587
yutaka 豊 870
yuu 結 390

ZAI 材 403
ZAI 在 613
ZAI 財 793
ZAI 罪 794
ZAN 残 409
ZATSU 雑 615
ZE 是 822
ZEI 説 654
ZEI 税 826
ZEN 前 102
ZEN 全 267
ZEN 然 450
ZEN 善 831
zeni 銭 656
ZETSU 舌 827
ZETSU 絶 828
ZŌ 雑 615
ZŌ 造 662
ZŌ 象 663
ZŌ 像 664
ZŌ 増 665
ZŌ 蔵 833
zosuru 蔵 833
ZOKU 族 455
ZOKU 続 456
ZOKU 属 835
zokusuru 属 833
zon 存 836
zonzuru 存 836
ZU 図 261
ZU 頭 294
zukuri 造 662
zure 連 538
zuri 刷 405

KATAKANA

ア a	サ sa	ナ na	マ ma	ル ru
イ i	シ shi	ニ ni	ミ mi	レ re
ウ u	ス su	ヌ nu	ム mu	ロ ro
エ e	セ se	ネ ne	メ me	ワ wa
オ o	ソ so	ノ no	モ mo	ヲ o
カ ka	タ ta	ハ ha	ヤ ya	ン n
キ ki	チ chi	ヒ hi	ユ yu	
ク ku	ツ tsu	フ fu	ヨ yo	
ケ ke	テ te	ヘ he	ラ ra	
コ ko	ト to	ホ ho	リ ri	

HIRAGANA

あ a	さ sa	な na	ま ma	る ru
い i	し shi	に ni	み mi	れ re
う u	す su	ぬ nu	む mu	ろ ro
え e	せ se	ね ne	め me	わ wa
お o	そ so	の no	も mo	ゐ o
か ka	た ta	は ha	や ya	ん n
き ki	ち chi	ひ hi	ゆ yu	
く ku	つ tsu	ふ fu	よ yo	
け ke	て te	へ he	ら ra	
こ ko	と to	ほ ho	り ri	

Katakana and hiragana are used in Japanese writing to supplement the kanji. Katakana are used to represent sounds in foreign languages. Hiragana are used with the kanji to conclude verbs, for postpositions, or when no word in kanji exists.

About the Author

DR. ANDREW DYKSTRA has always been fascinated by the Japanese *kanji* or the Chinese characters used in reading and writing and even thinking by nearly one billion of the earth's peoples. These volumes of *The Kanji ABC* are his first publications on that subject.

The *kanji* have usually been the difficult part of an Oriental language course. Dr. Dykstra hopes to make the *Kanji* a subject of intense interest to everyone.

The pictographs, the *Kanji* are an international language intelligible to all of us human beings. Many scientists and humanists have assumed that ancient minds are primitive, lacking the ability to associate and reason logically. But Dr. Dykstra believes that the ancient minds are in no way inferior to our own, and that we have not had the acumen to understand what they are telling us.

Dr. Dykstra was born in the historic Lushan (mountains) of Kiangsi Province and spent his youth in China where he graduated from the Shanghai American School. During World War II, he received his commission from Columbia Midshipman School, and his diploma from the Navy Oriental Languages Postgraduate School at Colorado University and Oklahoma State University. He was later promoted with a speciality in Psychology in the Medical Service Corps.

After the war, Dr. Dykstra was employed by the State of California and also taught courses for Lassen College in Psychology, Humanities, History, Political Science, and German. He was awarded fellowships in Law at Boalt Hall, in Interpersonal Relations at Immaculate Heart College in Los Angeles, in Chinese at Claremont Graduate School and San Francisco State University, and in Japanese at UCLA.

Another of Dr. Dykstra's interests, Oriental humor, has produced *Sexy Laughing Stories of Old Japan,* printed by Japan Publications, Inc., 1255 Howard Street, San Francisco, California 94103. "Laughing stories" are literally what the Japanese call the sexy and humorous tales that for centuries have been retold by travelling story tellers who accompanied words with vivid facial expressions, gestures, and sounds.

Dr. Dykstra hopes to transmit his pleasure in the *kanji* by his writings. His purpose is to promote understanding between American and Oriental peoples through enjoyment of the *kanji*. Strangely enough, even the Japanese and Chinese often have done little more than to memorize the meanings of the *kanji*, practice their writing, and enjoy their beauty. The *kanji* deserve far more than this.